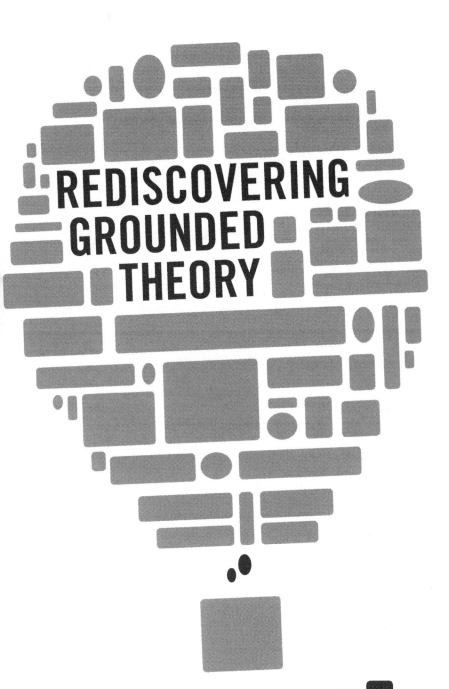

REDISCOVERING GROUNDED THEORY

REDISCOVERING GROUNDED THEORY

Barry Gibson / Jan Hartman

⑤SAGE

Los Angeles | London | New Delhi
Singapore | Washington DC

Los Angeles | London | New Delhi
Singapore | Washington DC

SAGE Publications Ltd
1 Oliver's Yard
55 City Road
London EC1Y 1SP

SAGE Publications Inc.
2455 Teller Road
Thousand Oaks, California 91320

SAGE Publications India Pvt Ltd
B 1/I 1 Mohan Cooperative Industrial Area
Mathura Road
New Delhi 110 044

SAGE Publications Asia-Pacific Pte Ltd
3 Church Street
#10-04 Samsung Hub
Singapore 049483

Editor: Jai Seaman
Editorial assistant: Lily Mehrbod
Production editor: Nicola Marshall
Copyeditor: Sarah Bury
Proofreader: Derek Markham
Marketing manager: Ben Griffin-Sherwood
Cover design: Francis Kenney
Typeset by: C&M Digitals (P) Ltd, Chennai, India
Printed in Great Britain by Henry Ling Limited at
The Dorset Press, Dorchester, DT1 1HD

MIX
Paper from
responsible sources
FSC
www.fsc.org   FSC™ C013985

Library of Congress Control Number: 2013937332

British Library Cataloguing in Publication data

A catalogue record for this book is available from
the British Library

ISBN 978-1-4462-4870-6
ISBN 978-1-4462-4871-3 (pbk)

Contents

List of Tables   ix
List of Figures   x
List of Boxes   xi
List of Skills and Tips   xii
Preface   xiii

1 Introduction   1
Why is theory so important anyway?   2
Why this book?   3
The sociological context   5
The philosophical context   13
Outline of the book   20
Summary   23
Further reading   23
Notes   23

PART 1   WHAT *IS* GROUNDED THEORY?   25

2 What Kind of Theory is Grounded Theory?   27
Existing views on what a grounded theory should
    look like   30
The core aspects of grounded theory   32
Concluding comments   41
Summary   42
Further reading   43
Notes   43

3 Constructivism in Grounded Theory   44
What is constructivist grounded theory?   45
Grounded theory and constructivist grounded theory   47
Combining constructivism with grounded theory   50
Concluding comments   62
Summary   64
Further reading   64

**4 Disentangling Concepts and Categories in Grounded
Theory**   65
The entangled nature of concepts and categories in
    contemporary grounded theory   66

The contemporary view of categories in grounded theory   68
Concepts and the discovery of grounded theory   70
Categories and the discovery of grounded theory   75
Concluding comments   78
Summary   80
Further reading   80
Notes   80

5 Coding in Grounded Theory   82
   Coding in the literature   83
   The theoretical context of coding in grounded theory   86
   Coding in *Discovery*   88
   The elaboration of coding in *Theoretical Sensitivity*   90
   Open coding   91
   Concluding comments   95
   Summary   99
   Further reading   99
   Notes   99

PART 2   DOING GROUNDED THEORY   103

6 How to Develop Theoretical Sensitivity   105
   What is theoretical sensitivity?   106
   Coding families and relations between categories   109
   Diversity, sampling, integration and modifiability   110
   Developing theoretical sensitivity: learning to think
      theoretically   113
   Reading the literature: skills and tips   114
   Exploring prior interests and preconceptions: skills
      and tips   116
   Key points about theoretical sensitivity   117
   Summary   120
   Further reading   121
   Notes   121

7 Rediscovering Skills for Theoretical Sampling   122
   General principles of sampling in grounded theory   123
   Slices of data: data analysis for the generation of theory 125
   From slices of data to theoretical sampling   128
   Theoretical sampling and coding in grounded theory   131
   Key points about theoretical sampling   133
   Summary   134
   Further reading   134
   Notes   134

8 Theoretical Pacing and the Process of Doing
   Grounded Theory   136
   The pacing and process of doing grounded theory   139
   Pacing the techniques of grounded theory   140

Pacing the process of grounded theory 142
Key points about theoretical pacing 148
Summary 150
Further reading 151
Notes 151

9 **Rediscovering Coding in Grounded Theory** **153**
Open coding 154
Selective coding 163
Key points about theoretical coding 168
Summary 170
Further reading 170
Notes 170

10 **Thinking Theoretically and Writing Memos in**
Grounded Theory **171**
When to memo 173
What to memo 175
How to write memos in grounded theory 179
A brief note on the use of computers 180
Key points about memoing 182
Summary 183
Further reading 184
Notes 184

11 **Theoretical Integration and Sorting in Grounded**
Theory **186**
Theoretical integration and sorting 187
Key points about sorting 197
Summary 198
Further reading 199
Note 199

12 **Integrating, Challenging and Contributing to**
the Literature **200**
Why is there a debate about the literature in grounded
theory? 202
How to handle the literature in grounded theory 203
Practical ways to use the literature in grounded theory 205
Key points about integrating the literature 209
Summary 210
Further reading 211
Note 211

13 **Understanding How to Write Theoretically** **212**
Preparing to write: read for structure 213
Avoiding obscure language 214
Writing the research monograph 215

Writing up PhDs   217
Writing journal articles   219
Key points about writing up   220
Summary   221
Further reading   222
Note   222

14 **Rediscovering Formal Theory**   **223**
Generating formal theory   226
Some preliminary conclusions   232
Key points about formal theory   234
Summary   235
Further reading   236
Notes   236

15 **Rediscovering Grounded Theory: Back to the Future**   **237**
The sociological imagination and rediscovering grounded
    theory   238
Can we speak of a 'grounded theory' perspective?   241

Glossary   243
Bibliography   246
Index   254

List of Tables

2-1 The main tenets of grounded theory   42

3-1 The main tenets of constructivist grounded theory   61

List of Figures

4-1   The contrast between definitive and sensitising concepts   72
4-2   Terms associated with 'concepts' in the original iteration
      of grounded theory   74
4-3   Terms associated with 'category' in *Discovery* and
      Theoretical Sensitivity   77

5-1   Coding in *Discovery*   89
5-2   Rules of coding in *Theoretical Sensitivity*   92
5-3   Selecting the core category   94

8-1   The stages of doing grounded theory derived from
      Discovery   137
8-2   The elaborated process of doing grounded theory in
      Theoretical Sensitivity   138
8-3   The basic techniques of doing grounded theory   140
8-4   The process of doing grounded theory   143
8-5   Example of a chart to aid project planning   150

9-1   Example of line-by-line coding in grounded theory   158
9-2   Coding data in the dental lifestyle study: focusing on
      what is being done   159
9-3   Alternative technique for coding data in the dental
      lifestyle study   161
9-4   Scripting and formality in dental clinics   166

14-1 Strategies for developing formal theory   225

List of Boxes

1-1   The link between the comparative method and grounded
      theory   9
1-2   Discontinuities between grounded theory and comparative
      methods in sociology   12

3-1   The main tenets of constructivist grounded theory   47
3-2   Epistemology: constructivism contrasted with objectivism   52
3-3   The problem of universals: essentialism and nominalism   55

6-1   The key elements of theoretical sensitivity   107
6-2   Reading the structure of a grounded theory   114
6-3   Evaluating adherence to the constant comparative method   115

8-1   Typical open questions suitable for doing grounded theory 145
8-2   Questions not suitable for doing grounded theory   146

10-1 An example of a memo from *Discovery*   172
10-2 The experience of memoing in grounded theory   174
10-3 Memo example   175
10-4 What to write memos on in grounded theory   178

11-1 A summary of the analytic 'rules' for sorting in grounded
      theory   190
11-2 Additional questions to consider asking when sorting for
      a PhD thesis   193

12-1 Suggestions for the critical use of the literature in
      grounded theory   207

List of Skills
and Tips

7-1	Data slicing	127
7-2	Theoretical sampling	132
8-1	Asking the right question	146
8-2	Project planning	150
9-1	Open coding	162
9-2	Selecting the core category	164
10-1	Writing memos	180
10-2	Writing conceptually	183
11-1	Planning for sorting	190
11-2	Memoing while sorting	197
12-1	Suggestions for the critical use of the literature in grounded theory	208
12-2	Integrating the literature	210
13-1	Reading for structure	214
13-2	Writing up	220
14-1	Formalising strategies	227
14-2	Moving categories	234

Preface

It is hard to remember, let alone describe, the many conversations that have taken place over the last eight years that have led to the writing and subsequent publication of this book. What we can say is that it all began as a chat in a pub, The Sun and Doves, in Denmark Hill in London. We had been introduced to each other by Hans Thulesius; otherwise the meeting would have been pretty improbable. What became apparent after that initial conversation was that not only did we see different things in grounded theory, but we also had a lot that we needed to learn about how each other saw grounded theory. In some respects the more we began to understand each other's background perspectives the more we began to understand grounded theory. Sometimes we agreed easily, other discussions took longer.

As you can tell, given the length of time over which these conversations have taken place, we have both enjoyed the discussions immensely. This is not least because a large proportion of the conversations took place at key locations around where we both lived and worked. They happened in Lund and Malmö in Sweden in Allegro with Giannis, The Bishops Arms, Malmö Brygghus, Nya Tröls, among others. They also took place in Sheffield in the UK after Barry was appointed as a Lecturer in Medical Sociology at the School of Clinical Dentistry. There we spent time debating and discussing grounded theory in The Bath Hotel, The University Arms, The Hallamshire, The Nottingham House, The Gardiners Rest and The Rising Sun. We could name a few others but we think you can get the idea.

Apart from discovering that we both have a passion for Real Ale, several things happened in these conversations. First, we began to understand that an essential component of the legacy of grounded theory as a method *was its sociological origins*. In some respects, we felt, this legacy has been lost or at the very least underplayed. Our dilemma was that on the one hand the originators promoted grounded theory as a general method, one that could transcend disciplines, but on the other hand grounded theory is also *inherently sociological*. We felt there was a real need to revisit this context. Although in this book we seek to highlight the sociological origins of grounded theory, there is of course a risk that we might compromise its openness. As a consequence, we attempt to make sure we always point to the openness of grounded theory in the book. We would also like to stress that when you learn to see grounded theory as a method that has its roots in sociology, when you fully understand the implications of this, we feel you can do grounded theory better. We hope you can see this as you read the text.

Second, we could see that it can also be situated within the context of philosophy of science in order to clarify its similarities to and differences from other theoretical perspectives. It became very apparent that not only was this view valuable, but it could make grounded theory more accessible and this might definitely enable us to do better grounded theory. Indeed, we believe that if the philosophical assumptions had been clarified from the start, the mess grounded theory now seems to be in could have been avoided. We hope that the philosophical parts of this book will redeem the situation somewhat.

Third, during this time we have both been supervising PhD students attempting to do grounded theory. We have both witnessed just how challenging it can be for some to get to grips with building a theory that goes beyond description. We have both been helping them understand how to conceptualise, how to do constant comparative analysis and also how to engage with theoretical sampling, coding, memoing and, of course, integrating their theory. As our students encountered different problems we would discuss these problems and how to overcome them. We have talked about the parts of our advice that worked and the parts that didn't. From these conversations we began to see what worked in terms of giving advice to students and what didn't. In this respect, a third goal for our book was to enable a way for students to do grounded theory better.

This book would just not have happened if it had not been for the very generous study leave that was granted to both of us from our respective departments, the School of Clinical Dentistry at the University of Sheffield, UK, and the Department of Philosophy at Lund University, Sweden. We are both indebted to these departments for giving us the time to write. We are also indebted to the Department of Sociological Studies at the University of Sheffield for hosting us in the Interdisciplinary Centre of the Social Sciences during our study leave and, in particular, to Allison James for making this happen. Others have taken on teaching and administrative duties on our behalf and this was no small job; indeed we are both very grateful for their support. Erik & Gurli Hultengrens Foundation at Lund University has made it possible for Jan to go to Sheffield regularly, and Jackie Benson deserves thanks for arranging for his stay over the years. Apart from this, there are a number of individuals who need to be mentioned because they have supported us throughout the development of this book. We are indebted to our families, who have had to tolerate significant absences as the book was being written. Our thanks therefore go to Lucy, Alex, Cornelia, Christel, Jazz, Kelly, Nicolas and of course Ingar, who has been ever present throughout these discussions. We are also grateful to a number of others for their support and friendship throughout this project and so we would like to extend our thanks to Dean, Natalie, Sarah, Peter and Werner.

Finally, a few caveats. In writing this book we in no way claim special insight or that somehow our understanding of grounded theory is more authentic or better than anything else that has been written. It simply is what it is. Neither do we wish to participate in a kind of 'tyranny of grounded theory' that argues that only one way is the right way, whether this might be the classical or constructivist form. All we wish to do is to take you through our intellectual journey as a sociologist and a philosopher both encountering the same phenomena. We hope you can see that we have a lot of admiration for the method, for its originators and for those who have been working on it since it was developed. Our intention, then, is to engage constructively and vigorously with these contributors wherever we can with the aim of providing a meaningful and helpful contribution to the grounded theory literature. We hope that you gain something from undertaking this journey with us.

Barry and Jan

1

Introduction

Aim: To explore the context and reasons for rediscovering grounded theory

Learning outcomes

After reading this chapter you should be able to:

- identify and appreciate the need to rediscover grounded theory
- outline and appreciate the sociological context of grounded theory
- have a critical awareness of the need to understand the philosophical context of grounded theory
- develop a clear understanding of the outline and overview of the book

Grounded theory has become one of the most widely applied research methodologies.[1] You will find reference to it in fields as disparate as medicine, education, architecture, marketing, business management, psychology and sociology. This variety of uses is testimony to the success of grounded theory. So what is this widely applied methodology and why should we pay attention to it? Put simply, grounded theory is a method for the generation of theory from data. It is a method that seeks to produce theory that is practical and useful and closely related to the field in which the theory has been developed. It seeks to achieve this by building theory that is 'grounded' in the perspectives of the people who are trying to work in the area being studied as they resolve the problems with which they are confronted.

Grounded theory was developed to try to address what had become an embarrassing 'gap' in sociology in the 1950s and 1960s. This 'gap' was effectively a 'gap' between theory and empirical research. On the one hand, there were sociologists developing 'grand theories' that sought to explain everything in society, but who conducted very little in the way of empirical research. On the other hand, there was a large literature of empirical studies that did not say very much that was theoretical.

Why is theory so important anyway?

Theory is important for several reasons. First, it reduces the complexity of the world as we study it by selecting the most important and relevant aspects of that world and highlighting those in detailed descriptions. Second, it involves specifying how the relevant aspects of the thing being studied relate to each other. Third, because a theory can enable us to know how things in the world are related, it can enable 'predictions' about the world. How theory achieves this can be highly variable and nuanced, depending on the field in which you are working. So, for example, in some fields relationships are described in mathematical formulas; in others these kinds of descriptions will be rare. Fourth, if theory enables us to predict how things are related in the world, it then allows us to intervene in that world to control or change it in some way.

Some fields, public health, for example, are characterised by a desire to change things for the better. Public health scientists often develop theory that reflects their interest to improve the health of whole populations. This goal means that public health professionals have tended to develop research that tests the predictions that they make concerning why certain groups of people in the population get ill or remain healthy. They often use the predictions derived from their view of the world to pressure governments to make changes to society to promote better health. So, for example, they might predict that high levels of alcohol consumption can predispose groups of people to a range of diseases. A whole series of studies might demonstrate that this prediction appears to be correct. Public health scientists have gone further, however; they have also sought to try to change the situation. Some research has tested the prediction that if we increase the price of alcohol by a certain amount that people will tend to consume less. They have subsequently recommended to governments that there should be a minimum price per unit of alcohol. They have been successful in changing government policies to some extent. This kind of theory, when accompanied with accurate predictions borne out by empirical research, can be used as an important political tool.

The kind of theory that results from grounded theory methodology, as we shall see, is not like the kind of theory which you find in public health. Why is this? First, grounded theory is developed with a different purpose in mind. Grounded theory is developed mostly to explain 'what is going on' in a particular field or area of human endeavour. This is a more general starting point than beginning with the desire to improve population health. The kind of theory that public health leads to tends to be developed from the top down; 'deduced', if you like, from a few general ideas. So, for example, one proposition is that people are directly influenced by their environments. A consequence of this proposition is the deduction that the remedy for problems such as the over-consumption of alcohol might be to change the environment in some way. This has been achieved by increasing the minimum price of a unit of alcohol and therefore attempting to price groups of people 'in society' out of over-consumption. Theory that is developed in this way is often developed from outside the situation to which it is applied. In this case, it is developed by a group of professionals who, for the most part, will not be affected *as much* by the results of their research. As a consequence, public health research *often acts against groups* in society in some way *with the goal of being for them in other ways*. After all, the goal of public health research is to promote health.

Grounded theory is not like this. Grounded theory is a perspective on how to build theory that is grounded in the perspective of those in the field. It is problem-focused because it involves studying how people experience and resolve their everyday problems. The theory that is developed through the method is focused on explaining how those problems are resolved. How grounded theory does this is what this book is about.

Why this book?

In recent years there have been a number of new books on grounded theory. Why, then, yet another book on the subject? More specifically, why a book about *rediscovering* grounded theory? What does that mean? Our reasons are as follows. First, some years ago we looked at the state of the discussion about grounded theory. We saw that over time there had been numerous adjustments and changes to grounded theory methodology, and this had led to increased variability and complexity in what grounded theory is. This increasing complexity has had the effect of threatening key aspects of the methodology. It has also frequently masked very different understandings about how to do grounded theory. Some have argued that there are probably as many different versions of grounded theory as there are grounded theorists (Dey 1999). You don't need to look too far to see evidence to support this position. Apart from Barney Glaser's version, which is said to cling to the original ideas, we have Strauss and Corbin's (1990) version, and we have a group of versions belonging to what has become known as the 'second-generation grounded theory'. The most important of these is the 'constructivist grounded theory' of Charmaz (2000, 2006, 2008).

This increasing variability in grounded theory has led to a confusing variety of procedures and 'rules' for doing grounded theory. These rules are not always compatible and can conflict with each other. So, for example, Charmaz (2000) argues that we should be studying and conceptualising meaning. In contrast to this, Anselm Strauss and Juliet Corbin (1990) argue that we should be studying social phenomena, while Barney Glaser says that we should look for core categories and social processes. Someone who reads all of these books might be more confused than enlightened.

There is a third argument for this book. The increasing complexity of grounded theory has tended to mask the fact that the method was developed at a time when there was a debate in sociology in the 1950s and 1960s. This debate has had important consequences for why grounded theory was written the way it is. By rediscovering these debates we can have a much more critical awareness concerning why grounded theory is the way it is. This takes us to a stronger point. As the complexity of grounded theory has increased, different approaches have developed that contradict each other. In some cases today, approaches to grounded theory have, in fact, been deliberately constructed *in opposition to each other*. The question then arises to what extent can we talk of grounded theory in a general sense? It is for this reason in particular that we feel it is important to engage in the process of *rediscovery* that is at the heart of this book. The only way to come to terms with the variability of views on grounded theory, we believe, is to go back to the method in the context in which it was developed because there you have something that is stable. We feel that this approach can be used to enable us to embrace the more recent versions of the methodology.

With this in mind, the purpose of this book is to try to cut through the current debates on grounded theory by seeking out grounded theory in the context in which it was produced. In doing so we will be able to focus on defining what grounded theory is. We feel this is important because it will help to protect a core set of ideas around which variations in approaches to doing grounded theory can be justified. Our position, then, is to encourage methodological pluralism, but at the same time to protect the core identity of a methodology that is clearly valued.

There is more to this book, however. The book has developed out of a long conversation between a philosopher and a sociologist. As you will see, this conversation in itself entails a new kind of *discovery*, a discovery that grounded theory can also be situated within the context of the philosophy of science. This discovery can be conducted in an entirely positive and constructive way, a way that can clarify the similarities and differences between grounded theory and other theoretical perspectives. When these comparisons are made, we begin to see how grounded theory handles important philosophical problems, what is unique about the method and also what remains to be said about it. At all points we have tried to produce an engaging and positive discussion of these issues. It is in no way meant to be comprehensive but, as you will see, there are some very important philosophical discussions that we can have about grounded theory. Our desire is therefore to stimulate further discussion.

Finally, grounded theory is a practical method, a way of generating theory from data. At times this way of doing something is unnecessarily shrouded in mystery. We would like to enable you to discover how to do grounded theory and how to do it well. This is the third aspect of our *rediscovery*. Having gone back through the original texts we wish to take you through what the *rediscovery* of grounded theory means for *doing* grounded theory. Our reasons for thinking that this might be possible are because we feel that a careful analysis of the original texts has produced some surprising findings, all of which we will reveal to you in what follows. As we have indicated above, we have gone beyond this initial analysis and have drawn on the perspective of analytical philosophy to seek out positive statements about what grounded theory is. Part of our *rediscovery*, then, is about bringing you to these statements.

In the next sections we will explore the theoretical contexts of grounded theory. Our goal in this exploration is to highlight that grounded theory developed out of the background of the comparative method as a general method in sociology. In this analysis you will discover the important continuities and discontinuities that exist between grounded theory and comparative sociology. This analysis presents an alternative account of the origins of grounded theory than you will find in the current literature on grounded theory. After doing this, we will go on to consider what this means for grounded theory. The chapter then introduces the philosophical context and shows the important philosophical issues to which grounded theory relates. After this, we provide an outline of the book.

The sociological context

Grounded theory has its origins in sociology. That grounded theory originated from sociology is well known; what is less well known are the specific influences on the method as it was developing. The original text, *The Discovery of Grounded Theory* (Glaser and Strauss 1967; hereafter called *Discovery*), is radical and, at times, polemical. To students who try to read it today it can be daunting and impenetrable. It has a certain style of argumentation that can be difficult to follow. This is especially the case for those unfamiliar with the context in which the book was being produced. This is unfortunate because it means a lot of the debates and arguments within the book will be lost on today's reader. Indeed, there is a strong possibility that the text will obscure more than it reveals. But there is something exciting about the text. There is a real sense that in *Discovery* the authors had hit on something new. You get a feeling that Glaser and Strauss (1967) were mapping out new directions for sociologists that would free them from the domination of the 'theoretical capitalists' of sociology.[2] Not only would grounded theory free the sociologist, we are told it might even promise a new kind of sociology. What we want to do in this book is take you back through these debates to enable you to grasp something of the 'spirit' of grounded theory. This is one of the elements of *Rediscovering Grounded Theory*.

Origins: *Sociologists at Work* and comparative sociology

As we have already said, the original texts of grounded theory – *Discovery* and, in some respects, *Theoretical Sensitivity: Advances in the Methodology of Grounded*

Theory (Glaser 1978; hereafter called *Theoretical Sensitivity*) – were written as a new approach to doing research. They were written *against* something and *towards* something new. To be more specific, *Discovery* was very much written *against a particular form of theory generation in favour of another form of theory generation*. In addition, the text was directed at a particular audience. Understanding this is critical to understanding and discovering what grounded theory is all about.

In our study of the original texts, looking closely at the footnotes and the direction of the writing, we discovered that significant sections of *Discovery* are written both against and beyond various contributions to an edited collection by Philip Hammond, entitled *Sociologists at Work* (Hammond 1964). *Sociologists at Work* is a remarkable text. It was an important landmark in the development of research methods in sociology. This is because it was one of the earliest attempts to describe the processes involved in doing research, with one other text acting as another example (Hanson 1958). Of course, prior to this, sociology did discuss methods. You only need to look at the work of Weber and Durkheim to realise that quite a bit of debate had taken place (Weber 1904/1949a 1904/1949b; Durkheim 1938). The debate to which *Discovery* appears to be directed was a debate happening in North America, supported by Lazarsfeld, Merton, Whyte, Gouldner and Mills (Hammond 1964). Glaser and Strauss (1967) took many of their main points of departure from *Sociologists at Work*. It is important to understand what *Sociologists at Work* was trying to achieve before we can begin to understand grounded theory.

In the introduction to *Sociologists at Work*, Hammond (1964) makes a number of revealing points. We discover that the book was an attempt to explore what was termed the 'logic of discovery' in relation to the 'logic of justification' in social science. We will discuss what this means in more detail in Chapters 2 and 3. The key thing we would like you to realise, then, is that the first book on the grounded theory method, *Discovery*, was not the only book concerned with discovering theory. It was *another* approach that was being suggested at the time. From Hammond's perspective, the process of discovery was 'disorderly', often circumstantial, non-rational *as well as* logical and systematic (Hammond 1964). The nature of this 'disorderly process' meant that often the contributors to the volume were reluctant to specify too much about the process of doing research. Indeed, Hammond stated that it would be 'an error to expect of these essays on the "context of discovery" a set of rules to follow' (Hammond 1964: 13). As you can see, the very idea of *discovering theory* was not new; rather, this idea was part of a broader debate at the time.

Glaser and Strauss's *Discovery* (1967) clearly develops from this general debate. Indeed, the parallels between *Discovery* and *Sociologists at Work* do not stop there. Many of the themes of discussion from *Sociologists at Work* were later developed and extended in grounded theory. For example, in the introduction to the book it was made clear that each of the researchers writing in the volume was also struggling with the distinction between theory and research.

Every research question had some form of structuring idea or preconception, and the distinction between research and theory was problematic. Hammond argued against the view that research involved the classification of facts:

> when, in reality, as science it is concerned with 'evolving conceptual schemes.' Indeed, research by induction is patently not what scientific discovery typically involves but rather what has been called abduction, or 'leading away,' that is 'theorising'. (Hammond 1964: 4)

Many of the problems common to social research to this day form part of the focus of this text. Common problems included the problem of how to deal with huge amounts of data, how to select and integrate data in research and how this process is related to or dominated by pre-existing ideas (Coleman 1964). As you will see, all of these themes became central to grounded theory. Some of the problems were reformulated, others were not. Take the example of Geer, who discovered an 'integrating principle' (Hammond 1964: 5) in her field work. A very similar idea occurs in grounded theory (see Chapter 9). Finally, many of the writers cited in *Sociologists at Work* were grappling with the problem of refining theoretical insights so that they could adequately explain reality (Hammond 1964). The main discussion at the time was that this process was gradual and iterative. There is, of course, a remarkable parallel between this idea and the processes associated with doing grounded theory.

So while many of the problems discussed in *Sociologists at Work* eventually found their way into *Discovery*, a key question is the degree to which *Discovery* either advances or incorporates solutions to these problems. Let us take an example. The concept of 'forcing' can be located in *Sociologists at Work*:

> A common experience, then, of these social researchers is the sense of struggling with data so that conceptual schemes can be imposed. It is this imposition of conceptual order that distinguishes research from cataloguing. And imposing conceptual order is what the thoughtful reader sitting behind a desk is also trying to do. (Hammond 1964: 5–6)

Dalton (1964) went on to discuss this imposition of conceptual schemes at length. He argued that a premature hypothesis can become a real burden by binding 'one's conscience and vanity'. Preconceived ideas about what is happening in the social world can make the researcher selective and blind to what is actually happening. Dalton went on to state that researchers were 'professionally bound to understatement rather than overstatement' (1964: 54). This problem became a central theme in grounded theory, where it is discussed under the theme of 'forcing'. Forcing, as we shall see, is when the researcher imposes their own ideas on to the social world, forcing it to comply with their conceptual schemes about what is happening in the social world.

Several of the contributions to *Sociologists at Work* have become significant *points of departure* for *Discovery*. Of particular relevance to the development of grounded theory appears to be the work of Coleman (1961, 1964), who articulated how his interest in the macro structures of society and, in particular, pluralism developed (Coleman 1961, 1964). His discussion was focused on how sociology had amounted to nothing more than an aggregate psychology rather than a discipline that studied the social system as a thing in its own right (Coleman 1964). In order to overcome this psychological bias he focused on roles and statuses as his 'units of analysis'. His interest was not on individuals (Coleman 1964: 191) but on truly 'social' phenomena. Coleman felt it was possible to separate and identify parts of American society. Nonetheless, the problem he was interested in at the start of his study did not fit the main problems that he discovered in the data and as a consequence he had to switch the focus of his analysis. This is also something that would later become an important theme in *Discovery* where it is discussed that any theory that we develop must 'fit' the data we are analysing. The similarities do not stop there. Coleman stated:

> Suppose that we first identified the major roles and role relations in the system, sampled these, and then obtained data on the types of response made by a person in a given role when faced with a given situation. This might be done quite precisely or quite loosely, but the important point is that the result would be an inventory of contingent responses for each role. (Coleman 1964: 239)

This process of selectively sampling around the 'contingent responses for each role' is remarkably similar to what would later become 'theoretical sampling' in grounded theory (see Chapter 7, Rediscovering Skills for Theoretical Sampling). It was well known that research interests develop both prior to and during research, so this should be expected. Glaser and Strauss (1967) also sought to develop ways to handle 'preconceptions' productively during data analysis. In fact, time and again, if you explore these texts you will find the same problems and concerns that were later to become central to grounded theory. In some instances it appears that these problems were lifted directly from the experiences of these researchers; in others, Glaser and Strauss (1967) were clearly trying to go beyond these experiences and provide some solutions.

Glaser and Strauss (1967) referred directly to Coleman's work when they later discussed the problem of studies that start out with one interest but ended up having to focus on what was in the data. They also relate to Coleman's experience that a preconceived theory can often be irrelevant to the data and changes in one's approach to a study are often necessitated as a consequence. Glaser and Strauss (1967) went on to suggest that their approach, subsequently called the 'constant comparative method', presumably to distinguish it from the 'comparative method', could often be blocked because a researcher got tied to a few pet concepts. Coleman (1964) was, on the one hand, commended for providing a good example of how an interesting and engaging theory can break through 'both preconceived and verificational schemes' (Glaser and Strauss 1967: 187). On the other hand, he was also an example of a researcher who was said to have started out on the right path only for the comparative method to be blocked (Glaser and Strauss 1967).

The extent of the discussion in *Discovery* with the problems described in *Sociologists at Work* does not stop there (Lipset 1964; Udy 1964). One author, Lipset (1964), is discussed in *Discovery* as an example of a researcher who used different 'slices of data'[3] to reflect on the differences between his findings and other theories (Glaser and Strauss 1967: 66, footnote 24). Lipset (1964) described how, in 'Union Democracy', he was interested in challenging the 'iron law of oligarchy'. He had carefully selected the International Typographical Union (ITU) as an important negative case in order to challenge the dominant theory. His inside knowledge of the ITU suggested that it was so different that it could act as a source to challenge many of the existing assumptions of theory on trade unionism. His intuition to explore what worked in one place and not in others was later called a 'deviant case analysis' (Lipset 1964: 99). Glaser and Strauss (1967) would describe such negative comparisons as especially useful for discovering theory and incorporated such techniques into the grounded theory method (Glaser and Strauss 1967: 172).

So far in this chapter we have established that grounded theory was developed out of a response to existing approaches to conducting comparative research at the time. What we have found is summarised in Box 1-1. From this analysis it should be clear that the influence of *Sociologists at Work*, and *comparative methods*[4] in general, on the development of grounded theory is considerable. As we shall see, many of these points of connection were subsequently incorporated into grounded theory. There are also some very important differences and it is to these we will now turn.

Box 1-1

The link between the comparative method and grounded theory

1. The idea and logic of discovery was recognised within comparative methods before grounded theory was developed.
2. The process of discovery was frequently non-rational and not to be subject to rules. This became an important feature of the spirit of grounded theory.
3. Controlling ideas frequently hampered the discovery of new ideas and relationships within the data. In particular, the problem of dominating preconceptions

(Continued)

(Continued)

in research was recognised. An awareness of these problems became central to grounded theory.

4. Prior interests could inform the development of comparative methods and grounded theory. These were to be distinguished from controlling interests because they often acted as starting points rather than controlling ideas.

5. Theoretical sensitivity was first conceptualised in *Sociologists at Work* and was cited as a solution to the problem of forcing. It is a central theme in grounded theory.

6. Abduction or 'leading away' into theory was frequently recognised as an important dimension of comparative research, the idea of leading away from data is a core approach in grounded theory.

7. The idea that we should focus on units of analysis, specifically social units of analysis,[5] can be found in comparative methods and also became central to grounded theory.

8. The exploration of new lines of enquiry *during the study* was a characteristic of the process of doing comparative analysis. This process also became crucial to the process of constant comparative analysis in grounded theory.

9. Obtaining 'slices of data' was part of the comparative method and was incorporated as a practice within grounded theory.

10. Negative cases were used in comparative methods to challenge established hypotheses. The use of such negatives was also said to be useful in grounded theory and negative cases were termed 'deviant cases'.

When it comes to the differences between grounded theory and the comparative method, it is apparent that Glaser and Strauss are responsible for several key innovations (Glaser and Strauss 1967; Glaser 1978). The principal difference appears to be grounded theory's emphasis on generating theory over verifying hypotheses. From the outset (in the preface in fact), Glaser and Strauss (1967) are very clear that this was to be one of their main points (Glaser and Strauss 1967: viii). Take, for example, the following passage, which follows a critical evaluation of the work of Coleman:

This standard, required use of comparative analysis is accomplished early in the presentation of a study for the purpose of getting the ensuing story straight. This use is, of course, subsumed under the purpose of generating theory. However, when the analyst's purpose is only the specifying of a unit of analysis, he stifles his chances for generating to a greater degree than with any other use of comparative analysis. The distinctive empirical elements distinguishing the units of comparison are kept in the level of data, to insure clear understanding of differential definitions. As a consequence, the units' general properties in common, which might occur to the analyst as he compares, are carefully unattended. No ambiguity of similarity, such as a general underlying property pervading all of them, is allowed between the competing units. Comparative analysis, then, is carefully put out of the picture, never to 'disrupt' the monologue again. (Glaser and Strauss 1967: 26)

An important feature of comparative methodology is comparisons between large-scale social units, such as nation states or trade unions. These comparisons were usually made between units that were in the main identical in everything but the key aspects that were being explored. So observations between large-scale units were carefully 'controlled' to test the effects of the absence or presence of certain key characteristics of the unit or organisation. As you can see, this method often had the explicit goal of verifying a few general hypotheses rather than developing theory. But if you look carefully, you can see that Glaser and Strauss (1967) were in fact arguing against the carefully controlled technique of the comparative method. Coleman (1964) was being criticised for not using the comparative method to its fullest extent. In other words, comparisons within the comparative method were neither rigorous nor extensive enough. You can see why Glaser and Strauss then labelled their method 'the *constant* comparative method'. A label designed to emphasise the rigorous application of comparisons throughout the new method of grounded theory.

Another central feature of the break between grounded theory and the earlier form of comparative sociology was the shift in emphasis and direction on how researchers should work on the relationship between ideas and data. Glaser and Strauss's (1967) basic innovation was to relax this relationship. In order to illustrate this point it is worth exploring one of Glaser's examples. In *Theoretical Sensitivity*, Glaser (1978) begins with a comparison between diarrhoea and perfume, which seem at first glance to have nothing in common. But in this comparison he went on to show how both can be related to the more general idea of 'body pollution', one favourable and the other not so favourable, one sought-after the other avoided. For Glaser (1978), the principle of interchangeability brought 'out enriching differences on the same idea'. In this example the comparisons between two highly diverse indicators should not be ignored, 'until thoroughly checked by constant comparative analysis' (Glaser 1978: 33). Comparison in the constant comparative method therefore involved comparisons from different, often diverse examples to new encompassing ideas or categories. In grounded theory, comparisons are not made to test hypothesis; they are exploratory and creative.

In this book you will discover that there are several important consequences of the switch from verification to generation in grounded theory. Glaser and Strauss (1967) were to argue that rather than forcing a few pet ideas on to their data, researchers should discover order and indeed develop their ideas from the data. As you can see, they knew from the work of Dalton (1964) and others that the data in any particular study was hugely variable and that in some ways this should be used positively. The other discontinuities between grounded theory and comparative methods in sociology are outlined in Box 1-2 below.

Box 1-2

Discontinuities between grounded theory and comparative methods in sociology

1. Grounded theory was developed with a different purpose in mind – to generate theory as opposed to verifying hypotheses.
2. Grounded theory seeks to explore general underlying properties across social units of analysis as opposed to carefully delineating differences across units without enough comparison.
3. Grounded theory was extended to permeate the whole of the method. Comparisons were to be made not just between units, as in the more general comparative method, but between data slices and categories within the developing theory (see Chapter 9).
4. In grounded theory the relationship between ideas and data is relaxed and the process of verification becomes subject to the process of induction from the particular to the general.
5. In grounded theory we should avoid forcing pet ideas on to the data and exploring relationships that develop from the analysis of the data – in contrast to the way those in *Sociologists at Work* (Hammond 1964) were working.
6. Grounded theory sees negative cases as examples to be integrated into the theory rather than challenging the theory in some fatal way.

What does the constant comparative method of grounded theory involve?

Before you start to do a grounded theory, it might be worthwhile understanding that grounded theory is a 'building process'. This 'building' happens through the rigorous application of what Glaser and Strauss (1967) called the constant comparative approach. It involves seeking to establish the general nature of various 'facts' to help generalise the emerging theory and establish its boundaries.[6] This happens through a more radical approach to data comparison than previously existed at the time grounded theory was developed. What kinds of comparisons were outlined in the original version of grounded theory? In what follows we will take you through what the constant comparative method *involves* and to do this from the perspective of the original texts.

As we have said the constant comparative method involves a building process from facts to theory. The emphasis in this process is, however, on being open and flexible. So although Glaser and Strauss (1967) indicate that one of the purposes of grounded theory is to establish the generality of 'facts' (i.e. 'does the incest taboo exist in all societies?'), the status of a 'fact' as an 'accurate description'

(Glaser and Strauss 1967: 24) is always open and subject to revision in the light of further evidence. Often what you think is a central 'fact' can later become marginal with further observations. Within grounded theory the relationship between concepts and facts was relaxed, with emphasis being placed on the concept that was in the process of being generated. Throughout the original texts the emphasis is always away from claims of accuracy of data analysis towards exploring the generation of 'conceptual categories' and their properties. We are told, for example, that one case can generate a category, one or two more cases can verify it (Glaser and Strauss 1967: 30). In this sense, the constant comparative analysis was developed with the goal to generate and delimit a theory. More specifically, as part of this overall goal you will find it is the core approach to the generation of categories and their properties in your theory.

The main techniques that you will use when doing grounded theory will be to find similarities in your data and using these to generate statements that can be generalised across different units of analysis (Glaser and Strauss 1967: 26 and 230). The constant comparative method of grounded theory also entails finding groups that are more comparable than incomparable. This is because grounded theory emphasises generating theory that is clearly focused on broad comparisons rather than constrained and exclusive verification (Glaser and Strauss 1967: 51). It is through the broad comparison of groups that grounded theory generates clusters of variables that eventually become the building blocks of a specific theory.

As you can see, grounded theory involves comparing broadly similar observations that can be related in some way to the problem you wish to study. You should expect to be building from careful comparison of observation to observation[7] while developing categories related to these observations. Within this process the analyst is urged to compare different 'data slices'.[8] This process involves writing memos about the data and how these relate to ideas that were to be used as the basis for the emerging theory. This focus – on the play of ideas in the research process – is often overlooked. Indeed, some claims have been made that grounded theory comes to the data *tabula rasa*. Such claims are patently untrue.

The philosophical context

So far we have tried to explain some of the roots of grounded theory by putting it in its original sociological context. But, as was mentioned above, another thing that also needs to be done is to study the philosophical context of grounded theory. The first thing to address is the philosophical situation, especially related to science, during the 1960s. It is well known that philosophy of science was dominated in the twentieth century by a philosophy that goes by the name 'logical positivism'. Logical positivism has its origins in the British empiricist philosophy of the 1600s and 1700s, the sociologist Comte in the early 1800s, and the progress made in the philosophy of language and logic of Frege and Russell at the turn of the twentieth century. It was not until the twentieth century that 'logical positivism' was developed. This happened in Vienna, by a group of philosophers and scientists who met regularly to discuss basic questions in science. The group is often referred to as the 'Vienna Circle'. Their views were influenced in large part by Wittgenstein's *Tractatus*, a strange book written by an enigmatic philosopher (Wittgenstein 2001). The main idea for the members of the Vienna Circle was that there are propositions that lack truth value, that is, they are neither true nor false. Therefore they are, as Wittgenstein puts it, meaningless.

The logical positivists used this idea to find a criterion of demarcation, a criterion that would make it possible to distinguish between science and non-science. The idea is simple. In the sciences, knowledge is constituted by theories which are sets of propositions that are meaningful: they can be true or false. Non-scientific theories, on the other hand, consist of propositions that lack truth value, and therefore are meaningless. That is, they are not false, they are meaningless, which is infinitely worse. What makes propositions meaningful is, according to the logical positivists, their verifiability. This is their principle of verification: a statement is meaningful if, and only if, it can, in principle, be verified by sense experience.[9] From this it follows that much of what was earlier regarded as science really wasn't. Marxism, Freudian psychoanalysis, astrology and the interpretive sciences, were no longer real sciences but 'pseudo-sciences' because you could not have a sense experience to verify the existence of such a thing as the unconscious. The natural sciences, quantitative social sciences and economics, on the other hand, lands on the 'right' side. Psychology, formerly seen as the study of the mental, had to be converted to the study of behaviour, which is a study of something observable.

The principle of verification indicates that the logical positivists were empiricists – knowledge has its foundation in sense experience. But when it comes to scientific methodology, they were rationalists. They argued that it was possible to develop methods that should be used in all the sciences. If this was done, scientific research would be objective, because the researcher would not influence research and make it subjective and arbitrary. The idea is called 'the methodological unity of science'. Research done with other methods was simply not scientific research. Much of the discussion within the Vienna Circle of course concerned the nature of research and there were different views. But the standard view was something like this: studies must begin with observations. Statements that describe such observations are highly verifiable and almost infallible. From these observation statements would then inductively derive a theory, a theory which would then be verified by further observations. That is, from the premise 'All observed A are B' (which are the observation statements) you infer 'All A are B' (which is a general hypotheses), and you verify the conclusion by making more observations. The idea was that when doing research you should make more and more observations, derive more and more theories, and finally it would generate theories describing everything that exists. There were even those who believed that all theories could be combined into one big theory with the help of so-called 'theory-reductions'. Anyway, one would thus ensure that we get a cumulative growth of knowledge: we constantly learn more and more about reality.

The Vienna Circle dissolved in the 1930s because of the looming war. Most of the members travelled to the USA, where they had a huge influence. One of the universities where the positivist influence was strong was Columbia University in New York, and it was there that Glaser received his education and wrote his thesis. An example of the positivist influence can clearly be seen in the Swedish sociologist Hans Zetterberg's *On Theory and Verification in Sociology* from 1954. Zetterberg also worked at Columbia and the book is referenced in Glaser and Strauss's *Discovery*.

The influence of logical positivism would eventually wane, and this would happen in the 1960s, when Glaser was in California and collaborating with Strauss. There are many explanations for why the logical positivism disappeared, and why it disappeared so rapidly: there are, first of all, internal problems with it, for instance with the formulation of the verification principle; there were problems with the inductive argument; there were problems about how to construct physical reality from sense experience; and so on. Second, it was disliked by many because it ruled out much of what is traditionally considered to be scientific work, for example in the human sciences. Also, one cannot ignore the fact that the social situation at the universities in the United States played a role, with its increasingly anti-authoritarian attitude towards the end of the 1960s, which led to regular student uprisings.

In the philosophical context, it is clear that there are two works that influenced the view of science more than others. The first work we think of is Karl Popper's *The Logic of Scientific Discovery*, which was first published in 1934 entitled *Logic der Forschung* but was not translated until 1959 (Popper 1959). Popper (1959) started what was perhaps the most influential department of philosophy of science in Europe, the London School of Economics, and his view is often called critical rationalism. He did not believe in anything the positivists said. He did not believe that induction worked to prove anything important. He did not believe in verification as a demarcation criteria or in verification in general. He did not think science should start by doing observations, and he did not believe there were infallible observation statements. Scientific knowledge does not grow in a cumulative fashion. Instead, he believed that science should grow by scientists making guesses (conjectures, the wilder the better) and then test them by logically deriving test implications. These tests should be efforts to falsify hypotheses, and as long as you do not succeed in doing so, it is corroborated and you should hold it for true. But it should be rejected immediately when a derived test shows that the hypothesis does not hold.

The other work we think of is Thomas Kuhn's *The Structure of Scientific Revolutions* in 1962. Just as Glaser and Strauss, Kuhn was working in California: he had moved to Berkeley University in 1956 and became a full professor there in 1961. His *Structure* is one of the most sold academic books ever, and one that has been cited the most (Kuhn 1962). What Kuhn does is even more radical than what Popper did. Popper believed, after all, in scientific rationality, just as the positivists did: it was just that they had got it wrong. Kuhn believes instead that there can be no ultimate reason for how to work rationally in science. All theories are developed in so-called paradigms and paradigms contain general assumptions about reality and science. The point is that the paradigm provides its own criteria of rationality. One can therefore not use rationality criteria found in one paradigm to criticise another paradigm because they do not accept the criteria. It follows from this, according to Kuhn, that the choice between paradigms cannot be made rationally; it is social, psychological, economic, and political factors that determine how a scientist thinks and what problems they try to solve. This provides immediate opportunity for a scientific pluralism. It need not be that all researchers must work on the same problems and in the same way. Instead there may be research done with different problems and different methods which are conducted simultaneously. Naturally, this had been a possibility earlier also, but only in a small scale. Now there was suddenly a way to show that it is perfectly acceptable to go one's own way and develop one's own methods. This is what Glaser and Strauss did in the 1960s, and they were not alone: Garfinkel, who also was in California, developed ethnomethodology (Garfinkel 1967) and interest in Schütz's lifeworld sociology gained momentum (Schütz 1967). These examples can easily be multiplied. It is difficult to say whether Glaser and Strauss were directly influenced by Kuhn, but they do reference him in *Discovery* (see Glaser and Strauss 1967: 28).

The important thing is that the scientific climate changed in the 1960s. Logical positivism, which said that everyone should work in the same way in all the sciences, was gone. Instead, the possibility to pursue science in many different ways, and in different ways in different disciplines, developed. The strong requirements for verification by observation disappeared, which again allowed for psychological and qualitative studies in sociology. No longer was one, and only one, way to conduct science considered more rational than any other, because each methodology itself contains criteria for rationality. Soon these ideas were radicalised. Anarchist ideas were presented (Feyerabend 1975) and it all led eventually to postmodernism and constructivism. Nonetheless, the perception of science changed in the 1960s and this made the development of grounded theory and other methods possible – although possibly Glaser and Strauss themselves did not study the philosophy of science, they found themselves in a context where these ideas undoubtedly played a role.

What can philosophy do for grounded theory?

The next issue we will discuss is what can philosophy, or rather philosophy of science, do for grounded theory? It is one thing to give an explanation of the conditions that made grounded theory possible, as we did above, but what more can philosophy do? There is something almost paradoxical when it comes to the relation between philosophy and grounded theory. First, the philosophical role in grounded theory has been downgraded, or even eliminated, by the 'classical' grounded theorists,[10] such as Barney Glaser. Classical grounded theorists tend to believe that to start digging in the philosophical assumptions behind grounded theory is a waste of time and effort. You should just get on with your research, and when you do it you will see that the most amazing theories will emerge. If bogged down in philosophical discussions, you will be less productive, less sensitive to what goes on in a social setting, and no theory will emerge. 'Just do it' is the mantra to which the researcher should adhere.

This view has some merit. Thomas Kuhn, in his *Structure* (1962) mentioned above, said very much the same thing. If a researcher pays too much attention to philosophical assumptions lurking in his or her research, he or she will be unproductive. He or she will start to think about philosophical issues and, as is well known, in philosophy there is no certainty, or even consensus, to be found so it will be a long journey. Still, Kuhn accepts that there always are philosophical assumptions behind research – he just does not believe that there is any advantage for the researcher to think about them. He, or she, should just accept them, often tacitly, and go on doing what he or she does best – collecting and analysing data, setting up experiments, and so on. But second, at the same time (and this is what is paradoxical), there are lots of philosophical discussions about grounded theory. In the last couple of years, three books about classical grounded theory have been published and what they say about philosophy is instructive. If we look at the first one, *Glaserian Grounded Theory in Nursing Research* by Artinian, Giske et al. (2009), there is no mention at all of philosophical issues and their possible relevance for grounded theory research. Clearly, they believe that philosophy is not worth knowing about when you do a grounded theory study (Artinian, Giske et al. 2009). No argument for this is provided, however, but the book holds to the Glaserian tradition.

Next, we have Stern and Porr's *Essentials of Accessible Grounded Theory* (2011). Here, in Chapter 2, philosophy is discussed to a large extent. It starts off with a brief table of 'Philosophical trends in science'. On four pages, it contains short descriptions of such 'trends' as 'Modern science' (Galilei and Descartes); Social science (John Locke); Hypothetico-deduction (Newton); Enlightenment (Voltaire); Positivism (Comte). Now, you can always argue with such a short description as the one which can be found in their book, and unfortunately, in this case, most of what is stated in this table is incorrect. But that is not the issue here. What is of interest is the view that such knowledge is of importance to the grounded theorists. But why is it? No argument can be found, it is just claimed that:

...it's important to be aware of the philosophical disputes predating *Discovery of Grounded Theory* because they persist within the social sciences (Bernard 2006) and within most scientific communities. (Stern and Porr 2011: 25)

So, it is important to know about philosophical disputes because they persist. But the reason why it is important to know about these persisting disputes is never explained. What we would like is a clear statement of what difference it would make for the grounded theorist to have a take on these issues. Anyway, it seems that they believe that it is important to know something about science itself, to know the history of science and also about how science has been viewed in different historical periods.

We believe that this indeed would be a good thing, just as Glaser recommends that researchers read about theories in social science, since it will enhance his or her understanding of theoretical issues. Knowledge about the development of the sciences will enhance their understanding of what it means to be doing science. Birks and Mills' *Grounded Theory: a Practical Guide* (Birks and Mills 2011) also has a chapter on philosophy but here the point is different. They believe that since grounded theory is an interpretative methodology, it is important for the researcher to 'discern a personal position'. Explaining what they mean by 'personal position', they refer to Denzin and Lincoln, who state that 'All research is interpretive; it is guided by the researchers set of beliefs and feelings [sic] about the world and how it should be understood and studied' (Denzin and Lincoln 2005: 22). So, it is suggested by Birks and Mills (2011) that we take the following four questions and think about them so that we know where we stand:

1. How do we define our self?
2. What is the nature of reality?
3. What can be the relationship between researcher and participant?
4. How do we know the world, or gain knowledge of it?

These questions are, of course, philosophical in nature, and they are not easy to answer or even to have a clear opinion about. Just to understand them is hard. But the problem here is this: if you do grounded theory the way it was originally thought, then you do not have to think about these questions. Grounded theory was developed as a method that will steer the researcher in the correct direction regardless of how he or she defined him or herself or what they thought about the nature of reality. Questions such as these are important when thinking about differences between different versions of grounded theory, but it is not clear that they will have any relevance once you have decided to use one of those versions. These are complicated questions, and we will have to return to them later in this book.

A fourth suggestion on the relation between philosophy and grounded theory can be found in Alvita Nathaniel's chapter on 'An integrated philosophical framework that fits grounded theory' (Nathaniel 2012). Nathaniel tries to 'propose an extant, integrated, philosophical framework that fits the classic grounded theory method and undergrids its rigorous scientific process' (2012: 187). She then goes on and tries to demonstrate that classic grounded theory is 'highly consistent with' C.S. Peirce's philosophy. Now, we do applaud that Nathaniel stresses the importance of being aware of philosophical frameworks, but, what she does in her paper is clearly dangerous for two reasons. First, there is no mention of Peirce or pragmatism in *Discovery* or *Theoretical Sensitivity* and to infer such a relationship on the fact that in some cases there are similarities is very weak. Indeed, many of the points she makes can be found in many other thinkers' work as well. Related to this is the fact that Nathaniel often says that Glaser and Strauss are influenced by Peirce, but it is very difficult to say anything about Glaser's and Strauss's minds. After all, their text is all you have. Second, a philosophical framework is what lays the foundation for research. You start with a philosophical framework (for instance, views in epistemology and ontology) and then you build your methodology on that. What Nathaniel does is the opposite: she tries to find a philosophy that fits with an already established methodology. But then the philosophy is of no use: it is intended to support the methodology, but it clearly does not if it is chosen just because it fits. We would need independent arguments for the truth of the philosophical framework, and to give that is to enter a highly complicated philosophical discussion. As it is now, the pragmatic framework is pointless.

These are just some of the more recent views about the relationship between philosophy and grounded theory. They are that: (a) there is none; (b) the history of philosophy of science is useful to know about; (c) philosophy can help identify your beliefs and feelings that guide your work; (d) philosophy can be used as a foundation for grounded theory. Regardless of their merit, we have another take on how philosophy can be of service to grounded theory. We think that it has two tasks.

First, many of the issues discussed in *Discovery* and *Theoretical Sensitivity* are philosophical in nature. *They are just not recognised as such.* Not all philosophical discussions are about the immortality of the soul, God's existence, the nature of free will, and how to live a good life. Indeed, those problems cannot be found in those two books. Instead, there are discussions about theory structure, that is, about things such as concepts, categories, properties, hypotheses, about the application of theory, and so on. Questions about the nature of concepts and properties, for example, and their relation to reality are clearly philosophical. They are a priori questions which cannot be solved by doing empirical research and they have been discussed by philosophers since antiquity.

Second, the emergence of different versions of grounded theory mentioned above often has philosophical implications. For instance, the difference between Glaser's 'classic' grounded theory and Charmaz's 'constructivist' grounded theory is foremost philosophical – it concerns the nature and origin of knowledge and the nature of reality and truth. Those differences lead to different methodologies. Therefore, in order to clarify the original version of grounded theory, we must take a closer look at those assumptions and also to some extent see how they differ from all the later versions. The approach we will adopt in this book will be to explore in some detail Charmaz's constructivist grounded theory while seeking to explain why this version has been developed and what is significant about it. This will enable us to demonstrate that methodological pluralism is something we should value in grounded theory, but it also provides us with an important justification for going back and rediscovering grounded theory from within its original context.

Outline of the book

This book is divided into two parts, the first part deals with what grounded theory is and the second part deals with how to do grounded theory. Our reasons for this division are clear. The fact that there are now a wide variety of ways of doing grounded theory means that there is a need to consolidate the core aspects of the method and to clarify these for today's audience. We need to show that this is the case and so we devote time and space in illustrating the variation in approaches to grounded theory in the contemporary literature. Likewise, we devote considerable time to teasing out positive descriptions of the method in the original texts. We then present our analyses of the original texts and at the same time seek to explore the philosophical issues associated with grounded theory. Our goal in this section is to *clarify* grounded theory. We begin this process in Chapter 2 by describing what kind of theory grounded theory is. This is important because you will need to know in advance what it is you are aiming to produce before you begin to do grounded theory. Having outlined the kind of theory you are looking to produce, we then go on to outline how to do grounded theory. The second section of the book is therefore largely practical in its focus.

Chapter 2 explores what a grounded theory should look like by outlining how it is described in the current literature and then explaining what you should expect to see when you develop grounded theory. Chapter 3 explores some of the central debates at the heart of grounded theory and how these relate to the philosophy of science. In this chapter we take one version of grounded theory, Constructivist Grounded Theory, and subject it to some scrutiny. Our reasons for doing this are to be able to demonstrate the importance of understanding that when grounded theory is combined with other approaches it is important to map out any compromises and changes that may need to be considered. We take existing views of constructivist grounded theory and seek to advance the current version of constructivist grounded theory.

Our goal is to demonstrate how grounded theory can be combined with other approaches, but how in doing so it has to be modified. Our position is that if grounded theory is to develop, such methodological pluralism should be encouraged. Nonetheless, we should also seek to preserve grounded theory as it was originally developed. The analysis of Chapter 3 provides an important justification for the rest of the book.

Chapter 4 seeks to disentangle the relationship between conceptualisation and categorisation in grounded theory. It highlights how these two terms are frequently mixed up and confused in the method and explores how the understanding of these terms can be traced back to important continuities and discontinuities with different traditions in sociology. We explore these issues in some depth and seek to clarify the use of the terms within the method. Chapter 5 then picks up the issue of coding in grounded theory. It begins with an exploration of how the term is referred to in the literature and then goes on to explore how coding was developed in *Discovery* and *Theoretical Sensitivity*. In particular, we explore specifically how grounded theory broke with the traditions of Blumer and Lazarsfeld and how specific procedures were developed for doing coding in grounded theory that were based on the techniques that were found useful when the method was being taught to graduate students. We point out the centrality of different positions on coding to current debates in grounded theory and hopefully clarify the reasons why these differences exist.

The second part of the book begins with an exploration of theoretical sensitivity as a central skill and attitude to grounded theory. It then goes on to outline and explore the nature of theoretical sensitivity in grounded theory. We seek to enable readers to be able to develop a greater awareness of the importance of this skill in doing grounded theory. In Chapter 7 we explore the important factors you will need to consider when sampling in grounded theory. This involves developing your ability to engage in something that was originally called 'data slicing' while relating this to the processes associated with sampling and theory development. In Chapter 8 we go on to provide you with an overview of the process of doing grounded theory. The goal behind this chapter is to prepare your expectations of what the overall process of grounded theory should look like to enable you to plan how to do your grounded theory study. The chapter makes an important distinction between the stages and techniques of grounded theory and outlines how the various techniques for doing grounded theory are distributed throughout the process. It then provides an overview of what each stage in the process of grounded theory might look like. It is important to note, however, that this process will vary considerably from theory to theory. Chapter 9 then picks up two central phases in grounded theory, the open coding and selective coding phases. In the discussion of open coding, we begin with a discussion of 'what is data?' and how the answer to this question might vary considerably. We then discuss the issue of coding line by line and in broader chunks or incidents and illustrate how different comparisons can generate different kinds of categories for your theory. Different techniques for generating categories that go beyond simple description are outlined. Central to this chapter is the use of comparisons and 'data slicing', which has become something of a lost art in grounded theory. We then go on to outline when you should finish open coding and move on to selective coding and choosing the core category.

In Chapter 10 we discuss the issue of writing theoretical memos. Theoretical memo writing is central to grounded theory. Without doing this, you are not doing grounded theory. It is a difficult skill to develop but it is at the heart of the method. We provide an explanation of when to memo and what to memo when doing grounded theory and give a list of things to think about that might enable you to reflect on what subjects you should be memoing on in grounded theory. We then go on to discuss the writing phase of grounded theory. This involves a discussion in Chapter 11 of the importance of theoretical sorting as a technique that can help you prepare parts of your grounded theory for a range of presentations. In this chapter we go through an analysis of the original texts, rediscover and present many of the hidden guidelines of sorting. This chapter then discusses how you might plan for sorting in advance so that you might be able to anticipate some of the problems you experience. It also includes a discussion of how these might be overcome in a range of different ways. In Chapter 12 we take many of the ideas about sorting forward into the controversial issue of how to handle the literature in grounded theory. In this chapter we discuss what has become something of a controversy in grounded theory, including why there is a debate about the literature. Having discussed these issues, we explain how you might engage with the literature in numerous ways when developing your grounded theory. Once again our goal is to prepare your expectations and enable you to develop a critical approach to the literature.

Having explored the process of doing a single grounded theory study, we then move on to consider the importance of thinking about formal theory in Chapter 14. Once more, we rediscover another important aspect of grounded theory that was originally intended to be a central goal of the methodology but which has fallen out of use as the method has been revised over time. In this chapter we explain the centrality of formal theory to grounded theory as a way of thinking about the world. We then take time to provide you with a series of practical strategies to enable you to do formal grounded theory. We hope, as you explore this chapter, that you will begin to see the importance of integrating formal theorising into your thinking throughout the grounded theory process. Finally, in Chapter 15 we outline some preliminary conclusions about what we think we have rediscovered about grounded theory.

Summary

This chapter took as its starting point what grounded theory is and why we felt this book was necessary. The chapter then proceeded to outline two key contexts for grounded theory, the sociological and philosophical. In the section on the sociological context of grounded theory, the chapter located key ideas that became central to grounded theory in a previous text by Hammond called *Sociologists at Work* (1964). Here we discovered that ideas such as the logic of discovery, theoretical sensitivity, data slicing, the problems associated with controlling ideas, prior interests and preconceptions pre-existed grounded theory. Important breaks with previous traditions were also explored. So, for example, the way comparisons were made between 'units' of analysis when generating theory was developed quite differently in grounded theory. The chapter then went on to outline the philosophical context of grounded theory. Here we discovered that grounded theory developed when logical positivism had collapsed, and the resulting vacuum enabled methodological pluralism to be developed in the 1960s. Grounded theory was one part of the emergence of this pluralism. While some of the language addresses positivism as its context, we have pointed out that it would be a mistake to say grounded theory was positivist as a consequence. The chapter then discussed what philosophy can do for grounded theory by reviewing the range of arguments for and against having a philosophical view of grounded theory. It then ended with a summary of the book.

Further reading

Chalmers, A.F. (1976) *What is This Thing Called Science?* Brisbane: University of Queensland Press.

Glaser, B. and Strauss, A. (1967) 'The discovery of grounded theory', Chapter 1 in B. Glaser and A. Strauss, *The Discovery of Grounded Theory*. Chicago: Aldine.

Hammond, P. (1964) 'Introduction', in P. Hammond (ed.), *Sociologists at Work: The Craft of Social Research*. London and New York: Basic Books.

Okasha, S. (2002) *Philosophy of Science: A Very Short Introduction*. Oxford: Oxford University Press.

Notes

1 It is important to keep in mind the distinction between 'resultant grounded theory', which is the theory you end up with, and 'grounded theory method', which refers to the use of different sets of procedures and techniques to produce a grounded theory, and 'grounded theory methodology', which is used when we

refer to the logic for the method. Often the context makes it clear what is meant by just 'grounded theory', but when there is the possibility of misunderstanding we try to make the intended meaning explicit.

2   Time and again they refer to different individuals but in particular they appear to be reacting against the authority of writers such as Parsons and Merton.

3   We will discuss the role of 'slices of data' in grounded theory later in the book. Please see the heading 'Slices of data: data analysis for the generation of theory' on page 125.

4   Very few authors have pointed out the obvious link between grounded theory and comparative sociology. Indeed, it seems that in some very important ways grounded theory is a break from comparative sociology. This break can be seen as both positive and negative. It can also perhaps explain why Dey (1999), who was reading grounded theory from the perspective of a comparative sociologist, might have been reacting the way he did.

5   A very important legacy of grounded theory is its sociological heritage. Part of this heritage involves an interest in social units. Throughout this book we will return to this idea. For now social units are defined as any unit where groups of people interact for a particular purpose. There are many types of social units; they can be organisational, bureaucratic, subversive, informal, familial and so on. Sampling social units to enable data collection and analysis seems to have been lost as part of the grounded theory process.

6   They state: 'Our goal of generating theory also subsumes this establishing of empirical generalisations, for the generalisations not only help delimit a grounded theory's boundaries of applicability; more important, they help us broaden the theory so that it is more generally applicable and has greater explanatory and predictive power. By comparing where the facts are similar or different, we can generate properties of categories that increase the categories' generality and explanatory power.' (Glaser and Strauss 1967: 24)

7   In grounded theory the comparisons are made from 'incident to incident', but we will develop this in more detail later in the book.

8   As we have seen, this sensitivity was related to their reading of Lipset (1964).

9   It is worth noticing that this means that logical positivism is not a realistic position, contrary to what many social scientists believe. The reason is simple: realism says that something exists independently of sense experience, but how can you verify something like that with sense experiences?

10 We use the term to refer to the group of people who believe that we should preserve grounded theory as it was developed in the 1960s.

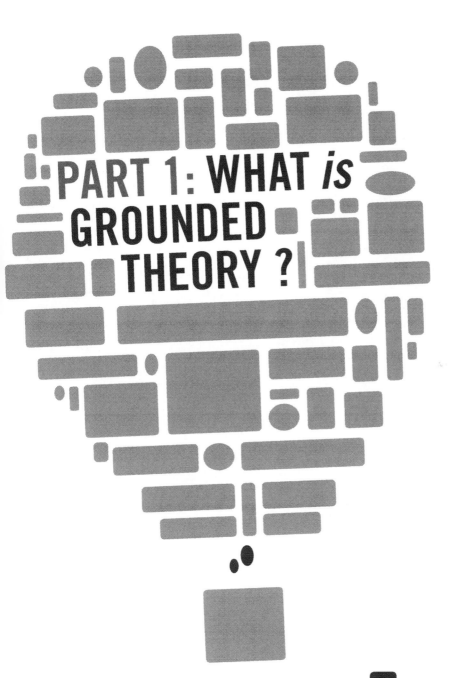

PART 1: WHAT *is* GROUNDED THEORY ?

2

What Kind of Theory is Grounded Theory?

Aim: To review and analyse what we mean by 'theory' in grounded theory

Learning outcomes

After reading this chapter you should be able to:

- criticise and evaluate current views on what grounded theory is
- be aware of the existing views on what a grounded theory should look like
- detail the core aspects of grounded theory in relation to its openness, explanatory power, the contrast between generation and justification, theory structure and research process

This chapter is about an interesting puzzle. This puzzle is that there is not a lot of information in *Discovery* and *Theoretical Sensitivity* on *what a grounded theory should look like* (Glaser and Strauss 1967; Glaser 1978). If we don't know what a grounded theory should look like, how can we discuss *what kind of theory grounded theory is*? There are a number of possible reasons for this. First, as we have seen, Glaser and Strauss (1967) were writing for a particular audience. That audience appeared to be familiar with what theory was and so it might have been possible that, because of the context in which grounded theory was written, there was no need to clarify what a grounded theory should look like. Second, as we have also seen, grounded theory was presented *as a new approach to doing theory*. So, for example, throughout the book Glaser and Strauss (1967) indicated that they were writing in opposition to 'verificational studies'. Grounded theory, then, was primarily described *as a process of doing something*. Less was said about what the outcome of this process should look like. Third, it is quite clear on reading *Discovery* that Glaser and Strauss (1967) were constantly at pains to avoid foreclosing alternative ways of generating grounded theory. Throughout *Discovery* they indicated that the project of grounded theory was just the beginning and that other ways of generating theory may be found and described. This and more can be gleaned from the beginning of *Discovery*.

> ...we offer this book, which we conceive as a beginning venture in the development of improved methods for discovering grounded theory. Because this is only a beginning, we shall often state positions, counter positions and examples, rather than offering clear-cut procedures and definitions, because at many points we believe our slight knowledge makes any formulation premature. A major strategy that we shall emphasize for furthering the discovery of grounded theory is a general method of comparative analysis. This puzzle is not the same as not knowing what your theory will be about. That is a different problem and one that is very well covered in grounded theory. (Glaser and Strauss 1967: 1)

Apart from the cautious humility of this quotation, you can see that grounded theory was meant to be a general method. *Discovery*, as a text, was only meant to describe Glaser and Strauss's starting position, and it was deemed 'premature' to be providing a definitive description of what grounded theory was at that time.[1] Finally, it is very clear that Glaser and Strauss (1967) were seeking to set grounded theory in opposition to other approaches. An important consequence of this is that within *Discovery* there would never be a set of clearly defined 'procedures and definitions'; the book is part argument, part presentation of their approach rather than what they perceive as the outcome of the approach. Understanding this is fundamental to getting to grips with the original texts and what they were saying.

All of this presents those new to grounded theory with a significant set of intriguing problems. Where am I going? What should I be aiming for? What is a grounded theory and if I am to produce a grounded theory what should it look like? Despite these questions much is promised in this approach. You get the freedom and ability to generate your own theory and do not have to remain enthralled to the grand theory of others. For many today, this might seem moot. After all, we have had over four decades of grounded theory and there have been many innovations in the method. Other research areas have moved on as well. The social sciences as a whole have had the crisis of representation, and have witnessed the increasing importance of post-structuralism. Medical science has also had its changes, with the development of evidence-based medicine with its emphasis on evaluation. It seems that

Discovery, as a book, represented the first tentative steps towards the development of a new method for generating theory from data. It was just a beginning. It was written as part of a debate in social science. As a consequence, the book is full of positions and counter-positions. It can be difficult to decipher the positive statements of the new method from the background debates. Nonetheless, it makes for highly rewarding reading as part of these debates.

every era has dominant approaches; this was no less true at the time when *Discovery*[1] was written.

When *Discovery* was produced, it was clear that the authors were excited by what they had found and were seeking to encourage readers to produce their own theory. The fact they were suggesting that authors could engage in producing their own theory indicates the high esteem that theory had at the time. In some respects, theory remains important in some fields but less important in others. Yet grounded theory did something that previous ways of doing theory did not. We feel that it opened up theory to a whole new generation of researchers and perhaps even opened up the possibility of doing theory to new areas of enquiry. The significance of grounded theory in successfully doing this remains today. In this chapter we aim to explore what a grounded theory should look like, and to explain the significance of understanding this question so that you have a good sense of what it is you should be trying to achieve before you start the process of doing grounded theory.

This is an important question for several reasons. It is important because anyone seeking to do a grounded theory should really know before they start what they are seeking to achieve. You need to have an overall sense of where you are going. This question is also important because grounded theory has become such a widely used approach. Indeed, aspects of it can be found in many qualitative studies. Since the influence of grounded theory has been so extensive, you will need to be able to identify ways to explore to what extent the method has been used or to what extent it has been compromised or modified and for what reasons. While the question of what a grounded theory should look like is an important question, there is no direct or obvious answer to it. Take, for example, *Discovery*, where Glaser and Strauss (1967) stated:

> The constant comparative method can yield either discussional or propositional theory. The analyst may wish to cover many properties of a category in his discussion or to write formal propositions about a category. (Glaser and Strauss 1967: 115)

But what does it mean to have a 'discussional' or a 'propositional' theory? They continue:

> The former type of presentation is often sufficiently useful at the exploratory stage of theory development, and can easily be translated into propositions by the reader if he [sic] requires a formal hypothesis. For example, two related categories of dying are the patient's social loss and the amount of attention he receives from nurses. This can easily be restated as a proposition: patients considered a high social loss, as compared with those considered a low social loss, will tend to receive more attention from nurses. (Glaser and Strauss 1967: 115)

Are these approaches simply different ways of presenting theory? Or are there different types of theory? What are the consequences for doing grounded theory? We are interested in answering these questions here and we are also interested in exploring if someone doing grounded theory can do better grounded theory knowing what it is they are seeking to achieve. These are the main questions behind this chapter. There are no obvious answers to these questions but we hope that by reading this chapter anyone seeking to do grounded theory may be enabled to start the process with a good idea of where they are going.

| Critical reflection 1 |

What is grounded theory?

Before reading any further in this chapter, take time to write down some brief notes[2] on the following questions:

- What do you understand by the word 'theory'?
- What is your understanding of the term 'grounded theory'?

Existing views on what a grounded theory should look like

Knowing what a grounded theory should look like is important because it is central to establishing the degree to which your own work can be called grounded theory. This issue has become central to recent debates within grounded theory. You will often find that a published article will claim that it is a grounded theory when, in fact, it has few of the characteristics that would recommend it as a grounded theory. This is a problem that the main commentators on the method agree with (Dey 1999; Charmaz 2000, 2006; Birks and Mills 2011). Glaser and Holton (2004) called this the 'remodelling' of grounded theory; others have called it 'method slurring' (Baker, Wuest et al. 1992; Glaser and Holton 2004). The problem is, of course, that any method should evolve. After all, the standards and criteria by which we evaluate other scientific methods are constantly changing. Grounded theory is no exception to this process (Yuen and Richards 1994; Annells 1996; Dey 1999; Bryant 2003; Bryant and Charmaz 2007; Denzin 2007; Lempert 2007; Reichertz 2007; Birks and Mills 2011). Adjustments and changes to all research methods are a sign that a particular field is characterised by lively debate and healthy evolution. These debates in grounded theory have certainly been lively. There is the by now infamous 'falling out' between Glaser and Strauss over the publication of *Basics of Qualitative Research* (Strauss and Corbin 1990). Others have gone on to develop their own versions of grounded theory, the most famous of which appears to be the 'Constructivist Grounded Theory' of Charmaz (Charmaz and Mitchell 1996; Charmaz 2000, 2006, 2008; Glaser 2002; Bryant and Charmaz 2007). This can make the task of understanding what a grounded theory should look like more complicated. Let us take a few brief examples.

What do you think a grounded theory should look like?

One recent iteration of grounded theory is produced by Melanie Birks and Jane Mills (2011) in their book *Grounded Theory: A Practical Guide*. In this book, Birks and Mills describe theory as 'an explanatory scheme comprising of a set of concepts related to each other through logical patterns of connectivity' (Birks and Mills 2011: 113). For them, overarching explanatory schemes are central to what a grounded theory should look like. Indeed, because such schemes lead to a high level of abstraction and integration, this is an important feature of grounded theory. We are also told that the theory must have something called a 'core category' and its major categories must be 'theoretically saturated'. We will go into more detail on the nature of these later in the book. While Birks and Mills (2011) provide lots of examples of how to go about doing grounded theory, they provide few other guidelines on what the theory should look like other than these positive statements. It is very much left up to the reader to decide what a grounded theory's core features should be. It seems that in the same way that grounded theory was originally produced against a background debate within sociology, others also bring to the method particular readings and interpretations. Such 'readings' often highlight different aspects of grounded theory and this can often be quite confusing.

Another form of revisiting and reinterpretation of grounded theory is to focus on the status of grounded theory as a form of knowledge production. A great example of this is without doubt the work of Charmaz (2000, 2006) and others, who have argued for a 'constructivist' turn in grounded theory (Bryant 2003). In these examples grounded theory is often first *recon*-structed as 'objectivist' and then *re*constructed as 'constructivist'. Many of the arguments that are used to sustain this approach are often made without much reference to the original texts. Many of the criticisms of grounded theory are imputed to grounded theory. So, for example, you will discover a new version of grounded theory called 'objectivist' grounded theory. Charmaz (2000, 2006) makes the following claims about this version. She claims that:

- it resides in the positivist tradition and is therefore objectivist (Charmaz 2000: 510; Charmaz 2006: 131)
- it 'erases the social context from which data emerge' (Charmaz 2006: 131)
- it erases 'the influence of the researcher' and
- it often erases 'the interactions between grounded theorists and their research participants' (Charmaz 2006: 131)
- it assumes an external reality waiting to be discovered (Charmaz 2006: 131)

This approach to grounded theory constructs it *as a form of positivism* and has been further reinforced by a historical reconstruction of the development of the method. Bryant and Charmaz (2007), while exploring the background of Glaser and Strauss's work, sought to trace how their respective influences impacted on the grounded theory project. Of particular note was the fact that Glaser and Strauss apparently gave grounded theory a 'positivist, objectivist direction' (Bryant and Charmaz 2007: 33) and that they did so because they were seeking to establish the credentials of grounded theory in opposition to a largely quantitative tradition at the time (Bryant and Charmaz 2007). They also stated that the 'early position (*of Grounded Theory*) can be interpreted as justification for what they called a naïve, "realist" form of positivism, which holds that the veracity of theory can be determined simply by recourse to "the data"' (Bryant and Charmaz 2007: 33). Their whole argument seems to rest on the fact that Glaser and Strauss (1967) had a relatively unproblematic stance with respect to 'the data'. They do not acknowledge that perhaps the language Glaser and Strauss (1967) used was in fact addressing debates within research at the time and therefore in some respects reflected the views of the audience they were addressing. We shall return to this point time and again throughout this book. Needless to say, if you turn to this account of grounded theory, you will not find a detailed description of *what a grounded theory should look like*.

As you can tell, a central argument of ours is that very few interpretations of grounded theory can be seen as directly embedded in an analysis of the original texts. The only exception we could find was the work of Dey (1999), which presents itself as a sustained and careful critique of the original texts. Although here Dey (1999) was so concerned with building a sustained critique of grounded theory that you will struggle to find a comprehensive definition of *what a grounded theory should look like*. Dey (1999) begins his analysis by asking the expansive question 'what is grounded theory?' He then gives a reiteration of Cresswell's (1998) description of what grounded theory is before moving on to describe what grounded theory is in terms of how to do grounded theory (Creswell 1998; Dey 1999). These are all very engaging debates and discussions but they do not really help us to see *what a grounded theory should look like*.

The core aspects of grounded theory

We would argue that both strong and weak versions of the method can be identified. We take Glaser and Strauss's (1967) view and Glaser's (1978) perspective to represent the strong position. In doing so we will avoid the 'objectivist' label that Charmaz and others have used. We do this not to discount their position but to hold that issue as an open question. We believe that the five points discussed below represent some of the core tenets of grounded theory. We feel that by elucidating these points we will be better able to see the relation between grounded theory as it was originally intended and constructivist versions of grounded theory. The first point concerns the openness of the grounded theory method, the second, explanatory power, the third, the difference between generation and justification, the fourth, theory structure, and the fifth and last, the research process. These points overlap to some degree but it is still fruitful to look at them separately.

The openness of grounded theory

The grounded theory methodology is characterised by its openness. There are many aspects to this openness, but the main point is that the researcher shall not make use of preconceived concepts or ideas. Indeed, this idea was the major inspiration for Glaser and Strauss (1967): to enable researchers to escape from the ideas developed by grand theorists such as Marx, Weber, Durkheim and, of course, Parsons, whose 'structural functionalism' was predominant at the time. Glaser and Strauss discussed this in the section on 'Verification and Grand Theory' in a passage which discusses the grand forefathers of sociology (Weber, Durkheim, Simmel, Marx, Veblen, Cooley, Mead, Park, and so on). They indicate that only a few sociologists have since then managed to generate their own theories (Parsons and Merton). But what they had done had its flaws:

> But even these few have lacked methods for generating theory from data, or at any rate have not written about their methods. They have played 'theoretical capitalist' to the mass of 'proletariat' testers by training young sociologists to test their teachers' work but not to imitate it. (Glaser and Strauss 1967: 11)

As we have seen, grounded theory was in part a reaction against simply applying preconceived theory. If preconceived concepts were used in the method, this would constitute 'forcing', which would have been against the basic idea in grounded theory that concepts and hypotheses should emerge from the observation of 'data'. The formulation of the research question, then, is usually based on a social 'unit' of analysis. So, for example, in *Awareness of Dying* (Glaser and Strauss 1965; hereafter called *Awareness*), hospital wards were analysed as units specifically to see what was happening around people who were dying. That is not to say that individuals cannot be used for a grounded theory. Glaser and Strauss clearly stated in *Discovery* that individuals, as social units, could also be used as the basis for a grounded theory, but more importantly, so could 'social roles' and indeed school classrooms. It is a sad fact that since then the vast bulk of grounded theory, for example in medical disciplines, has been conducted on individuals as the unit of analysis and that the original inspiration to study 'social units' has gone.

In weaker versions of grounded theory it is not uncommon for research questions to be put like this: 'How does group G experience/perceive/understand

S?', where 'S' is a social phenomenon. For instance, Strauss and Corbin stated that the 'research question in a grounded theory study is a statement that identifies the phenomenon to be studied' (Strauss and Corbin 1990: 31). For example, Charmaz's research question in her book from 1991, sought to explore 'how chronicity affects ill people's self-concepts' (Charmaz 1991a). If the research question is put like this, two things are presupposed: that there is an identifiable group of people to be studied, and that the phenomena the study is to focus on, in this case 'self-concepts', is relevant in some way to that group. We should also note that the idea of drawing on social units *was only a starting point*. The mantra of Glaser and Strauss (1967) was always to be open and flexible in developing the theory. By limiting the unit of analysis to specific phenomena and individuals as social units, the consequence will be to compromise the openness of grounded theory. How the unit to be studied was to be delineated, and what phenomena to study, must emerge during research and must be grounded in the observation of data.

> The openness of grounded theory is designed to protect the theory-building process from becoming preconceived and forced. Grounded theory in its basic form just specifies a phenomenon and a location in which it exists and then begins to study that phenomenon. This does not mean that the researcher starts with no preconceptions.

To identify groups and phenomena from the start is of course possible in social research; it is often done, for instance, in phenomenological research. To do so, however, clashes with the original idea in grounded theory that everything from the research question to the concepts to be used in the theory should emerge from observation of data. It is important to be more specific. In *Discovery* it is stated that:

> The initial decisions for theoretical collection of data are based only on a general sociological perspective and on a general subject or problem area (such as how confidence men handle prospective marks ...). The initial decisions are not based on a preconceived theoretical framework. (Glaser and Strauss 1967: 45)

The idea is for the researcher to start off with a partial 'framework' of 'local' concepts. These are used to very loosely explore the 'structure' and 'processes' in the situations to be studied. In *Discovery*, Glaser and Strauss go on to use an example taken from their study of hospital wards, where they knew they would see doctors, nurses, patients, aides, wards and admission procedures. These concepts gave them a good start in the research process and had the effect of making sure that their theory was going to be developed from what was happening in the setting. By being open, they were also able to discover that a doctor could be called a 'therapist' and not a doctor under certain circumstances. As the researcher observed the setting, a distinction was made between local concepts and the theoretical repertoire which was developed from the professional background of the researcher. These theoretical repertoires were used as a resource to help fit appropriate categories to what was happening in the hospital wards.

If the research question is open in grounded theory, so is data collection and analysis. With respect to data collection, the mantra is that 'all is data', Glaser proclaims (Glaser 1978; see also Glaser and Strauss 1967), and this not only means that everything can be used as data, but that everything should be used as data. It is an imperative: do not exclude anything beforehand! The researcher is to collect data as diverse as possible, or their preconceived notions will make them see only what they already believe is relevant. This openness cascades throughout the research process. The implication is that the researcher should use a wide variety of sources of information. The researcher should not focus on what he or she is interested in but on what interests can be found in the area. Those interests are the concerns of participants and should not be prejudged. The collection of data is characterised by openness in two ways. Openness to the way participants see the main problem they are confronted with and openness to the relevance of local and professional theoretical constructs. This is called 'theoretical sensitivity' (see Chapter 6, 'How to Develop Theoretical Sensitivity') and was the subject of Glaser's later book on the method (Glaser 1978). Failing to remain open during data collection and analysis may well lead to the generation of a theory that has not emerged from the data but from applying ideas to the data. A consequence of this might be to generate a theory that will not work because it is irrelevant to the problems that are the main concerns of those in the setting.

QUESTION

The claim that grounded theory begins with as few preconceived notions as possible doesn't mean there are no assumptions about social reality. What do you think are the basic assumptions of grounded theory about social reality?

Openness has sometimes been misunderstood. It has, for instance, been suggested that such openness is impossible because no researcher can start off with an 'empty head'. Nothing like that was suggested in grounded theory. The opposite is in fact the case. The distinction we are looking at here is the distinction between *using preconceived notions* and *having preconceived notions*. Doing research without having preconceived notions is of course impossible. We all view the world in a certain way, and as soon as we have read some relevant books or have done similar previous research, that will give us a set of scientific notions. Glaser is quite clear about this. Indeed, he claims that it is important for researchers to be well-read in the literature on social theories, since this will help him or her to find what is relevant.

The point, then, is not to force our notions when data is collected and analysed. It is in some way like the *epoché* of the phenomenological method: preconceived notions should be bracketed. The method to do this is different, however. Researchers using the phenomenological method are to identify those notions, and make sure that they do not contaminate the pure description of a phenomenon. In grounded theory this is accomplished by the use of line-by-line coding and avoiding reading the literature on the area. Doing this will make the researcher open to words or phrases that indicate concepts that will be used in the resulting theory. Indeed, as we have said the term 'theoretical sensitivity' means that the researcher should be aware of the different theoretical codes that could be used to explain what is happening in the field and, more generally, they should also know what a theoretical code is (see Glaser and Strauss 1967: 46–47). This makes the researcher sensitive to known codes so that he or she recognises them when data is analysed. It also makes it possible for him or her to generate new ways of organising their data.

The explanatory power of grounded theory

A theory generated with the grounded theory method must work. This means that the resultant theory must be capable of explaining how the concerns of those in the area are resolved. In *Discovery*, Glaser and Strauss discuss the relationship between categories and their properties using the example of nursing care, which has two categories – 'professional composure' and 'perceptions of social loss' – of a patient who is dying. 'Perceptions of social loss' are said to explain nurses' 'view of what degree of loss his death will be to his family and occupation' (Glaser and Strauss 1967: 36). So the category explains their views. However, the situation is more complicated. A property of the category of social loss described above is 'loss rationales' and these are 'the rationales that the nurses use to justify their perceptions of social loss' (Glaser and Strauss 1967: 36). So the nurses' concerns are composed of a conglomeration of perceptions (their views), rationales and justifications. The theory of dying is then about how these different perceptions and views interact.

Grounded theory seeks to explain how social phenomena are organised. Its basic tasks are to discover what the relevant social phenomena are within a problem area and then to specify the relationships between the relevant social phenomena. It therefore presupposes two basic things about the social world. That the social world is organised around the problems people experience and that this organisation can be discovered and conceptualised.

A grounded theory is about the multitude of things that interact in a field of enquiry. Of course this means that the grounded theory method differs from phenomenology and hermeneutics. Grounded theory seeks to answer the question 'what is going on in this area?' This brings us to another feature of grounded theory, which involves describing the core category and how it varies. The core category is said to be related to the core concern(s) of those in the area and how these are resolved or organised. It cannot be assumed from the start. If it is taken for granted, we may be mistaken and the theory may not work. We will return to this point below.

Generation versus justification and grounded theory

The grounded theory method is a method that describes the process of systematically generating theories from data, and it must therefore be distinguished from methods used to justify theories. This goes back to the distinction between what Popper refers to as the 'context of discovery' and the 'context of justification' (Popper 1959). The context of discovery concerns how to develop a theory. There are different schools concerned with how to do this. One school, often associated with logical positivism, says that we are to proceed inductively. That is, we shall collect data as neutrally as possible, and then systematically analyse the data in order to find relationships between types of data. We are then to generalise those relations within a theory. This contrasts with Popper's critical rationalism, where it is claimed that it really does not matter how we come up with a theory. We can either find it by analysing data, or it may just be an ingenious creative idea, or even a bold conjecture. Indeed, the bolder the conjecture, according to Popper, the better.

Justification, on the other hand, concerns our reasons for believing that the theory is true and what we do to provide an argument for it. In this instance, there are different schools of thinking. According to verificationalism, we verify the theory by collecting more data that supports it. The argument will then be inductive and look like this: All known As are Bs: Therefore all As are Bs. In order to strengthen this inductive argument you are to make observations in different circumstances, make many observations, and no negative cases are to be found. According to the hypothetico-deductive method, on the other hand, you shall logically deduce consequences from the theory and see whether they occur. The argument will appear as follows: If theory T is true, observations O should occur in situation S, observations O did occur in situation S, therefore theory T is confirmed. If they had not occurred, the theory is falsified. We can test the theory that 'A causes B' by creating a situation where A is present and see whether B occurs. Indeed, according to strong versions of the hypothetico-deductive method, we are supposed to try to find situations where B does not occur despite the presence of A, that is, we should try to falsify the theory. This is, of course, the cornerstone of Popper's falsificationalism (Popper 1970).

> Grounded theory belongs to that part of science that is concerned with discovery of theory. Rather than dreaming up a theory or building a theory out of logical reason, it involves working out a theory that is 'grounded' on the perspective of those in the field. Since social phenomena behave differently from objects in the real world, being much more open and flexible, there is a need for a method that is also open and flexible in order to study them.

Think about the area you are working in. Is there a deficiency of theory? Why might there be a need for a 'grounded theory'?

In the philosophy of science there is a clear distinction between discovery and justification. You first discover a theory either by guessing or, alternatively, by analysing data inductively. Then you justify the theory either by verifying it inductively or confirming it by deducing observable consequences. These methods can both be used in qualitative research. You may, for instance, analyse data to find a theory, and then justify it by finding more data that verifies it. Or, if you use induction (Znaniecki and Thomas 1918/2007), you start by formulating a tentative hypothesis and then you try to find negative cases. If such cases are found, the hypotheses are reformulated, and you start looking for new negative cases. In this way you constantly reformulate your hypothesis until no negative cases are found. The hypothesis thus developed is therefore justified.

As you can see in the grounded theory method, there is no justification at all – there is only discovery. This means that there is no further attempt to test or verify the emerging theory by trying to find data that falsifies it and there is no effort to try to find data that would verify it. All that is done is to inductively and systematically generate ('discover') theories by trying to find data that give you more information, so that the generated theory becomes more comprehensive. But if the theory is generated in the right way, it will be grounded in data, or fit the data. So, it is not just a creative whim à la Popper. And when there is no fit anymore, perhaps because the group studied has changed or you get new data, the theory is not falsified. What you do is that you modify it so that it once again fits the data. So the theory can be constantly revised because of new data.

We have somewhat loosely talked about the kinds of theories grounded theory research results in. But what does such a theory look like? That question leads to another important feature of grounded theory.

Theory structure in grounded theory

Theories generated with the grounded theory method have a specific structure. In this section we will restrict our comments to one type of theory, substantive theory. Substantive theories are theories about a substantial, or empirical, unit (for more on the other kind of grounded theory, see Chapter 14, 'Rediscovering Formal Theory'). As we have seen, Glaser and Strauss (1967) argued that a theory can be presented 'either as a well-codified set of propositions or in a running theoretical discussion' (Glaser and Strauss 1967: 31). Since it is unclear how to present a 'theoretical discussion', we will opt here for the propositional version. After all, if you have a 'running theoretical discussion', what are you supposed to discuss if not propositions? This way of presenting a theory is of course not intended to diminish the content of the theory – the primary goal is to make its content clearer and to distinctly separate it from the way it was generated, the illustrations, and how these can be applied.

Somewhat simplified, this means that substantive theories would consist of propositions attributing to a unit a set of variable things usually arranged around a core problem which is labelled the core category. The theory describes the relationships between all categories. First, a resultant theory contains a proposition attributing a core category to a well-defined setting, role or group of people. A category for a setting, role or group is then the concept of a phenomenon shared by that setting, by the role or by the group, usually experiencing the same problem. So, for example, people in the setting may experience 'unemployment', 'marriage', or encounter 'power'.

A category that is core, then, is a category that is important because it can be seen as a central problem in the area being studied. Taking *Awareness* as an example, the central category around which everything – all the behaviours, views, perceptions and interactions – were organised was the awareness of everyone in the ward of whether the patient was dying or not (Glaser and Strauss 1965). This variable was the primary problem. It was the main focus of the book and it was the core problem that appeared to govern the views – behaviours and attitudes of those in hospital wards. The theory contains propositions attributing sub-categories to the setting, role or group of people. Such categories are also concepts of phenomena shared by that setting, role or group of people. The differences between the core category and sub-categories are that the latter are not directly related to the core concern, and they do not have as many properties as the core category. They also help to explain less of the activity in the field under study.

The theory will also contain propositions that relate to the core category and to the sub-categories. What such propositions do is to describe the categories and their relationships. For instance, in *Awareness* Glaser and Strauss (1965) discovered that dying in hospitals was a 'non-scheduled status passage', in other words people who were dying in hospitals were often not told or at least were not aware that they were dying. As a consequence, the interactions between patients, family and health care professionals became

> A grounded theory is composed of categories and propositions about those categories. It is also composed of propositions that relate categories to each other to produce an integrated whole. This is achieved by having a core category which acts as the integrating idea for the theory.

concerned with the primary question of establishing if the patient was dying or not. The core category, awareness of dying, had four different sub-categories that described different 'awareness contexts'; these sub-categories were called 'open awareness', 'closed awareness', 'pretence awareness', and 'suspicion awareness' (Glaser and Strauss 1965). The main property of 'open awareness' was that everyone knew the patient was dying. In contrast, during 'suspicion awareness' everyone may have known that the patient was dying except for the patient themselves, who did not know but suspected they may be dying. In this case, the intention wasn't to describe the essence of the phenomena.[3] Instead, the categories were described as richly as possible.

Finally, the theory contains propositions about the relations between the core category and sub-categories, and between sub-categories. Such relations in grounded theory are referred to as 'theoretical codes'. Theoretical codes are ways of demonstrating how the different categories are integrated and organised into explaining how the core concern is resolved. For instance, *Awareness* is a book about a grounded theory that is focused on the problems associated with health professionals' and patients' perceptions of dying in hospital wards in North America. The theory elaborates how the question of 'someone dying or not?' can become a central theme for interactions in hospitals. The problem of dying relates to the diagnosis of the patient and therefore there are two sub-properties of the core category – the certainty of death and the time of death. Certainty of death refers to the degree to which the defining person is certain that the dying person is going to die. The time of death can be measured in hours, days, months. Both of these variables are said to combine in different ways. For example, you can have a '(1) certain death at a known time, (2) certain death at an unknown time, (3) uncertain death but a known time when the question will be resolved, and (4) uncertain death and unknown time when the question will be resolved' (Glaser and Strauss 1965: 18–19). Uncertainty is a theoretical category that belongs to a particular type of category which in turn belongs to what he terms 'the degree family' later described in *Theoretical Sensitivity* (Glaser 1978).

Theories containing propositions such as these constitute the basic and simplest of grounded theory. It is also quite common to generate what are referred to as process-theories. Such theories describe temporal processes of different kinds. Temporal theories describe how categories change from one time to another, or even through a series of times. For instance, a theory may describe what happens to people going through some kind of change, like getting married or becoming a doctor or nurse. Glaser and Strauss later revisited their data on *Awareness* to produce a different account of the *Time for Dying* (Glaser and Strauss 1968). In this book, they analysed dying as a change in *status* over time and called this a change in *status passage*. They discussed different dying trajectories, such as sudden deaths or lingering deaths. Their analysis demonstrated the flexibility of grounded theory. In the original study, Glaser and Strauss had found two possible core categories, one focusing on awareness and the other on the time for dying. They decided to initially focus on awareness and then write their theory on the time for dying at a later date.

The final condition characterising grounded theory is that resultant theories must be generated in the correct way. In particular, they should be developed from a detailed analysis of the data and should not be 'forced'.

The research process of doing grounded theory

The research process of grounded theory differs from traditional research based on deduction and induction. Deductive work is based on the idea that we put forward a hypothesis, deduce consequences, and collect data in order to see if those consequences in fact emerge. If they do, the hypothesis is corroborated; if not, it is falsified. Induction is based on the idea that we collect data, analyse data in order to find a hypothesis, and then verify the hypothesis by collecting more data. Contrary to this, the grounded theory research process is interactive. This roughly means that we collect data, analyse it to generate concepts, collect more data, continue to analyse to generate more concepts and where necessary modify the evolving theory. We then go on to collect more data, and so on, until the finished theory has emerged. We could say that, borrowing a phrase from Nozick (1981), that this process is 'truth-tracking'. During this process we write memos to document emerging ideas, and we repeatedly choose comparative places to sample more data. This process is interactive because we let what we find when we analyse data affect what data we look for next. For instance, if a category has emerged, we then try to find more data that helps us understand what properties it has.

So, the research process becomes more and more theoretically controlled not by preconceived notions but by ideas that have developed in our research. By doing this we make sure that we get relevant data and avoid masses of

> A lot is said about the process of doing grounded theory in terms of the way in which it uses induction, deduction and abduction. Another way of understanding the process is to see it as a simple process of 'truth tracking'.

data which are irrelevant. All this is quite abstract and somewhat vague. To help you understand how this is achieved we have provided a detailed discussion of the overall process in Chapter 8, 'Theoretical Pacing and the Process of Doing Grounded Theory'.

Concluding comments

A key problem that has emerged in the literature on grounded theory is that frequently an article will claim that the method of grounded theory has been employed when, in fact, the research being reported has few of the characteristics that would recommend it as a grounded theory. The main commentators appear to agree on this as a central problem (Dey 1999; Charmaz 2000, 2006; Birks and Mills 2011). In this chapter we have sought to provide you with an initial outline of what a grounded theory is. In doing so, we have focused on describing some initial core tenets of grounded theory (see Table 2-1). This list is designed to introduce you to an initial outline of the method. What we shall do in the rest of this book is to revisit the original texts in some detail in order to *clarify what grounded theory was when it was first written*.

Table 2-1   The main tenets of grounded theory

Main tenets of grounded theory	Consequences for doing grounded theory
(1) Openness	- the research question should be open, usually starting with a unit of analysis (setting, role or group of people) - neutral data collection, along with openness, to new area to explore - avoid preconceptions by keeping in check what the researcher thinks will be relevant
(2) Explanatory power	- the grounded theory must work - the grounded theory must fit the problems being experienced by people in the area under question - the grounded theory must be relevant to people in the setting or performing the role - the grounded theory must remain modifiable in the light of new information
(3) Generation versus justification	- grounded theory is a method for discovery, not justification - there are no techniques for justification; if new information emerges, the theory is adjusted to accommodate the information
(4) Theory structure	- the theory must have a set of propositions organised around a core problem (core category) - there will be sub-core categories that are not directly related to the core concern but nonetheless modify it indirectly in some way - the theory will attribute properties to the core and sub-core categories - the theory will have propositions relating core category to sub-core categories; these propositions are achieved through theoretical coding
(5) The research process	- the research process is interactive; you collect data, analyse it and collect more data, then analyse it - there are three phases: the open, selective and theoretical phases

---

Critical reflection 2

What is grounded theory?

Now go back to your brief notes and respond by writing about how your perspective on grounded theory has changed after reading this chapter. You might also want to make some notes on any further questions that have arisen while you have been reading this chapter. This could include notes concerning any further reading you might like to make.

Summary

In this chapter we have addressed the question about what kind of theory grounded theory is. We achieved this by exploring some of the contemporary views on what grounded theory is. We discussed the fact that because of the success of grounded theory much of what passes as grounded theory in some fields of research actually bears little resemblance to the method. We outlined how some of the contemporary scholars have constructed grounded theory. Of particular note was the fact that there has been a tendency to construct different versions of grounded theory, some of which could not be sustained on more careful analysis. We then proposed what the core aspects of grounded theory are. Here we reviewed grounded theory as an open and flexible method for doing research that seeks to base theory on the analysis of carefully collected data. Likewise, we discussed the explanatory power of grounded theory and the fact that any particular grounded theory should fit and work in relation to the field being studied. Here we discussed the fact that grounded theory must be relevant to people in the setting. Another important aspect of a grounded theory is that it must remain modifiable in the light of new information. We then went on to discuss how grounded theory compares to other approaches in science, specifically those that seek to justify their theory. Here we found that grounded theory was more about the context of discovery than the context of justification. After this, we discussed the key features of a grounded theory by briefly exploring what a grounded theory should look like. Finally, we talked about the distinctive approach that grounded theory adopts to the research process.

Further reading

Birks, M. and Mills, J. (2011) 'Essentials of grounded theory', Chapter 1 in M. Birks and J. Mills, *Grounded Theory: A Practical Guide*. London: Sage.

Bryant, A. and Charmaz, K. (2007) 'Grounded theory in historical perspective: an epistemological account', in A. Bryant and K. Charmaz, *The Sage Handbook of Grounded Theory*. London: Sage.

Charmaz, K. (2006) 'Reconstructing theory in grounded theory studies', Chapter 6 in K. Charmaz, *Constructing Grounded Theory: A Practical Guide through Qualitative Analysis*. London: Sage.

Glaser, B. and Strauss, A. (1967) 'Generating theory', Chapter 2 in B. Glaser and A. Strauss, *The Discovery of Grounded Theory*. Chicago: Aldine.

Notes

1 If *Discovery* was just the starting point, we might reasonably conclude that further developments in the method were necessary. After all, Glaser felt the need to write *Theoretical Sensitivity* (1978). There is no reason to assume that the developments should stop there, is there?

2 We would suggest keeping your reflections short and to the point so perhaps use small yellow 'sticky notes' or Post-its.®

3 In this sense, then, there is no such thing as eidetic reduction in grounded theory.

3

Constructivism in Grounded Theory

Aim: To explore the meaning and nature of constructivism in grounded theory

Learning outcomes

After reading this chapter you should be able to:

- summarise the main tenets of constructivist grounded theory
- appreciate the consequences of bringing constructivism to grounded theory, including the compromises that may need to be made when doing constructivist grounded theory
- evaluate the epistemological and ontological consequences of constructivism for grounded theory
- appreciate the practical consequences of adopting constructivist grounded theory in your study

As we have seen from the previous chapter, grounded theory is often presented in quite different ways. By now you should know that there are several versions of grounded theory in the literature. This should not be surprising. As we have seen, grounded theory developed at a time when methodological pluralism in social science was emerging. This presents us with a bit of a problem. The proliferation of different versions of grounded theory can be confusing. One of the reasons for this confusion is that when authors are building new approaches to grounded theory, they often feel they must justify their method against a previous version of grounded theory. In providing such a justification they may or may not paint a picture of grounded theory that can be distorted. This can then result in some confusion. This does not mean that their 'version' of grounded theory is incorrect or wrong. On the contrary, some methodological innovations have been extremely useful. One such approach has been the development of what is now known as constructivist grounded theory. In this chapter we will explore constructivist grounded theory. In our analysis we seek to highlight how some aspects of the way in which constructivist grounded theory was presented was misleading, but we will go beyond this. We also seek to clarify what a constructivist grounded theory should look like. In conducting this analysis, we seek to provide further justification for *rediscovering* grounded theory.

| Critical reflection 3 |

What is constructivist grounded theory?

Before reading any further in this chapter, take time to write down some brief notes on the following questions:

- What do you understand by the word 'constructivism'?
- What is your understanding of the term 'constructivist grounded theory'?

What is constructivist grounded theory?

Probably the most frequently quoted expression of constructivist grounded theory is Charmaz's seminal chapter 'Grounded theory: Objectivist and constructivist methods' (Charmaz 2000). Most other statements of this view tend to draw heavily on this chapter. We will focus on this in our analysis. In this chapter there are several very useful positive statements about constructivist grounded theory. These passages of text contrast constructivist grounded theory with something called 'traditional' grounded theory. They can be divided into three sub-groups: there are statements about 'meaning', 'mutual creation of knowledge', and about 'perspectives'.

A focus on meaning

According to Charmaz, constructivist grounded theory 'aims toward interpretive understanding of subject's meanings' and she claims that a 'focus on meaning while using grounded theory furthers, rather than limits, interpretative understanding' (Charmaz 2000: 513). Working within an individualist methodology, social phenomena can be reduced to intentional states of people. Such intentional states are meaningful in the sense that within them people attribute meaning to behaviour, organisations, and so on. The focus on meaning is part and parcel of a phenomenological agenda. The problem is that grounded theory, when it was originally developed, also thinks of social phenomena as meaningful. To the constructivist, however, this meaning is the focus of research. This contrasts with grounded theory when it was developed. Back then, the focus was much more on providing an explanation for why things mean what they do, including the consequences such meanings have for those acting in the setting.

Categories developed in a grounded theory must, as we have seen, be attributed dimensions – to do so is to describe the meaning they have. It follows from this that in grounded theory, when it was originally developed there was no direct focus on meaning. This was a secondary concern. In this respect, we have a fundamental difference between the two versions. In addition to this, Charmaz (2000) states that, in contrast to the objectivist grounded theorist, when the constructivist grounded theorist researches phenomena such as the experience of pain, they 'start by viewing the topic of pain subjectively as a feeling, an experience that may take a variety of forms. ... 'What makes pain pain? (that is, what is essential to the phenomenon as defined by those who experience it?' (Charmaz 2000: 526). We will return to this later in our analysis.

> Constructivist grounded theory can be distinguished from grounded theory, when it was first developed, because it focuses on meaning and how meaning is constructed. Grounded theory, when it was developed, also thinks of social phenomena as meaningful. However, it tends to focus on explaining why things mean what they do and the consequences these meanings have for those in the setting.

QUESTION

Focusing on meaning and how it is constructed rather than on why things mean what they mean, including explaining the consequences of such meanings, has an effect on how we do grounded theory. Discuss.

The mutual creation of knowledge

Charmaz (2000) claims that constructivist grounded theory 'recognizes the mutual creation of knowledge by the viewer and the viewed' (p. 510), that it 'recognizes that the categories, concepts, and theoretical level of an analysis emerge from the researchers interaction within the field and questions about the data' (p. 522), and that 'the "discovered" reality arises from the interactive process and its temporal, cultural, and structural contexts' (p. 524). She also states that the 'viewer then is part of what is viewed rather than separate from it' (p. 524). These points are epistemological in that they say that knowledge is gained by a dialectical, interactive process in which both the researcher and the researched take part. *A clear difference, then, between constructivist grounded theory and 'objectivistic' grounded theory is that the researcher in constructivist grounded theory in some way identifies themselves with the researched.* This is similar to Gadamer's view about the 'fusion of horizons', where the horizons of the researcher and the researched meld together and generate understanding (Gadamer 1976). This is, of course, a hermeneutical way of doing science and is quite different from grounded theory as it was originally intended.

The use of different theoretical perspectives

Charmaz says that 'researchers starting from other vantage points – feminist, Marxist, phenomenological – can use grounded theory strategies for their empirical studies' (Charmaz 2000: 511). It is unclear if she means that different vantage points can be used while conducting a grounded theory, or if grounded theory strategies could in fact be used in other kinds of research. The second point would be trivial. Of course other researchers can use theoretical sampling, or memo-writing, or interact between collecting and analysing data whatever method he or she uses. But that does not make such studies grounded theory. The statement can be interpreted differently, however. It might, in fact, be saying that different vantage points can be used legitimately in a grounded theory study. We will return to this question throughout this book. In attempting to clarify what constructivist grounded theory is by starting with the seminal work of Charmaz (2000), we can say there are three basic tenets to constructivist grounded theory (see Box 3-1).

Box 3-1

The main tenets of constructivist grounded theory

(a) a focus on meaning,
(b) the mutual creation of knowledge, and
(c) a legitimisation of using various well-established theoretical perspectives in sociology.

In the next section we will explore the differences between Charmaz (2000) constructivist grounded theory and grounded theory as it was originally presented. We will then look at constructivism in science in order to move beyond Charmaz's (2000) version of constructivist grounded theory. We will seek to formulate a view that we feel could adequately be called 'constructivist grounded theory'. The next section seeks to compare and contrast the original version with constructivist grounded theory.

Grounded theory and constructivist grounded theory

In the following comparison, we are seeking to highlight differences and spell out the consequences of adopting a constructivist grounded theory approach. To make this comparison we will use the five essential tenets of grounded theory presented in Chapter 2 (see page 32).

Openness

As we saw in Chapter 2, openness means that the researcher should not use preconceived notions when he or she formulates the research question, collects data, or analyses data. As we shall see, he or she can have pre-existing motivations and interests and, indeed, he or she may have preconceptions about what is going on in the area of interest. But the idea is that these should not drive the collection and analysis of data. The reason for this is that the theory must emerge from data. In grounded theory this is achieved by using a general and flexible research question, open line-by-line coding, avoiding reading the literature on the area, and trusting the sensitivity of the researcher and the emerging theory. In constructivist grounded theory, the researcher may focus on essential meaning, as in phenomenology, use a theoretical perspective, such as Marxism, and start out thinking that the researcher's own understanding of the world will always affect the research. Research is, and must always be, contextualised. Let us discuss the consequences of this.

One consequence of adopting a constructivist approach to grounded theory is that it asks a more direct but closed question. Charmaz formulated her research question by asking 'how chronicity affects ill people's self-concepts' (Charmaz 1992). This means that she presupposed two things: that there is an identifiable group of people to be studied (people with chronic illness), and the relevance of people's 'self-concepts'. In some respects this represents an element of what Glaser (1992) called 'forcing'. In doing so, the openness of grounded theory is being compromised. Such a compromise might be advantageous; it is up to you as the researcher to decide.

QUESTION

What advantages might we accrue from being more closed in the way we ask our research questions?

Another consequence of this process is that it may result in a more closed process of data analysis. Analysis of data, in grounded theory as it was originally presented, involves starting with open coding. You code line by line, find incidents and generate categories and their properties, you seek to discover the core concerns of your participants. If, however, other perspectives are allowed to influence this process, then some data may be taken to be important while other data may be ignored. There may be a risk that what is deemed important and what is counted as data might be shaped by preconceived ideas.

Explanatory power

The second tenet of grounded theory is that the resultant theory must *work*. This means that the theory should be able to explain what goes on in a substantive area. In grounded theory such explanations are provided through the delineation of the core concerns, categories and theoretical codes. Now, what happens when you do constructivist grounded theory? Let us look at the options again. Combining grounded theory with the study of meaning means that the phenomenon to be researched is decided beforehand. A set of categories generated in this way may well have very little explanatory value. Suppose we research the essential meaning of experiences of pain (Charmaz 2000). It may well be that such experiences do not have anything to do with what is going on. What really matters may be concerns about the future for employment, family, and so on, and the process of resolving those concerns. Therefore, although interesting as it may be, the meaning of pain will be pretty irrelevant to those concerns and how they are resolved.

The same is true if a theoretical framework or the pre-understanding of the researcher is used. For instance, if we research dying patients, we may investigate whether they are alienated, and we may investigate what it is like to be a woman dying in hospitals. However, it may be that their main concerns are elsewhere, and all references to alienation and womanhood are irrelevant in order to explain why they do what they do. Again, such theories may very well not work to explain what is happening because too much is presupposed from the beginning.

Generation and justification: the use of the constant comparative method

The third tenet of grounded theory is that the theory must emerge by using the constant comparative method, and there is no effort to justify it. It does seem that constructivist grounded theory may well be conducted without any extra effort to justify. For instance, if grounded theory is combined with an interest in meaning, there does not necessarily have to be any effort to justify this. You can also generate a theory using a preconceived theoretical framework or a pre-understanding without justification. Of course, there is still a difference – if any of the combinations are used, the preconceived ideas will aid the generation, but that does not mean that there is any justification.

Theory structure in constructivist grounded theory

The fourth tenet concerned theory structure: what kind of propositions make up the resultant theory? As we shall see, grounded theory, as it was originally presented, contains propositions attributing to a substantial area a core category, sub-categories, properties to them, and relations between them (theoretical codes). What, then, would a resultant theory look like if grounded theory is combined with different perspectives? If grounded theory is combined with the general study of meaning, the resultant theory will categorise the meaning of the phenomenon being studied. Such categories perform a very different purpose from approaches to grounded theory when it was originally developed.

The research process

The fifth and final tenet of grounded theory involves the logic of the research process. In grounded theory we have open, selective and theoretical phases. But, once again, if grounded theory is combined with the general study of meaning, it seems difficult to see how this logic can be maintained. It is unlikely that we will be able to end up with a fully integrated theory.

QUESTION

What are the key compromises involved in adopting constructivist grounded theory?

Combining constructivism with grounded theory

It should be clear from our review of constructivist grounded theory that the status of the field is less than clear. On the one hand, it was set out as an alternative to 'objectivist' grounded theory. The constructivist method of Charmaz (2000) does have a positive approach with its focus on meaning, an emphasis on the mutual creation of knowledge and legitimisation of using well-established perspectives in sociology, such as Marxism and feminism in qualitative research. The problem, however, is that these key aspects of constructivist grounded theory in no way correspond to what we consider to be the core aspects of constructivism in general. This does not mean, of course, that constructivist grounded theory is fatally flawed. To the contrary, it simply means that the task of clarification is not yet finished. Before moving on to clarify what we think constructivism in grounded theory should look like, it is worth exploring what we think constructivism is.

Constructivism in science

Generally, 'constructivism' is a label used to refer to the view that reality is constructed. There are strong versions of constructivism, such as Kant's view that reality is constructed by transcendental a priori forms of the mind, or a phenomenalist view that external reality is logically constructed out of sense experience. Such views are often foundationalist; they say that knowledge has an infallible foundation in pure reason and that we can deduce a priori forms, or in basic beliefs about sense-experience. The version of constructivism relevant for this chapter is not the same. It points to social factors as being at least partly responsible for how scientific research is conducted and therefore for how reality is constructed. Those who call themselves 'constructivists' are not a homogeneous group. Indeed, some have remarked, there is not much more than a 'family resemblance' between their views (Burr 2003). Nevertheless, there are two tenets that we must accept in order to belong to that group. One tenet is epistemological and concerns the rationality of the research process. The other tenet is ontological and concerns the nature of scientific facts.

Constructivist and objectivist epistemology

Constructivist epistemology is based on the idea that the practice of doing scientific research depends on social factors. The researcher will take certain beliefs for granted, conceptualise the world in a certain way because of his or her language, and use certain methods because that is the way he or she was taught to think about science. In this book, we will call these sets of factors preconceptions, as we shall see they are very relevant for grounded theory. Preconceptions result in the fact that the researcher will frequently formulate certain kinds of questions and look for certain kinds of answers. Because observation is 'theory-laden' some of those preconceptions will be validated and some, at least sometimes, will not be considered at all. This in itself does not give us constructivism. Constructivism is a position inferred from this point. It is argued that since research practices depend on external factors, no scientific practice is superior to any other. Constructivists deny that there is just one rational way to do science. The reason for this is that standards of rationality are always contained within research practice. There is no overarching, fully universal and neutral theory about how science should be done that can be used in order to show that one research practice is better than another. This does not mean that scientific work is completely irrational. It means that standards of rationality are relative to the research practice.

In contrast to this, objectivism about the scientific method says that there is one, and only one, way science should be conducted. Such an overarching theory about the scientific method can be developed and applied without being constrained by external factors. Methods used in the past that did not follow the correct research practice were simply bad methods. Logical positivism was such an objectivist view, based on the principle of verification and part of the programme referred to by Hempel as 'the methodological unity of science' (Hempel 1965). It has been the goal of normative philosophy of science since the time of Aristotle to find such universal methods. Scientific rationality, within this perspective is therefore objective and independent of external factors. Relativism and objectivism about scientific rationality are epistemological issues (see Box 3-2 below for a summary). We now turn to the ontological tenet of constructivism.

Constructivist ontology

Constructivism argues that the products of scientific research, such as theories and explanations, depend on external factors. The reason given for this is that these theories and explanations are products of scientific research which itself depends on external factors. As a consequence, then, our theories and explanations also depend on external factors. This means that the way research is conducted partly determines what is believed about the world. This is hardly surprising, and a quick glance at the history of science will confirm that scientists have believed very different things about the world because of their research practices. Taking 'scientific beliefs' to include theories, hypotheses, explanations, and so on, to be held for true, then it can be argued that scientific beliefs do indeed depend on research practice. This does not give us constructivism. Constructivism concludes from this *that there simply are no independently existing 'scientific facts' that can be discovered.* There are no objective truths, only truths relative to what scientific practice leads you to believe in. All scientific beliefs are dependent on research practices, and therefore all the facts that science can come up with are constructed by, and dependent on, those practices.

Against this we have realists, who believe that there are independently existing facts, and it is the goal of science to give us knowledge about these facts. What has happened in history, and often still happens, is that scientists have got it wrong. If this is the case, then scientific beliefs do not describe what the world actually is like. Despite this, the *goal* of scientific research remains the same – to discover such facts. So, according to the realist, scientific facts exist independently of research practice. This needs some further explanation. In what sense can we say that 'scientific facts' do not exist independently of scientific beliefs but are rather constructed by them? The easiest way to understand this is to realise that theorising always involves some kind of classification. We say that it is true for 'all metals that...', for 'all humans that...', for 'all people with a certain disease that...', and so on. That is, theories are about general facts, facts that involve some kind of classification. The question is: On what is such a classification based? This question goes back to the problem of universals.

| Box 3-2 |

Epistemology: constructivism contrasted with objectivism

Constructivism

There is no universal and neutral theory about how science should be done but rather standards of rationality are relative to the research practice.

Objectivism

There is one, and only one, way science should be conducted, and scientific rationality is objective and independent of external factors.

The problem of universals

The problem of universals is best explained by considering that in the world there are individual objects, such as rocks, chairs and human beings. These objects are located in space and time, and can only be in one place at the same time. The chair in this room, for instance, cannot be both here in this room and in the next room at the same time. All such objects have properties which make them what they are. Properties, however, seem to function differently from objects. The object in this room is a chair, and the object in the next room is also a chair. Those objects are distinct, that is they are both different chairs, but they do, however, have the same property, the property of being a chair. Properties therefore, it seems, can be located at different places at the same time. *The problem of universals is the problem of what such properties are, and what the relation is between them and the individual objects.* This problem is very relevant to grounded theory.

Plato's solution to this puzzle was his theory of ideas or forms (Plato 1966). It is worth going through the basic arguments because they are relevant to our discussion about grounded theory and constructivism. First, Plato maintains that there is an abstract, transcendent world of ideas, which is eternal, not located in space, and unchanging. Such ideas must not be confused with ideas we have in our minds. Plato's ideas exist outside the human mind and are independent of them. Indeed, if all thinking beings vanished, the ideas would still continue to exist. Next, he says that individual objects have properties in virtue of participating in, or being copies of, such ideas. For instance, the chairs are chairs because they participate in the idea of a chair, just as we are human beings because we participate in the idea of a human being. So, Plato manages to explain how properties can be in many places at the same time by relating all objects that have the same property to the same transcendent, abstract, idea. Plato is therefore a realist, since properties, as abstract ideas, exist independently of human thought. His disciple, Aristotle, was also a realist about universals, but gave his realism a different slant (Aristotle 1924). He believed that ideas do not exist in a transcendent,

The problem of universals relates to how properties behave and can help us explain the difference between constructivism and realism. On the one hand, properties can be seen to exist independently from the human mind. This view is realist. On the other hand, some argue that properties do not exist outside our classification schemes. In this view, we always sort objects relative to our conceptual schemes and our concepts create essences. This is constructivism.

abstract, world of their own, but they exist immanently in the objects them-selves. Properties in this perspective exist in space and time and are located where the object that has the property is. Properties are, however, different from objects because they can be in different places at the same time. *In this approach, the ideas, contrary to Plato, are dependent on objects.* For instance, if all chairs vanish, then the idea, or property, of being a chair vanishes as well.

A consequence of realisms such as Plato's and Aristotle's are that the world we live in, which consists of such things as human beings, horses, chairs and rocks, have a nature that is independent of human thought. *Things are what they are in virtue of properties they have which are independent of what humans think and believe.* This view is sometimes also called essentialism. Things have essences which makes them what they are; if they lose their essence they will not be of that nature anymore. For instance, if the essence of being a human being is to be rational, and someone loses that property, then he or she will not be a human being anymore. The fact that properties exist independently of human thought means that the world is objective – we all, independently of culture, history, gender, live in a world that is exactly the same. We will from now on refer to such essences as real essences.

QUESTION

Is it possible that there are some things that do not exist outside our classification schemes? Can some things be *non-real* whereas other things are real? What might these be?

The opposite view of essentialism is called nominalism. Nominalism says that everything that exists is located in one, and only one, place in space and time. There are no Platonic or Aristotelian ideas, only individual objects located in space and time. The view that there is something that exists in many places at the same time is either incomprehensible or at least superfluous. Because of this, we should not postulate such entities, using the principle of parsimony often referred to as 'Occam's razor'. Of course this seems to be a good idea. Why accept a kind of entity when it isn't strictly necessary to do so? However, it is still a fact that we use general concepts, such as 'chair' and 'human being', and we use them about many different objects. How can this be if there really is no such thing as the property of being a chair or being a human being? Or to put it differently: How can the proposition 'this is a chair' and 'that is a chair' both be true at the same time if they attribute the two objects the identical property?

Nominalists have worked out different answers to that question. Some have tried to explain it by saying that the concept 'chair' applies to many objects because they resemble each other, some that it is because they are members of the same class, and so on. Nevertheless, the version of nominalism that interests us most, since it can be directly related to constructivist grounded theory, is called conceptualism. Conceptualism also has a long history, but it could be argued that it was perhaps first put clearly forward by John Locke (Locke 1632–1704). The main idea in this perspective is that the classification of things into different kinds of things is a product of human conceptualisation (Locke 1732). An object is a certain kind of object because we have created ('constructed') the concept under which the object falls. Such concepts are constructed by a process of abstraction. This means that properties differing between individual objects are disregarded, and only properties had by all objects of a certain kind remain. For instance, a chair in one room and a chair in the next room are both chairs because we have the concept of a chair and the object falls under that concept. This concept expresses which properties a thing must have in order to be a chair. All other properties are irrelevant to its being a chair, for instance its colour. So, we all have conceptual schemes. These schemes make us categorise the world in a certain way, sorting objects into different kinds of objects. Indeed, those concepts affect not only how we think; they 'impregnate' our sense-impressions so that we immediately see what kind of object stands before us. But, and this is the important point, *there really are no kinds of objects or essences independently of our classification.* The sorting of objects is always relative to our conceptual schemes, and such schemes can differ. *It is not the case that essences make us have the concepts that we have; it is the other way around – our concepts create essences.* Such essences are nominal and are to be distinguished from Plato's and Aristotle's real essences. The problem and these differences are summarised in Box 3-3.

Box 3-3

The problem of universals: essentialism and nominalism

The problem of universals states that there are individual objects, such as rocks, chairs and human beings. These objects are located in space and time, and can only be in one place at the same time. Properties, however, can be located at different places at the same time. The problem of universals is the problem of what such properties are and what the relationship is between them and objects.

Essentialism	Nominalism
Things are what they are in virtue of properties they have, which are independent of what humans think and believe.	There are no objects or essences independent of our classification; rather objects are always sorted relative to our conceptual schemes.

Why do we conceptualise the world in the way we do?

According to social constructivism, there are social causes for the way we conceptualise in the way we do. By interacting with other persons from the time we are born, we learn how to use certain concepts, which also means that we learn to categorise reality in a certain way. For instance, we learn that certain objects are called human beings, and from that we create a concept of what a human being is. If we refer to the wrong kind of thing as a human being, we are corrected and we adjust our conception of what a human being is taken to be. This is not only true of objects, but also of other ontological categories, such as events and actions, states and processes. Regardless, the conceptual schemes we have are generated by our social environment.

Let's take the notion of 'health'. If you are an essentialist about health, you will believe that there actually is such a thing as health. This would be a natural property some people have and some lack and will be independent of any conception of what health is. If someone has health, he or she will have it independently of culture, society, gender, and so on. And if this is the case, it is quite possible to have a wrong conception of what health is, a conception that does not capture the real essence of health. In other words, a proposition such as 'S is healthy' is either true or false, and it is made true or false by facts existing independently of human thought.

If, on the other hand, you believe that there is no natural property such as health, you may be a conceptualist. You would then say that a person is healthy only relative to a certain conception of what health is. The proposition 'S is healthy' is therefore only truly relative to a certain conception of health. Indeed, it may be true according to one conception of health and false according to another. Normally, we may not see it this way – it may well be that in 'the present state of affairs, X is taken for granted, X appears to be inevitable' (Hacking 1999: 12). But there is no real essence here, the constructivist maintains (Hacking 1999). As a matter of fact, according to Hacking's constructivism, 'X need not have existed, or need not be at all as it is. X, or X as it is at present, is not determined by the nature of things; it is not inevitable' (Hacking 1999: 6). What this means is that it may even be that we would not have had the concept of health at all, and then there would not have been any such thing as health. Or we could have had a different conception of what it is (Seedhouse 2005). There is, of course, the possibility to believe in real essences in some cases and to be nominal when it comes to others. So, for instance, you can believe there are real natural objects, such as animals, rocks, and so on, but still believe that among phenomena such as 'health' and social phenomena generally only nominal essences can be found. Some essences, then, are constructed, others are real.

In sum, we may agree that research practice and scientific beliefs depend on external factors. The constructivist concludes from this, first, that no way of doing research is better, more rational than another, and as a consequence that many research practices should be tolerated. In other words, we should be pluralist in our approach to science. The objectivist, in contrast to this, believes that there is a way of doing science that is rational, and that all research ought to be done this way. The constructivist believes that scientific beliefs do not describe independently existing facts since there are no such facts that can be described, because such general facts involve classification and classes are constructed. It is against this that realists would insist that there *are* independently existing facts and it is the goal of science to give us knowledge about such facts.

It should be noted that the two points – the epistemological about scientific rationality and the ontological about scientific facts – are independent of each other. You can believe that there are independent facts, but not just one objectively rational 'best method' to get knowledge about those facts. Or it is possible to believe that there is one, and only one, scientific method that is rational, but there are no real facts to get knowledge about. We take constructivism to hold both the belief that there is no objectively more rational way to do science, *and* that there are no independently existing scientific facts.

<hr>

QUESTION

Do you believe different things about different kinds of objects and categories? Are you realist about natural objects such as rocks but constructivist about categories such as love?

<hr>

Constructivism in everyday life

Apart from constructivism about scientific knowledge, there is also constructivism about our everyday life. Here our beliefs about the world, and how we conceptualise it, depend on contingent factors, such as which society we live in. For instance, we conceptualise the world in a certain way, taking there to be such things as chairs, tables, friendships and families, and we have beliefs about those things. We believe that chairs are made to sit on, that friendships can take different forms, and so on. We do this because we have learned to do so in the society where we grew up. Therefore, phenomena such as tables and friendships are socially constructed; they only exist relative to different societies. This is a trivial point. Indeed, the statement that social phenomena are socially constructed is almost a tautology: how would it be possible for social phenomena to exist independently of society? Nevertheless, it is important to keep the distinction between everyday social facts and scientific facts in mind. It is not, for instance, possible to argue that if everyday social facts are constructed, then scientific facts about society are also constructed. Indeed, there is nothing logically odd with the view that everyday constructions exists independently of the researcher and that the researcher may describe them correctly. This is, for instance, John Searle's view (Searle 1998).

Constructivism and grounded theory

Following this discussion, we would like to suggest that constructivist grounded theory will be:

1. **Nominalist about everyday life.** Such an approach will focus on how people use categories to construct what problems mean to them in their everyday life. This ontological relativism represents a significant change from classical forms of grounded theory. We will explore the consequences of this for the method in more detail in the next section.

2. **There will be a belief following (1) that knowledge is co-created in the research process and that the categories being used in constructivist grounded theory will have a focus on what things mean to people.** As we have seen, this is one of the big strengths of the current form of constructivist grounded theory and can be readily seen in papers produced from this perspective (Charmaz 1991b, 1994, 2000, 2009). Glaser has termed this the 'worrisome accuracy' of qualitative data analysis, something which is typical of his realist interpretation of constructivist grounded theory (Glaser 2002). In some ways, we would contend that there is little to be gained from complaining that constructivist grounded theory is not realist.

3. **Given the nature of constructivism, we suggest that a constructivist grounded theory, like the method as a whole, will be epistemologically relativist in a general sense.** Grounded theory is compatible with the view that there are many ways to do science, constructivist grounded theory is also relativist in this way. This itself is not a problem. The problem emerges when constructivist grounded theory shows a marked tendency towards operational relativism. What we mean by this is that constructivist grounded theory drops certain techniques and procedures. We argue that constructivist grounded theory *should not be operationally relativist*. We recognise that, and this is a bit of a problem, constructivism as a whole is relativist. We do not think constructivist grounded theory can be afforded the same luxury. If constructivist grounded theory is to be able to carry the label 'grounded theory', we feel it must in some way carry with it some of the procedures and techniques associated with grounded theory. Otherwise the 'slide into postmodernism' will become a reality (Mills, Chapman et al. 2007).

4. **Various theoretical approaches can be used, and indeed ought to be used, in constructivist grounded theory.** In order for this version of grounded theory to achieve the political emancipatory vision of constructivism, some degree of normative interpretation and critique ought to be included to the method. This has implications for the practical steps and processes associated with doing constructivist grounded theory.

The method of constructivist grounded theory

We have outlined what we think are the main components of grounded theory when it was originally developed and the main elements of constructivist grounded theory as it currently stands. In this section we would like to attempt to indicate where a synthesis of all three components could be achieved and what the consequences of combining all three elements will be for grounded theory.

Before beginning we need to be very clear. Grounded theory, for us at least, is a general method. Constructivist grounded theory will always act as a subset of the general method. It will not be as general, or as broad, for the reasons we have discussed. *We have no problem with this difference. In fact, in many ways the variation should be encouraged, so long as the differences are made clear.* It should also be clear that we reject any claim that constructivist grounded theory is not grounded theory. It is, however, a very different proposition from grounded theory as it was originally developed.

As we have seen, constructivist grounded theory is based on something of a paradox. The paradox, simply stated, is between being both open and closed at the same time. It is nominalist in its outlook. It is not completely open in the sense that grounded theory was open because of its focus on meaning. It seeks to study the constructs people use to understand 'their' everyday experience. It will focus on these constructs and how these vary. Data collection is no longer a neutral process. It is negotiated between the researcher and the researched. The process of doing constructivist grounded theory involves the extra burden of checking how the researchers' interests may or may not be acting to shape their interpretation of participants' perspectives.

This is a significant shift from grounded theory as it was originally intended. There are some compromises. Gone is the ability to focus on settings, roles and people, among other things. Constructivist grounded theory no longer seeks to describe 'what is going on' in the field but instead explores how people construct their experiences. This shift cascades throughout the method and has consequences for the main features of constructivist grounded theory. This can be seen in Charmaz's (1991a) work on chronic illness. In this work, she began with an interest in the relationship between how a serious chronic illness related to individuals' self-concepts and their experience of time (Charmaz 1991a). While, on the one hand, this question has several relationships already presupposed, Charmaz (1991a) did acknowledge her research interests at the outset. Although this might be seen as a compromise in openness, it would be a mistake to say that she has 'forced' her analysis. To the contrary, Charmaz remained very much open to the meaning and the constructs that her participants were using to articulate these relationships. This brings us to the interpretative power of constructivist grounded theory.

One of the major features of constructivist grounded theory is its interpretative power. By this, we mean it has a focus on linking the constructs of researchers to what things mean for participants. This is not a trivial point. If we take, for example, Charmaz's (1991a) work, we find that the style of her text very carefully works out how each of her constructs relates to the meaning chronic conditions have for her participants. In the following example the construct of 'informing' is linked with 'decreasing emotional risks' and the feelings participants might have:

> ...informing decreases emotional risks. Compared to disclosing, informing permits greater control over emotions, over others' responses, and over possible negative labels. For example, her friend recalled how Helen Bartlett informed her about having leukemia. The friend said, 'Helen got very technical but there was no crack in her voice. That's Helen. She doesn't even give you a chance to think she's going to die.' (Charmaz 1991a: 121)

In this example, the construct 'informing' is contrasted to 'disclosing' and this is linked to the social science on labelling. However, Charmaz (1991a) goes on to illustrate what informing meant *for* Helen's friend. The example is used to show what informing means for participants. It is not used as a general illustration. This is what we mean by 'interpretative power'. Throughout her work, Charmaz (1991a) compares and contrasts how different constructs mean different things to different individuals. She also goes on to explore how her constructs fit the descriptions of her participants. The theory does not seek to explain the descriptions or the constructs, but rather to explore how they vary *for* participants.

'Any research is a product of the interaction between the observer and the observed and for that matter, between the observer and his or her discipline. Stripped of meaning the research process deals with creating the data, compiling it, and conferring meaning upon it.' (Charmaz 1991a: 281)

Constructivist grounded theory is also based on the co-generation of theory. The theory is quite different from grounded theory when it was developed. A constructivist grounded theory is based on the careful analysis of participants' descriptions, which have in turn been stimulated by the interests of the researcher and which are subsequently explored in the context of existing social science in the field. The theory consists of constructs and their interrelations. The requirement is that the constructs should be meaningful to both the researcher and the participants. Following this, constructivist grounded theory makes no special claims for the status of its findings. The theory is not a privileged point of observation. Charmaz (1991a) is very clear about this from the outset in her work. She describes her work as a 'sociological story' (Charmaz 1991a: 7). The sensitivity of constructivist grounded theory is on theory building as an interaction between the observer and the observed. It is not hard to see how this contrasted sharply with what she later called 'objectivist' grounded theory. What is more, added to the interpretative theory-building stage is an analysis of the status of each of the constructs in relation to social science in general.

Yet in many ways this is not that different from grounded theory when it was originally developed. The claims made for constructivist grounded theory, seem to us at least, to exaggerate the differences with grounded theory as it was intended. For a start, grounded theory must be 'grounded' in the data. This means it must be grounded in observation. That is not so different. Likewise, if new observations challenge the emerging grounded theory, in grounded theory the theory is modified. This is also not that different. Where the big differences develop is that constructivism generates constructs, relates them and then critically evaluates them in the light of the social science on the subject. The same is also the case when it comes to theory structure. Grounded theory, as it was originally developed, was intended to be composed of propositions attributing to a substantial area a core category, sub-categories, properties to them and relations between them (theoretical codes). Constructivist grounded theory is not presented as an integrated set of propositions and there is obviously no real need to define a core construct or a core category.

Finally, the research process varies for both approaches. Constructivist grounded theory is not as prescriptive. It does, however, have the same interest in building theory. This is crucial. While the theoretical products between the two approaches are quite different, the interest is the same – to build a theoretical discussion about an area or problem that is important in some way. At this stage, their interests separate. We have summarised the main tenets of constructivist grounded theory in Table 3-1.

Table 3-1 The main tenets of constructivist grounded theory

Main tenets of constructivist grounded theory	Consequences for doing grounded theory
(1) A paradox between being open and closed	- an 'open' focus on meaning but focused on definite problems - the research question will be focused on what certain things mean to people, specifically on their constructs and how they are used - data collection is not a neutral process but negotiated - researchers constant check on how their perspective shapes their interpretation of participants' explanations and categories
(2) Interpretive power	- the constructivist grounded theory must link researchers' and participants' constructs of what a problem means for participants - constructivist grounded theory will seek to capture how meaning varies for the group and the individual - constructivist grounded theory will tend to focus on individuals and meaning, although 'constructs' are ultimately the unit of analysis - constructs should 'fit' the descriptions of participants - constructivist grounded theory has less emphasis on explanation
(3) Co-generation of theory	- constructivist grounded theory is a method for the discovery of meaningful 'constructs', not justification - the theory will be about the constructs, and exploring what they mean both for participants and for social theory in general

(Continued)

Table 3-1 *(Continued)*

Main tenets of constructivist grounded theory	Consequences for doing grounded theory
(4) The theory will categorise, define and explore a set of problems associated with a problem area	- constructivist grounded theory will propose a set of categories that will define a range of problems associated with an area - these categories will be defined and carefully grounded in the meaning the area or problem has for participants - the problems thus described will be critically explored using existing social scientific approaches to similar problems
(5) The research process	- there is no one singular way of doing constructivist grounded theory, although some general principles are important for it to be called constructivist grounded theory - like grounded theory, the research process is interactive and open; you collect data, analyse it and collect more data, then analyse it - the process is characterised by a focus on making sure what the researcher thinks the problems mean to participants is what they mean to participants; there is, however, room for interpretation - emergent categories will be described then subjected to social scientific critique, with an interest in promoting a broader interpretation of the data

Concluding comments

In this chapter we have taken a version of grounded theory that has emerged in recent years and explored how this version of grounded theory differs from the original version. Not all versions of grounded theory are the same. Important differences exist. There are, however, some problems with constructivist grounded theory that may need to be resolved. First, if constructivist grounded theory does not have the same product or the same steps involved in the research process, what specifically makes it 'grounded theory'? Second, to what extent is constructivist grounded theory different from qualitative research in general? Is constructivist grounded theory just one step along a slippery slope into incoherence? We think each of these questions can be very briefly discussed in summing up this chapter.

What makes constructivist grounded theory grounded theory?

Constructivist grounded theory is interested in developing a theory about the everyday construction of meaning. Theory building is the goal of the approach and, as a result, it involves the development of categories and specifying their interrelations. In this sense, it produces its own 'constructivist' grounded theory.

The product that it produces is very different, but we feel it is sufficiently inspired by grounded theory to be recognised as a variation of grounded theory.

What makes constructivist grounded theory different from qualitative research as a whole?

Constructivist grounded theory is different from qualitative data analysis because it seeks to build theory. The theory it produces is not claimed to be as dense or as integrated as grounded theory, but it certainly carries with it a greater degree of conceptualisation and categorisation of qualitative data analysis as a whole. It shares all of the same concerns as qualitative analysis in general to document participants' perspectives, but it does so by trying to produce a loose set of constructs along with a critical discussion. In this respect, constructivist grounded theories are more than simply a re-description of qualitative data. They should be, or ought at the very least to be, theories about constructs, their relationships and how they relate to everyday meaning.

Does constructivist grounded theory represent a slippery slope?

When we started to analyse this problem we were concerned that it did represent a slippery slope. As our analysis proceeded we became more and more encouraged that this problem can be avoided and that we can encourage methodological pluralism in grounded theory. In a small way we hope this chapter can help others see that a way out of the controversies about grounded theory can be found. Indeed, we would argue that much can be gained by doing so.

This brings us back to our book. Clearly, those new to grounded theory will be confronted with the fact that there are frequently different approaches at the heart of grounded theory. These approaches can be profoundly different. One problem remains, however, and that is that in building constructivist grounded theory Charmaz constructed a version of grounded theory as 'objectivist'. We feel this can be confusing and somewhat unnecessary. It raises a question about the nature of the method as it was originally intended and somewhat justifies our task of rediscovery.

Critical reflection 4

Developing a perspective on constructivist grounded theory

Go back to the notes you have made while reading this chapter and detail what you now think about constructivist grounded theory. You might also want to make some notes on any further questions that have arisen while you have been reading this chapter. This could include notes concerning any further reading you might like to make.

Summary

In this chapter we have picked up the challenge of methodological pluralism in grounded theory through a critical evaluation of constructivist grounded theory. Here we have discovered that constructivist grounded theory is in fact very different from grounded theory as it was originally intended. We have explored the consequences of adopting constructivism in grounded theory by noting the important compromises that have to be made. Finally, we outlined how a stronger version of constructivist grounded theory can be developed. This was achieved by exploring the paradox between being open and closed, its interpretive power, the co-generation of theory, and how the theory categorises and explores a set of problems. Finally, we have discussed how the research process in constructivist grounded theory is different from grounded theory in general.

Further reading

Armstrong, D. (1978) *Universals and Scientific Realism*. Cambridge: Cambridge University Press.

Bryant, A. and Charmaz, K. (2007) 'Grounded theory in historical perspective: an epistemological account', in A. Bryant and K. Charmaz, *The Sage Handbook of Grounded Theory*. London: Sage.

Charmaz, K. (2000) 'Grounded theory: objectivist and constructivist methods', in N. Denzin and Y. Lincoln (eds), *The Handbook of Qualitative Research*. Thousand Oaks, CA: Sage.

Kukla, A. (2000) *Social Constructivism and the Philosophy of Science*. London: Routledge.

4

Disentangling Concepts and Categories in Grounded Theory

Aim: To critically evaluate the status of concepts and categories in grounded theory

Learning outcomes

After reading this chapter you should be able to:

- outline and explore the entangled nature of the relationship between concepts and categories in contemporary grounded theory
- discuss why it is important to clarify the difference between concepts and categories in grounded theory
- articulate what concepts and categories are in grounded theory and be able to establish why these are different

As you read about grounded theory, two key processes will be talked about You will also find lots of references in the literature to the key objects of these processes, concepts and categories. But what do the processes involve? More importantly, what exactly are concepts and categories? How do they relate to each other in grounded theory? The answer to this question is more complicated than it might at first seem. The first problem you will come across is the tendency to see concepts and categories as the same thing. The second problem is that concepts and categories actually do mean different things and disentangling their respective meaning in grounded theory can be difficult.

┌──────────┐ Critical reflection 5 ┌──────────
│
│   **What are concepts and categories?**
│
│   Before reading any further in this chapter, take time to write down some brief notes
│   on the following questions:
│
│   • What are concepts in grounded theory?
│   • What are categories in grounded theory?
│
└──

The entangled nature of concepts and categories in contemporary grounded theory

Much of the literature on grounded theory describes categories and concepts as being more or less the same thing (Dey 1999; Charmaz 2006; Birks and Mills 2011). However, when looking closer at the literature these terms often have different meanings. Let us take a few examples. Strauss and Corbin (1990) talk a lot about concepts[1] as do Birks and Mills (2011), who follow a similar approach. This approach begins by defining concepts as the 'building blocks' of 'categories', which are then described as being more general. They described concepts as follows:

> **Concepts are the basic building blocks of theory**. Open coding in grounded theory method is the analytic process by which concepts are identified and developed in terms of their properties and dimensions. The basic analytic procedures by which this is accomplished are: the asking of questions about data; and the making of comparisons for similarities and differences between each incident, event, and other instances of phenomena. Similar events and incidents **are labeled and grouped to form categories**. (Strauss and Corbin 1990: 74, emphasis added)

As you can see, the definition of concepts as the building blocks of theory is entangled with how you discover them during open coding. What we would like you to note is that in this respect concepts are being discussed as the building blocks of theory *in a general sense*. In other words, concepts are what all theories are made of. The following quotation is a good example:

> Recollect that concepts are the basis of analysis in grounded theory research. All grounded theory procedures are aimed at identifying, developing, and relating concepts. ... certain concepts are deemed significant because (1) they are repeatedly present or notably absent when comparing incident after incident, and (2) through the coding procedures they earn the status of categories. (Strauss and Corbin 1990: 177)

In this description we can see that concepts are significant in as much as they earn their way into becoming 'categories' *in grounded theory*. They are therefore somehow less powerful than categories (Strauss and Corbin 1990). This is obviously a bit confusing. Here we have something called a concept, which seems to have two uses. One is a general use: that concepts are something that we work with in all theory. The other is very specific: in grounded theory concepts are the building blocks of categories which are, in turn, a more general type of concept. This distinction is not very clear in the literature on grounded theory and yet it is very important.

It isn't hard to see just how confusing this whole state of affairs can get. Strauss and Corbin (1990: 65) talked about how it was possible to generate 'dozens' or 'hundreds' of concepts that had to be subsequently grouped. This process was described as the process of *categorising*. They also, rather confusingly, stated that:

> The phenomenon represented by a category is given a conceptual name, however this name should be more abstract than that given to the concepts grouped under it. Categories have conceptual power because they are able to pull together around them other groups of concepts or subcategories. (Strauss and Corbin 1990: 65)

As you can see, categories are built from concepts but they also have to be conceptual. Ian Dey, in *Grounding Grounded Theory* (1999), attempted to sort this confusion out. For him, categories and categorisation were clearly related to how to do grounded theory. Concepts, on the other hand, are part of the general discussion about conceptualisation in science. In this sense, then, Dey (1999) seems to have reversed the relationship between categories and concepts that you can see in others (Strauss and Corbin 1990; Birks and Mills 2011). Dey's discussion in fact moved the whole problem of categorisation in a different direction from that

'According to Glaser and Strauss, categories and their properties are concepts that must have two essential features. ... [T]hey have to be analytic, designating not entities *per se* but their characteristics. In other words, categories are not merely labels used to name different incidents, but involved conceptualization of some key features.' (Dey 1999: 7)

of Strauss and Corbin (1990). His primary concern was to define what a category was and in turn to specify how categories and properties were in fact *very different types of concept*.

In summary, there tend to be three different ways of relating concepts and categories in the general literature on grounded theory. One is to conflate the two terms and to take them as synonymous (Charmaz 2006; Birks and Mills 2011). Another approach is to separate concepts and categories, and focuses on categorising while keeping concepts to refer to something more general than categories (Dey 1999). In this view, concepts become ubiquitous elements of the theory, to be found everywhere. In turn, the processes of building concepts and categories, conceptualisation and categorisation, become the basic processes of doing grounded theory. Another strategy is the 'building blocks' approach. In this approach, concepts are developed from the data and are worked over and over to produce categories. In this view, categories are more general than concepts (Strauss and Corbin 1990). In each of these views it is really only the work of Dey (1999) that acknowledges the universal and ubiquitous nature of concepts and how this might be relevant to building theory. It is to the nature of categories in contemporary grounded theory that we will now turn.

The contemporary view of categories in grounded theory

There are different aspects to defining categories in grounded theory. The consensus is that categories are distinct because they have properties and dimensions (Strauss and Corbin 1990; Dey 1999; Charmaz 2006; Birks and Mills 2011). What exactly are these features of categories? Birks and Mills (2011), follow Strauss and Corbin (1990) very closely when they state the following:

> Categories and their sub-categories also have properties that need to be identified in the data and explained fully in order to develop conceptual depth and breadth. Strauss and Corbin (1998) define a property as a 'characteristic of a category, the delineation of which defines [the category] and gives it meaning' (p. 101). Properties of categories and sub-categories should be considered in terms of their dimensions, or the range of variance that the property demonstrates. (Birks and Mills 2011: 98)

This statement is not entirely clear. Properties are defined in relation to other things, so, for example, they are a 'characteristic of a category'. It is also not clear if properties can also have dimensions or if it is sub-categories that have dimensions. In contrast to this, Dey (1999) produces a much more complex exploration of the relationship between categories, properties and dimensions. His perspective is informed by the conventional wisdom that grounded theory represents a marriage between two very different traditions, the largely quantitative School of Paul F. Lazarsfeld at Columbia University, which is said to have influenced Glaser,[2] and the Chicago School, which is said to be the main influence on Strauss. Dey (1999) argues that Glaser and Strauss may have been trying to combine variable analysis (i.e. Glaser and the Columbia School) with a naturalistic mode of enquiry (i.e. the Chicago School). Dey argues that perhaps the solution Glaser and Strauss developed to the underlying tensions between these approaches was to develop two strategies. The first was to treat 'concepts' (or categories) as though they could fulfil both modes of enquiry. In this approach, categories could provide rich description and be well defined in the same way as variables. The second strategy was to argue that the theory could become more and more grounded as it was generated. This was not without its problems. In some senses, categories had to be initially 'fuzzy' or 'fluid', gradually becoming fixed in the process of analysis (Dey 1999). He goes on to explore the original texts and eventually settles on the following definitions:

Category: Class, division, or any relatively fundamental concept.

Property: Owning, being owned; attribute, quality, characteristic; quality common to a whole class but not necessary to distinguish it from others.

Dimension: Measurable extent of any kind (e.g. length, breadth). (Dey 1999: 52)

Once again, categories are defined as a particular type of concept, although they are also defined as a whole class or division. Properties are defined as an element of a class or as an element of a category, but they are not needed to mark the category out from other categories. Finally, we can see that dimensions are a measurable extent of any kind and therefore, within his scheme, might be related to both properties and categories.

For Dey (1999), the principal thing about categories was that they grouped similar things together (see Dey 1999: 52). Properties, on the other hand, seemed to refer to how an entity interacted with its environment. In contrast to properties, dimensions remained internal to the thing being measured, and indicated something about its scale. He went on to make a number of points with respect to properties, dimensions and categories. First, he argued that we tend to speak of something having properties or dimensions but we do not talk about it in terms of it possessing categories. Phenomena tend to belong to different classes of categories and are assigned to different categories for the purposes of comparison. In this respect, categories are part of how we construct phenomena and how we classify them. Second, we are told that properties and dimensions are discovered by studying how something interacts with its environment. Categories, on the other hand, are not observed or discovered, they are constructed.

QUESTION

Going back to some of the things we discussed in our previous chapter, is Dey realist about phenomena and constructivist about grounded theory as a scientific method?

Dey (1999) then goes on to argue that you will be involved in three different analytical processes. Categories will be built through comparison and classification. Properties will be developed by analysing or paying attention to the interaction between a phenomenon and its environment, and you should expect to specify dimensions through the use of various scales (Dey 1999: 56). The multiple distinctions he explores when clarifying what categories, properties and dimensions represent are a significant attempt at clarifying the meaning of these aspects of grounded theory. We can envisage two problems with this. The first is the degree to which this approach actually constitutes a clarification of the method, and the second is whether this way of specifying these elements of grounded theory are practical. We will now turn to the process of conceptualisation and categorisation within the original texts.

There are several other features of categories in grounded theory. Charmaz stated that categories should have abstract power, general reach, analytic direction and precision. Others, such as Dey (1999) and Birks and Mills (2011), have added that categories should also be saturated, and they should contribute to the integration of the theory.

Concepts and the discovery of grounded theory

An important theme of this book has been the degree to which grounded theory owes its origins and development to the Columbian and Chicago Schools of sociology (Dey 1999; Charmaz 2000, 2006).[3] *Discovery* and *Theoretical Sensitivity* make numerous references to these traditions. There is no more acute point at which these traditions become relevant than in the way grounded theory handles conceptualisation and categorisation. It is more or less accepted in the literature that there is an important distinction between the Columbian and Chicago Schools of sociology and that there is a tension within grounded theory as a result of the influence of each tradition. This tension, we are told, eventually ended up in acrimony in the split between Glaser and Strauss. This is a particular reading of grounded theory that can be justified by referring to the recent works of Glaser (1992, 1998, 2002; Glaser and Holton 2004). But what do the texts actually state? What is the context within which they are embedded? Can we locate the different treatment of concepts and categories in the original texts?

As we have seen previously, Glaser and Strauss (1967) distinguished their constant comparative method from methods that were primarily interested in verifying theory. They stated that their concern was to develop concepts from data in contrast to verifying pre-existing concepts (Glaser and Strauss 1967). The following passage of text appears to provide the clearest outline of what they mean by concepts in grounded theory:

> The type of concept that should be generated has two, joint, essential features. First, the concepts should be analytic – sufficiently generalized to designate characteristics of concrete entities: not the entities themselves. They should also be sensitizing – yield a meaningful picture, abetted by apt illustrations that enable one to grasp the reference in terms of one's own experience. To make concepts both analytic and sensitizing helps the reader to see and hear vividly the people in the area under study, especially if it is a substantive area. (Glaser and Strauss 1967: 38–39)

The first thing to notice about this quotation is that concepts are part of a more general set of entities from which there can be different types. We can then expect there to be many different types of concept. In addition, concepts will have two major features. They will be linked to concrete entities and, as such, will define general 'characteristics' of those entities; this was called their analytic function. Concepts should also be 'sensitising'. This feature means that concepts should enable the reader to have a direct link to the area under question. In *Theoretical Sensitivity*, Glaser (1978) added the fact that a concept should have dimensions. He also argued 'that the standard sociological way of defining a concept is too restrictive when compared to the specifying of its operational distinctions relevant to the emerging theory' and that 'conceptual specification' should be the focus of grounded theory rather than 'conceptual definition'. His reasons for this were related to the necessity to be flexible and the fact that constantly changing a conceptual definition was difficult to do. In contrast, constantly modifying the way we talk about a concept was easier (Glaser 1978: 64).

In this respect Glaser favoured the process of specification of concepts. In doing so he was extending and developing ideas that were originally outlined in *Discovery*. The curious phrase that 'Conceptual specification is the focus of grounded theory, not conceptual definition' refers to a process that involves the increasing refinement of concepts by specifying their links with the empirical world and, indeed, other concepts in the theory. Now if Glaser (1978) was heavily influenced by Lazarsfeld, perhaps we would expect his extension and development of grounded theory to draw heavily on the Columbian school of sociology. Others have claimed that this is the case. For example, Dey (1999) argues that this was the variable approach of Lazarsfeld (1958) creeping into Glaser's use of grounded theory. Yet can this claim be sustained?

It seems that the reality behind this aspect of grounded theory is quite complex. In order to clarify it we need to take you through a detailed analysis of what Lazarsfeld actually said. Lazarsfeld said that 'concept specification' involved taking the 'original imagery' of a concept and dividing it into components (Lazarsfeld 1958). 'The concept', we are told, 'is specified by an elaborate discussion of the phenomena out of which it emerged. We develop 'aspects', 'components', 'dimensions' or similar specifications. They are sometimes derived logically from the over-all concept, or one aspect is deduced from another, or empirically observed correlations between them are reported. The concept is shown to consist of a complex combination of phenomena, rather than a simple and directly observable item' (Lazarsfeld 1958: 101). As you can see, for Lazarsfeld, *the concept can be logically derived*. It can be *deduced* from an 'over-all concept' or it can be used to report observed correlations.

> Conceptual specification can be done deductively according to Lazarsfeld. This involves deducing different aspects of the concept from the original imagery associated with the concept. This is primarily achieved through a process of logical elaboration.

The problem is Glaser (1978) departs from this in significant ways. His approach is much more focused on the specification of concepts through the careful manipulation of observation. An approach that is much more in keeping with that of Blumer (1954), who argued that:

> Theory is of value in empirical science only to the extent to which it connects fruitfully with the empirical world. Concepts are the means, and the only means, of establishing such connection, for it is the concept that points to the empirical instances about which a theoretical proposal is made. If the concept is clear as to what it refers, then sure identification of the empirical instances may be made. With their identification, they can be studied carefully, used to test theoretical proposals and exploited for suggestions as to new proposals. Thus, with clear concepts theoretical statements can be brought into close and self-correcting relations with the empirical world. (Blumer 1954: 4–5)

Definitive concepts	Sensitising concepts
A definitive concept refers to a class of objects on the basis of benchmarks or well defined attributes.	A sensitising concept lacks the specification of attributes and benchmarks.
The clear definition enables the researcher to identify individual instances.	A sensitising concept lacks specification and so the user cannot move directly to specific instances and its content.
Individual instances of the concept are 'covered' by the concept.	Sensitising concepts are not covered by individual instances.
Definitive concepts prescribe what to see.	Sensitising concepts direct us where to look.

Figure 4-1 The contrast between definitive and sensitising concepts

It is therefore the nature of concepts to be refined. Blumer refers to specification in a very different way from Lazarsfeld:

> Careful scrutinizing of our concepts forces one to recognize that they rest on vague sense and not on precise specification of attributes. ... Formal definitions are of little use. ... Our concepts come to be taken for granted on the basis of such a sense. It is such a sense and not precise specifications that guides us in our discipline in transactions with our empirical world. (Blumer 1954: 5)

Blumer (1954) went on to discuss the principal problems with definitive concepts that were operationalised through specification and contrasted these with sensitising concepts (see Figure 4-1).[4]

Clearly, when it comes to working with concepts, the symbolic interactionism of Blumer contrasts with the approach of Lazarsfeld (1958). Yet in our earlier quotation Glaser and Strauss (1967) were drawing on Blumer. They were also carefully distinguishing the approach in grounded theory from that which could be found in Lazarsfeld.[5] Glaser (1992) later indicated that he was heavily influenced by the need to stick to the generation of theory in the field *through data analysis*. These, however, are not the only characteristics of concepts in grounded theory.

QUESTION

What are the practical differences between Lazarsfeld's approach and the approach that was subsequently adopted in grounded theory?

Apart from being analytic and sensitising, concepts in grounded theory are also linked to ideas,[6] something we can clearly see when it comes to the context of doing grounded theory and the influence of comparative analysis. Ideas were important because grounded theory involved 'lifting data into concepts'. By seeing the process of theory generation in this way, Glaser and Strauss (1967) attempted to go beyond Blumer's reflection on 'operationalism'[7] to provide clear procedures to generate theory from data (Glaser and Strauss 1967: 14).

By seeing grounded theory as a building process, Glaser and Strauss (1967) were proposing a particular relationship between concepts and data. It was here that their split from verification, but also Lazarsfeld, becomes especially acute. Glaser (1978) argued against all forms of *logical elaboration* in favour of something that he called *conceptual elaboration*. Conceptual elaboration involved working with the data by comparing similar instances and generating concepts that could capture 'characteristics of concrete entities: not the entities themselves'. Concepts should be worded in such a way that they 'yield a meaningful picture' and are elaborated through carefully directed explorations of the field. Building theory involves building concepts from the data. Such concepts had to have a cogent link with the data. The degree to which such links could be established would enable judgements about whether or not the theory fitted or worked. Glaser went on to talk about a specific type of concept called the category. He did this via something called the 'conceptual code'. There are several important points about the quotation in the box. First, Glaser (1978) specified the 'essential relationship' between data and the 'conceptual code'. This is the same problem that others were grappling with at the time (Blumer 1954; Bendix 1963). Second, concepts are also related to categories and are ubiquitous, that is they are the primary focus on doing grounded theory. Concepts link all of the elements of grounded theory together. It is not surprising to find that the term appears time and again throughout *Discovery* and *Theoretical Sensitivity*. The bewildering range of references attached to concepts in the literature appears to be well founded, and indeed justified from our study of the original texts. We have taken our analysis a step further and mapped all terms and ideas that are associated with the use of the term 'concept' in its various forms (i.e. conceptualisation, conceptual, concepts) in *Discovery* and *Theoretical Sensitivity*. We discovered a huge range of associated terms (see Figure 4-2).[8]

> 'The essential relationship between data and theory is a conceptual code. The code conceptualizes the underlying pattern of a set of empirical indicators within the data. Thus, in generating a theory by developing the hypothetical relationships between conceptual codes (categories and their properties) which have been generated from the data as indicators, we "discover" a grounded theory.' (Glaser 1978: 55)

In the original texts concepts are the building blocks of the method and understanding how they are used is fundamental to understanding grounded theory. The principal concern that appears to exist in relation to grounded

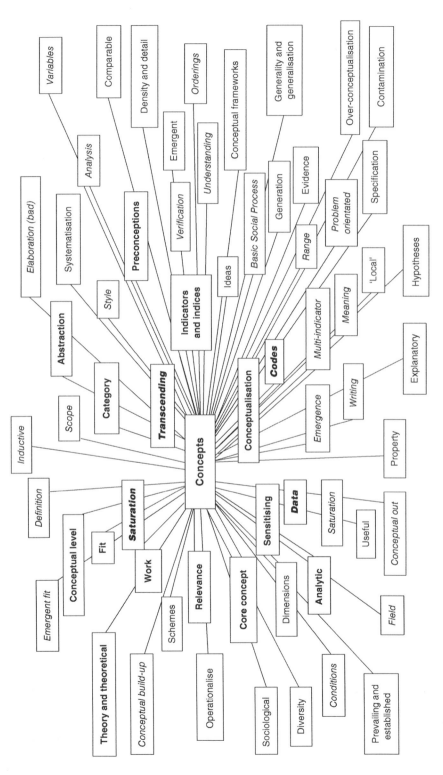

Figure 4-2 Terms associated with 'concepts' in the original iteration of grounded theory

theory is the relationship between concepts and data. As we have seen, a key aspect of grounded theory is the way it seeks to bridge the gap between theory and data. A close inspection of *Discovery* and *Theoretical Sensitivity* will readily uncover several references on how to do this. You will find reference to the perspectives of Blumer (1954) and Bendix (1963), both of whom were criticising social theory that appeared to deal with universal concepts that did not relate well to the empirical world. Such theoretical schemes, it was argued, were not that useful. There was a need to close the gap between theory and data. Both Blumer and Bendix proposed increasing the specification of concepts as a path to resolving this tension. Glaser and Strauss's (1964) specific innovation within this context was to suggest such procedures.

In *Discovery* and *Theoretical Sensitivity*, it is made quite clear that grounded theory involves a building process primarily through working with concepts and then with categories. *The essential link, then, between data and theory was the concept.* We can go further however. As we have already discovered in this section, *concepts in grounded theory need to have two essential features: they need to be sufficiently general (or analytic) and they need to be sensitising (i.e. useful).* In order to fully grasp the move from reading the data to thinking about general concepts, Glaser (1978) referred to the concept indicator model of Lazarsfeld (1958). But, *and this is important*, rather than specifying a concept and then seeking out indicators to illustrate it, in the manner of Lazarsfeld, Glaser (1978) reversed the relationship and argued that indicators indicate concepts. He then went on to argue that while one indicator might suggest a concept, another would not be enough to refute it but instead might modify it. In other words, the development of a gap in the one-to-one relationship between concepts and data was essential for the generation of theory. Concepts were to be 'specified' from the 'ground up' and the researcher *should expect a gap to develop between the data and concepts*. In this respect, *Glaser (1978) reversed the relationship between concepts and indicators as they were originally conceived by Lazarsfeld* – something that is overlooked in the contemporary grounded theory literature.

QUESTION

Is the discovery of theory from data unique to grounded theory?

Categories and the discovery of grounded theory

If concepts are ubiquitous in grounded theory, what are we to think about categories? We have mapped the terms associated with categories in *Discovery* and *Theoretical Sensitivity* in Figure 4-3 below.[9] For Glaser and Strauss, a category is 'a stand-alone element of a theory' (Glaser and Strauss 1967: 36). They went on to argue that categories had properties. Properties for their part were defined as 'a conceptual aspect or element of a category' (p. 36). This latter point, how-ever, does not seem to have been borne out by the example they gave at the time. Once more this is important:

> ...two categories of nursing care are the nurses' 'professional composure' and their 'perceptions of social loss' of a dying patient, that is, their view of what degree of loss his death will be to his family and occupation. One property of the category of social loss is loss rationales – that is, the rationales nurses use to justify to them-selves their perceptions of social loss. All three are interrelated: loss rationales arise among nurses to explain the death of a patient whom they see as a high social loss, and this relationship helps the nurses to maintain their professional composure when facing his death. (Glaser and Strauss 1967: 36)

If we follow their argument closely, we find that 'loss rationales' *are something nurses do* when making sense of dying in hospital wards. Such rationales can of course be related to the categories of 'professional composure' or the 'social loss' of the patient, *but they are not part of those categories*. In this respect there appears to be an inconsistency between what Glaser and Strauss (1967) claimed they meant by this relationship and what they were actually doing with it. We will return to this problem later in this chapter. Nonetheless, when Glaser and Strauss (1967) discuss categories it is here more than anywhere that they were outlining their perspective on the development of the gap between data and theory. Take the following statement as a key example of this:

> It must be kept in mind that both categories and properties are concepts indicated by the data (and not the data itself); also that both vary in degree of conceptual abstraction. Once a category or property is conceived, a change in the evidence that indicated it will not necessarily alter, clarify or destroy it. It takes much more evidence – usually from different substantive areas – as well as the creation of a better category to achieve such changes in the original category. In short, concep-tual categories and properties have a life apart from the evidence that gave rise to them. (Glaser and Strauss 1967: 36)

There we have it, categories and properties have a 'life apart from the evidence that gave rise to them'. Apart from being separated from the data by a gap, categories are also recognisably different from concepts in grounded theory. *Categories are a specific type of concept*; they also have specific functions. They form the basis of further sampling, they are the primary focus of hypothesis formation, the object of conceptual specification and the focus of theoretical integration. Categories also have the function that they group concepts together, typically under higher order ideas. They then bring these ideas together to form a coherent theory or explanation of what is happening in a particular area.

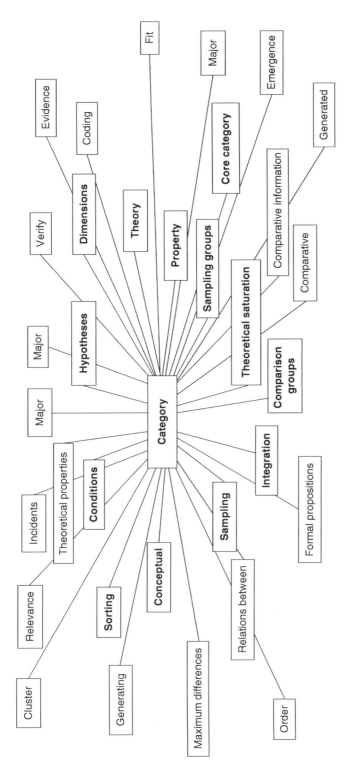

Figure 4-3 Terms associated with 'category' in *Discovery* and *Theoretical Sensitivity*

In the original form of grounded theory, categories and their specification are the central driving factor in sampling (see Chapter 7). It is the specification and delimitation of categories that the grounded theorist engages with in deciding where to go for more 'slices of data'. Take the example of Glaser and Strauss (1967) as they continued to specify the theoretical category 'social loss'. They identified different properties of different groups of patients and observed how these different groups received either better or worse care. Sampling is not discussed in relation to concepts. It is at the strategic level of theory development that we tend to see the development of sampling as a concern in grounded theory.

It is also at the strategic level of theory development that Glaser and Strauss tended to discuss the relationship between categories, especially in the form of hypothesis building. So concepts are chiefly used to build the link between categories and the data; categories relate to the overall status of the theory. Categories are much more important in giving the theory its direction and value.

Concluding comments

Understanding the nature of concepts and categories in grounded theory is not trivial. The difference between them is fundamental to the method. We have seen that for concepts to be useful in grounded theory they must have two major properties. First, they have to be sufficiently general, that is they have to capture characteristics of concrete entities, and second, they have to be related to the data. In the latter case, concepts that are in grounded theory should be seen to relate to observations in the field of study. They should be 'grounded'.

Another central theme of this chapter is that grounded theory was designed as an approach to remedy the complexity of the relationship between data and theory. In attempting to resolve this problem, we have seen that there are a series of subtle breaks between grounded theory and writers such as Lazarsfeld (1958) and Blumer (1940). Glaser and Strauss's (1967) use of conceptual specification was clearly more operational than that of Blumer (1940), but more 'inductive' than Lazarsfeld's (1958) 'deductive' use of the concept indicator model. In this respect the claim that grounded theory combines the Columbian tradition with that of the Chicago School should be questioned. It is *in the discontinuities from these traditions that we can begin to appreciate grounded theory as an innovative new direction in handling the theory data gap in sociology.* Lazarsfeld (1958) discussed the usual manner for specifying concepts by suggesting that we usually start out with an impression of general concepts that might be applicable, then specify dimensions, and subsequently search for indicators in a deductive manner. Glaser and Strauss (1967) draw on his inspiration but reversed the direction of the operations, beginning with indicators and building to more general categories through a careful comparison of indicators. The gap between the indicators, concepts and categories was clearly something that developed in the process of analysis.

One of the tensions Glaser and Strauss (1967) appear to have been faced with was the degree to which the researcher should engage with prior interests and preconceptions. Concepts did not emerge out of the air a priori. They were to be developed out of an intimate knowledge of the field of research achieved in a systematic manner, in contrast to the vague approach of Blumer (for more details on how this happens, see Chapter 5, 'Coding in Grounded Theory'). In this respect Glaser and Strauss (1967) were more operational than Blumer. Their conception of grounded theory as a building process involved the ubiquitous use of the term 'concept', which is central to doing grounded theory.

Less clear is the necessity of over-complicating this process by adding additional questions, such as coding for conditions and consequences (see Strauss and Corbin 1990). Or even the elaborate processes associated with Dey's (1999) attempt to clarify grounded theory. It has been argued that Strauss and Corbin over-specified new procedures and, as a consequence, ended up 'forcing' issues into grounded theory that were not necessary (Walker and Myrick 2006; Rich 2012). Walker and Myrick (2006) agreed with Dey's (1999) assessment that Strauss and Corbin's (1990) insistence on the use of new procedures, such as 'axial coding',[10] was really an *over-complication*. We would tend to agree. Equally, however, we think that Dey's (1999) respecification of the relationship between categories, properties and dimensions also seems somewhat over-elaborate. His approach to categorising doesn't seem to have become popular in grounded theory methodology.

In this chapter, we have also clarified that categories are a very particular type of concept in grounded theory. They are described as stand-alone elements of a theory. Categories are supposed to 'fit' and 'work'. They are supposed to explain how phenomena vary and also be directly related to the phenomena under investigation. One final point: in our analysis we discovered an inconsistency in the way that Glaser and Strauss (1967) specified the relationship between categories and properties. According to our analysis, while Glaser and Strauss (1967) were presenting their examples, properties were things possessed by participants and groups. They belong to real world entities. Not to categories.

Critical reflection 6

What are concepts and categories?

Now go back to your brief notes and respond by writing about how your perspective on the role of concepts and categories in grounded theory has changed after reading this chapter. You might also want to make some notes on any further questions that have arisen while you have been reading this chapter. This could include notes concerning any further reading you might like to make.

Summary

In this chapter we attempted to deal with the complex relationship between concepts and categories in grounded theory. We explored the current literature in grounded theory and outlined the range of ways that others have tried to understand the relationship between these key elements of grounded theory. The chapter went on to systematically examine the way concepts and categories were referred to in grounded theory. In this analysis, we discovered that concepts were ubiquitous within grounded theory and that they were linked to almost everything whereas categories had a very specific meaning. We discovered that categories are the main object of the method because they are the outcome of all of its processes, and that the relationships between categories are what give the theory its meaning and relevance. We then traced how, when it comes to conceptualisation and categorisation, grounded theory departed from the Columbian and Chicago traditions in sociology. In this respect, we have seen that some commonly-held assumptions about the origins of grounded theory can be questioned. The chapter has also argued that there has been a tendency in contemporary grounded theory to over-elaborate procedures and rules for the development of categories in ways that go well beyond the original approach of 'conceptual specification'.

Further reading

Birks, M. and Mills, J. (2011) 'Data analysis in grounded theory', Chapter 6 in M. Birks and J. Mills, *Grounded Theory: A Practical Guide*. London: Sage.

Blumer, H. (1954) 'What is wrong with social theory?' *American Sociological Review*, **19**(1): 3–10.

Dey, I. (1999) 'Categories', Chapter 3 in I. Dey, *Grounding Grounded Theory: Guidelines for Qualitative Inquiry*. London: Academic Press.

Glaser, B. and Strauss, A. (1967) 'Theoretical sampling', Chapter 3 in B. Glaser and A. Strauss, *The Discovery of Grounded Theory*. Chicago: Aldine.

Notes

1   In direct contrast to other writers, such as Dey (1999), who talk much more about categories than concepts.

2   This conventional wisdom is not without some justification. After all, Glaser (1992) has always claimed this was the case. What is less clear is if the Columbian School is in fact a central inspiration for the way that grounded theory subsequently developed categories.

3   Although, as we have seen, part of our *re*discovery has been that it also owes a lot to the comparative tradition in sociology.

4   We have adopted this diagram from an analysis of Blumer (1954).

5   We know this because of the footnote on page 14 of *Discovery* where Glaser and Strauss (1967) discuss Blumer's dislike of operationalism. Here they clearly agree with the idea of generating a data theory gap by working from the ground up. They go on to criticise Blumer for failing to develop a way of generating theory because he became preoccupied with attacking verification. In addition to this, what we have done here is to look closely at Lazarsfeld's discussion of conceptual specification. In doing so, hopefully you can see that his use of logical elaboration as part of the process of specification of concepts is something that Glaser and Strauss (1967) and later Glaser (1978) dropped. Rather, Glaser (1978) was to draw on Lazarsfeld in a very subtle way, making use of the concept indicator model to justify working from the ground up to develop concepts. These are quite subtle differences but they have significance for the way in which grounded theory is conceived.

6   Glaser (1978) stated 'Grounded theory is ideational; it is a sophisticated, careful method of idea manufacturing. The conceptual idea is its essence' (Glaser 1978: 7).

7   Operationalism here refers to the practice of defining concepts with reference to their quantitative or measurable correlations. Blumer was specifically objecting to the fact that such 'operational' definitions were reductionist and eliminated any reference to experience (see Blumer 1940).

8   Includes all references to 'concept', 'conceptualisation' and 'conceptual' in *Discovery* and *Theoretical Sensitivity*. Terms from *Theoretical Sensitivity* are in italics and important terms are in bold.

9   Includes all references to 'category' and 'categorisation' in *Discovery* and *Theoretical Sensitivity*.

10   Axial coding was defined by Strauss and Corbin as 'A set of procedures whereby data are put back together in new ways after open coding, by making connections between categories. This is done by utilizing a coding paradigm involving conditions, context, action/interactional strategies and consequences' (Strauss and Corbin 1990: 96). The way it was written into that text was as an essential strategy in doing grounded theory. Glaser (1992) later objected to this in a furious response and, as a consequence, there remains little or no consensus over what is or isn't grounded theory.

5

Coding in Grounded Theory

Aim: To explore and evaluate the meaning of theoretical coding in grounded theory

Learning outcomes

After reading this chapter you should be able to:

- outline how theoretical coding is discussed in contemporary grounded theory
- detail and explore how coding was elaborated in grounded theory
- formulate how to conduct open and selective coding in grounded theory
- describe the nature of the core category in grounded theory

If categorisation is a key goal of grounded theory, then coding is its key mechanism. It is also the place where most controversy can be located in the method (Dey 1999). But what is coding? What does it involve? Why is this important? As we shall see, coding is the principal set of techniques that are used in grounded theory to arrive at a set of well-developed categories closely related to the data and each other in a fully integrated theory. We will explore how these techniques are viewed in the literature on grounded theory. The purpose of this analysis is, of course, to evaluate what is said about coding in the light of our continued study of the original grounded theory texts. As with the previous chapters in this section, we begin by reviewing what is said about coding in the general literature on grounded theory. We then explore what is said about grounded theory in *Discovery* and *Theoretical Sensitivity*. As with our previous chapters, we go beyond those texts into some of the debates that were going on in the field at the time. Our goal is to clarify the meaning of coding in grounded theory in order to prepare the way for the second section of the book.

Critical reflection 7

What is theoretical coding?

Before reading any further in this chapter, take time to write down some brief notes on the following questions:

- What is theoretical coding in grounded theory?
- What does theoretical coding involve in grounded theory?

Coding in the literature

A key characteristic about coding in grounded theory is that it has become increasingly elaborate in the contemporary literature. This in itself should not be surprising. After all, any field of enquiry should demonstrate progress. It should not be surprising that when it comes to coding in grounded theory that a range of approaches are detailed in the literature. Coding is an activity that has two main purposes: (a) to secure categories from the data, and (b) to integrate these into a unified theory.[1] For some this process is divided into clear stages whereas for others these stages are less clear. Birks and Mills (2011) divide coding into two stages, referred to as initial and intermediate coding. Initial coding refers to the name used in *Discovery* (Glaser and Strauss 1967) and other iterations of the method as 'open coding' (Glaser 1978; Strauss and Corbin 1990; Charmaz 2006). We are told that coding involves asking the following questions of the data:

1. What is this data a study of?
2. What category does this incident indicate?
3. What is actually happening in the data?
4. From whose point of view? (Birks and Mills 2011: 96)

The last question, we are told, was added by Charmaz (2006). Birks and Mills go on to outline how Strauss and Corbin 'simplified' the process by reformulating the questions as follows:

1. There are conditions – why, where, how and what happens?
2. There are inter/actions and emotions.
3. There are consequences – of inter/actions and emotions (Birks and Mills 2011: 96).

Other writers, such as Charmaz (2006), illustrate how they do coding with detailed and helpful examples. According to these examples, coding involves rewording or summarising what is happening in a passage of text or set of observations. It involves 'fracturing the data' (Strauss and Corbin 1990) into categories and then reassembling it into a coherent theory. In this respect coding is often split into two or more stages, with different objectives for each stage. Take Charmaz (2006) as a good example. Her approach is to divide coding into two phases; there is an initial phase and then a more 'focused, selective phase'. In the former phase the researcher is involved in 'naming each word, line, or segment of data', whereas the focused phase involves using 'the most significant or frequent initial codes to sort, synthesize, integrate, and organize large amounts of data' (Charmaz 2006: 46). Charmaz goes on to describe coding as involving creating codes 'by defining what we see in the data' for her codes 'emerge as you scrutinize your data and *define meanings within it*' (Charmaz 2006: 46). We are told later that codes condense 'meanings and actions' (p. 48) and therefore the task of coding is to find codes that in some way cover meanings and actions.[2]

> How we specify coding has significant consequences for the kind of method we seek to develop. It relates directly to the kind of theory we feel we should be producing. Over time the procedures for coding have become increasingly elaborated. There are also huge differences, for example, coding meaning is completely different from coding conditions and consequences.

Charmaz (2006) goes on to provide numerous practical tips and clues to coding. As we discussed in Chapter 3, her emphasis is on getting at the meaning of the social world from the perspective of her participants and then fitting her codes closely to the meanings of those under study. Focused coding, we are told, requires you to make decisions about which of the initial codes 'make the most analytic sense to categorize your data' (Charmaz 2006: 58). The key thing, however, about Charmaz's understanding of coding is her emphasis on *understanding* and the promotion of *interpretation*. It is quite clear that for her, grounded theory is all about producing redescriptions of participants' lives. Such redescriptions need to be sensitive and must fit the lives they are describing. This is her constructivism.[3] The fact that Charmaz (2006) is more 'constructivist' in her approach can be discerned in her introduction and explanation of Strauss and Corbin's (1990) controversial coding procedure, 'Axial Coding', where she indicated that she felt it could either extend or limit your coding depending on 'your subject matter and ability to tolerate ambiguity' (Charmaz 2006: 61). She went on to contrast her approach to that of axial coding and demonstrates how the links between her categories are not really defined in terms of causes and consequences. For Charmaz, the links between categories are direct links made from the perspective of participants. So, for example, we can see how disclosing in chronic illness can be 'revealing and often "risky"'. She does not explain this link in any depth. Another important variation that Charmaz brings to grounded theory is in her approach to theoretical coding. While Charmaz (2006) appears to

> For Charmaz, the emphasis of research is on what things mean for people in the area under study. The purpose of coding is to fit codes closely to those meanings. The key to understanding her view of coding is her emphasis on the promotion of *interpretation*. In addition, the links between her categories are developed by looking at what the categories mean for participants and how they are linked by her participants.

support the use of theoretical coding, she does, however, challenge the use of these codes when they are used to lend an air of 'objectivity' to the grounded theory process. Her preference is to use such codes implicitly. On the other hand, she also claims that Glaser had failed to include important theoretical paradigms in his coding schemes, paradigms such as feminist and narrative theory.

QUESTION

Is there a relationship between the kind of theory you want to produce and the kind of coding you do when doing your research?

As you can guess, Strauss and Corbin (1990) have quite a different approach to coding. In contrast to Charmaz, they adopt a three-stage approach: open, axial and selective coding. You only need to read the following definition of open coding in Strauss and Corbin (1990) to see the differences:

> Open coding is the part of analysis that pertains specifically to the naming and categorizing of phenomena through close examination of data. (Strauss and Corbin 1990: 62)

In this definition there is an emphasis on 'phenomena' and 'data'. This is clearly different from what we can see in Charmaz, who focuses on meaning and perspective. Strauss and Corbin (1990) go on to talk about how the data are fractured during open coding and then suggests that axial coding be used to help put the 'data back together in new ways by making connections between a category and its subcategories' (Strauss and Corbin 1990: 97). It is well established that the presentation of this stage of analysis became a source of fundamental disagreement in grounded theory. We would like to make a few observations about Strauss and Corbin's (1990) account. First, this account does not appear to refer to the writing context within which grounded theory was developed. This is an unfortunate omission. Second, there is quite a distinction between open, axial and selective coding, as though these are separate phases of the research process. A key question is the degree to which the process of doing grounded theory can be separated into such phases?[4] This is precisely the criticism Dey (1999) makes of Strauss and Corbin when he discusses the problem of fracturing data into separate categories and then reconstructing these categories into holistic forms of knowledge. Dey's (1999) key criticisms of coding in grounded theory are reserved for two problems that he sees in the method. First, the distinction between substantive and theoretical coding is not very clear (Dey 1999). Second, Dey argued that Glaser (1978) did not talk about the difference between relationships that developed between categories during the process of doing grounded theory and the preconceived concepts that his theoretical codes represented (Dey 1999: 108).

Dey's principal observation was that most researchers who use grounded theory celebrate open coding as the hallmark of the creativity at the heart of grounded theory but are less inclined to engage with theoretical coding.

As you can see, there is variation in how coding is considered in the grounded theory literature. Over time the method seems to have become increasingly complex. Of course this is something we should expect. But the problem with this complexity is that the different approaches contradict each other. In some instances they have been deliberately constructed as such. What are we to make of this? The main problem with these debates is that it is actually very difficult to ascertain just how each of these approaches can be seen as an advance on grounded theory as it was written. A fundamental omission in this literature is that there is very little detailed discussion of the underlying principles or goals behind coding. Are we really just redescribing meaning (Charmaz 2000)?[5] Some of these answers can be derived by going back and having a closer look at what Glaser and Strauss (1967) actually said. Before we do this, however, let us turn to the theoretical context of coding in grounded theory.

The theoretical context of coding in grounded theory

We have discussed how grounded theory was developed in response to the embarrassing gap between theory and data in social theory (Chapter 2). If we pay attention to the sources cited in *Discovery* and *Theoretical Sensitivity*, it becomes apparent that this original problem of methodology was put forward by Merton at the American Sociological Association meeting in 1947 (Merton, Broom and Cottrell 1959). A debate developed about how people did sociology and this resulted in texts like *Sociologists at Work* (Hammond 1964). But these debates were also part of broader programmes of work. In *Sociology Today: Problems and Prospects* (1959), Merton, Broom and Cottrell discussed the idea of what a social problem is, including the problem of a 'social fact'. In this text, Merton and others appeared to be grappling with the core problem of how to produce generalisations beyond a particular institutional sphere or local problem. So, for example, one might observe the problem of deviance in different social organisations; it might be seen in hospitals, churches or taxi dance halls. Since similar phenomena could occur in different institutional spheres, this seemed to indicate that something more general could be said about the problem and social structure (Merton et al. 1959). A consequence of this thinking was the development of theory of the 'middle range' or theory that was focused on explaining how the substantive problems of people in everyday life were resolved. This approach was a direct inspiration for *Awareness of Dying* and the development of a detailed method called 'The constant comparative method of qualitative analysis' (Glaser 1965).[6]

Other problems discussed in *Sociology Today* relate to similar ideas and concepts that can be found in grounded theory. Parsons (1959) explored the problem of codification which related directly to the link between lower and higher levels of generalisation in a theory and was therefore closely related to the process of delineating schemes or sets of relationships between variables. Indeed, the process itself might involve building from empirical observations to mid-range and high-range theory. As we can see, many of the problems Glaser and Strauss were grappling with were common problems in research methodology at the time.

Another important background source for coding in grounded theory is Lazarsfeld's (1959) chapter on 'Problems in methodology' in *Sociology Today*. When citing the concept indicator model as a source of influence on coding in *Theoretical Sensitivity*, Glaser (1978) specifically cites the influence of this chapter (see Glaser 1978: 62). It is important to note that, on the whole, the authors of the book were concerned with closing the theory data gap. Lazarsfeld's main concern was with the problem of 'variates' or 'classificatory concepts'. Lazarsfeld (1959) outlined how such concepts are developed. It is worth quoting him at length:

> Behind any such classificatory effort stands what we shall call an originating observation: variations and differences exist which are to be explained. The 'explanation' consists of a vaguely conceived underlying or latent property in regard to which people or collectives differ. Four steps can usually be discerned in the translation of this imagery into empirical research instruments:
>
> 1. The original imagery, the intended classification, is put into words and communicated by examples; efforts at definition are made.
>
> 2. In the course of this verbalization, often called conceptual analysis, several indicators are mentioned, and these help to decide where a given concrete object (person or group or organization) belongs in regard to the new classificatory concept. As the discussion of the concept expands, the number of eligible indicators increases; the array of these I shall call the universe of indicators.
>
> 3. Usually this universe is very large, and for practical purposes we have to select a subset of indicators which is then made the basis for empirical work.
>
> 4. Finally, we have to combine the indicators into some kind of index. (Lazarsfeld 1959: 48)

Lazarsfeld went on to discuss the first three stages by asking how the original universe of indicators were established and what the consequences were of choosing one specific subset of indicators over another. The main thrust of Lazarsfeld's (1959) discussion, however, concerned the distinction between *expressive* and *predictive* indicators for a variable. He cited several texts to illustrate his point. He drew on Adorno et al.'s (1950) *Authoritarian Personality*, where he discussed

In Lazarsfeld's perspective, expressive indicators should express what a variable is about – they should express its link to the phenomenon under investigation. Predictive indicators should express the link between the variable and other variables.

the purpose of items on the instrument to measure an authoritarian personality. Such items appeared to have two purposes. One was to serve 'as "giveaways" of underlying trends in personality' (Adorno et al. 1950, cited in Lazarsfeld 1959: 49). This was termed the expressive function and referred to the fact that some items on the scale should express or describe what an authoritarian personality was. The second function of items on the scale was to be predictive. In this respect some indicators on the scale ought to be related to the connection *between* the authoritarian personality and other variables, such as prejudice. In the course of his discussion it becomes clear that the process of generating a classification scheme involves observing variations in empirical indicators and these in turn might point to a more general phenomenon, a latent construct. We are told to be sensitive to the fact that there will be indicators that are expressive of the construct and indicators that are predictive of the relationship between the construct and another construct. A particular problem sociologists were experiencing at the time was that they were using too many expressive indicators at the expense of more predictive indicators. These ideas have some relevance for coding in grounded theory.

Coding in *Discovery*

In *Discovery*, two types of coding are compared and contrasted. On the one hand, in quantitative theory coding was conducted to ensure accuracy of evidence. Indeed, there had been significant strides in the development of quantitative sociology. Glaser and Strauss (1967) sought to enable those looking to generate theory to have similar levels of sophistication.[7] They stated that:

> The path to systematization was guided (as this book has been) *by the pressure that quantitative verifications had put on all sociologists* to clarify and codify all research operations, no matter what the type of data or the content of the research report. (Glaser and Strauss 1967: 16, emphasis added)

A main goal of *Discovery* was to enable the systematisation of collection, coding and analysis of *qualitative data* with the explicit purpose of generating theory. In this purpose it was contrasted with other procedures which were aimed at verifying theory.

For Glaser and Strauss (1967), coding was embedded in a tripartite relationship between collection, coding and analysis. These processes were to be kept together, with the researcher being heavily involved in each. They clearly stated at several points that the coding of data is closely bound to sampling and data collection:

> Research aimed at discovering theory ... requires that all three procedures go on simultaneously to the fullest extent possible; for this, as we have said, is the underlying operation when generating theory. Indeed, it is impossible to engage in theoretical sampling without coding and analyzing at the same time. (Glaser and Strauss 1967: 71)

One of the puzzling aspects of *Discovery* is the distinction between coding and analysis. Coding appears to relate to the mechanical process of grouping indicators for categories in the theory. In contrast, analysis seemed to be related to the process of writing memos, specifying the theory and guiding theoretical sampling (Glaser and Strauss 1967). Glaser and Strauss (1967) developed explicit procedures in *Discovery* by outlining two current approaches to the analysis of qualitative data (page 101*ff*). The first approach involved coding the data so it could be analysed quantitatively in a very crude manner. Here the 'analyst' coded the data and subsequently analysed it in order to provide 'proof for a given proposition' (p. 101). In contrast to this, Glaser and Strauss (1967) argued for:

> a third approach to the analysis of qualitative data – one that combines, by an analytic procedure of constant comparison, the explicit coding procedure of the first approach and the style of theory development of the second. The purpose of the constant comparative method of joint coding and analysis is to generate theory more systematically than allowed by the second approach, by using explicit coding and analytic procedures. While more systematic than the second approach, this method does not adhere completely to the first, which hinders the development of theory because it is designed for provisional testing, not discovering, of hypotheses. (Glaser and Strauss 1967: 102)

Glaser and Strauss (1967) were arguing for a closer relationship between coding and analysis than had existed in other approaches. They sought to develop an approach that was much more iterative than coding, then analysing, and systematically coding everything and analysing separately. The risk, of course, was that the two operations might become confused. There was also an associated risk that the distinction between coding and analysis was unnecessary. Coding was subsequently outlined in detail in *Discovery* (see Figure 5-1). It involved reading data and coding each incident in the data into as many categories of analysis as possible. Coding, then, related to several operations. These operations formed the basic processes the analyst would be involved in while coding in the early stages. The analyst was told that they ought to expect conflicts in coding (Glaser and Strauss 1967: 107) and, when these occurred, to

---

a) Exploring the full range of types or continua of the category.
b) Delimiting the dimensions of a category.
c) Outlining the conditions under which it was either pronounced or minimised,
d) Exploring the category's major consequences.
e) Outlining the category's relation to other categories, and detailing its properties.
f) Involved integrating categories and their properties through comparing incident to incident, to the category and attributing properties, including how these vary in the groups under study.
g) Developed to reduce and concentrate the theory around its major categories.
h) Aimed at the development of the theory by coding new information into the theory.

Figure 5-1   Coding in *Discovery*

resolve them by writing down the solution in a memo or note. In *Discovery* there was no mention of *'selective coding'*.

Despite these purposes for coding, there is a further distinction in *Discovery* between categories that describe the 'processes' and 'behaviours' in the field and those aimed at explanations (Glaser and Strauss 1967: 107). While there appears to be no direct link between *Discovery* and earlier debates in *Sociology*, the distinction between the codes located in the field and those articulated by participants appear to be distinguished from those generated by the analyst.[8] They went on to give the example that social loss stories were found to exist (the expressive aspect of the code) and that these were then eventually related to a calculating and recalculating process (the predictive aspect of coding). They also discussed the fact that the story had 'ingredients' and these were related to balancing out which were, in turn, related to nurses' coping strategies to deal with the upset caused when someone died in their care. In the following example it should be noted that social loss was also related to professional composure. You can see through this example what they meant by integration and the task of relating different categories to each other.

> While *Discovery* did not contain the distinction between the expressive and predictive function of indicators, codes can fulfil both functions. During the process of integration emphasis was placed on predictive coding. As we shall see, these aspects of coding became central to the development of grounded theory described in *Theoretical Sensitivity*.

> we soon found that the calculating and recalculating of social loss by nurses was related to their development of a social loss 'story' about the patient. When asked about a dying patient, nurses would tell what amounted to a story about him. The ingredients of this story consisted of a continual balancing out of social loss factors as the nurses learned more about the patient. Both the calculus of social loss and the social loss story were related to the nurse's strategies for coping with the upsetting impact on her professional composure of, say, a dying patient with a high social loss (e.g., a mother with two children). This example further shows that the category becomes integrated with other categories of analysis: the social loss of the dying patient is related to how nurses maintain professional composure while attending his dying. Thus the theory develops, as different categories and their properties tend to become integrated through constant comparisons that force the analyst to make some related theoretical sense of each comparison. (Glaser and Strauss 1967: 109)

We will now turn to the elaboration of coding that can be found in *Theoretical Sensitivity*.

The elaboration of coding in *Theoretical Sensitivity*

One of the most significant changes in grounded theory between *Discovery* and *Theoretical Sensitivity* is the way Glaser (1978) went on to specify coding in more depth. He did this in response to appeals from students. We know he and Strauss had been supervising students all this time and that through this supervision they had both developed their approach (Gilgun 2010). In *Theoretical Sensitivity*, coding is described as conceptualising the underlying pattern of a 'set of empirical indicators within the data'. More critically, Glaser (1978) argued that it was through the development of relationships between these codes that we discover a grounded theory. In this account of coding more emphasis is placed on coding for ideas in order to escape the data and at the same time to *conceptually account for processes occurring in the data* (Glaser 1978). The process of coding was described as the process of condensing disparate data into something similar by tying such phenomena together. In plain English, this means you take a lot of different examples that seem to be quite similar and you summarise them by *calling* them the same thing. You label them with a word or set of words that typically captures the content they have in common. It is not complicated.

Glaser (1978) went on to make a distinction between substantive and theoretical codes, the former conceptualising the empirical substance whereas the latter related the substantive codes to each other. In *Theoretical Sensitivity*, it was argued that the 'analyst' would focus much more on substantive coding when developing the theory at the start and more on theoretical coding when integrating the theory. The formulation of this distinction is very specific to Glaser's development of the method in *Theoretical Sensitivity*. Having developed the distinction between substantive and theoretical coding, Glaser went on to specify two stages of coding: open coding and theoretical or selective coding.

Open coding

The goal of open coding, it was argued, was to produce a set of categories that fit, work and are relevant for the purposes of theory. This approach was contrasted with developing a theory that was preconceived or working with preconceived categories and data in order to specify the categories. For Glaser, open coding forced the analyst 'to think and transcend' the data. Coding was then aimed at getting out of the data into the realm of ideas.[9] For Glaser (1978), constant comparison literally forced the generation of codes. In *Theoretical Sensitivity*, Glaser (1978) went further and specified several rules for coding. The first rule was to ask a set of questions of the data. These were to be kept in mind and used while coding (see Figure 5-2).

While the first rule of coding was to ask these questions, a further rule was to analyse the data line by line (Glaser 1978: 57). Coding was therefore a meticulous process that involved going through the data thoroughly. The overview approach – an approach that involved reading through the data as a whole and then writing down some general themes or comments – was not recommended on its own. In addition to this line-by-line process for coding, Glaser (1978) argued for a third rule: the analyst ought to do their own coding.

- What is this data a study of?
- When looking at an incident of data one should ask what category does it indicate?
- When thinking of incidents one should ask what property of a category, or what part of the emerging theory, does this incident indicate?
- Reading the data involved asking what was happening in the data (in the words of Lazarsfeld, looking for a latent construct)?
- Open coding also involved asking what the basic social psychological problem(s) faced by participants in the action scene might be?
- One should also ask what is the basic social psychological or social structural process that processes the problem to make life viable in the action scene?

Figure 5-2   Rules of coding in *Theoretical Sensitivity*

In addition to these rules, Glaser argued that, while coding, the analyst ought to always interrupt coding for memoing ideas. This was his fourth rule. He also stated that the analysis wherever possible should remain within the confines of the substantive field of study until the analysts were sure of the 'relevance, fit and workability' of their theory. In this description Glaser referred to the work of Lazarsfeld (1959) and, if we are to link the two texts, it seems that open coding was characterised by a greater emphasis on expressive coding whereas Lazarsfeld's predictive coding may have been eventually reformulated into something called theoretical coding.

QUESTION

How will you code in your study? Think carefully about what you are trying to achieve when coding and write down the practical things you may need to do to prepare yourself for coding.

The final rule of coding in grounded theory was that it was important not to assume the relevance of any 'face sheet' variable, such as race, sex or age, until it emerged as relevant. Related to this was the fact that coding carried with it three phenomenon – verification, correction and saturation (Glaser 1978: 60). Grounded theory involves discovering categories and verifying that they persist in the field. Any gaps between the category and the data are subsequently checked and the category is corrected. Coding is about establishing those categories that describe what is happening and making sure that they fit the problems being explored. As a result, it was described as a process, the goal of which was to generate variables. The outcome of coding was to produce codes which described and grouped together data (Glaser 1978). In vivo codes were taken directly from the data and are usually generated in the field. It was argued that they would have good fit. A good code was described as a code that had good imagery and analytic ability. They must illustrate what they mean and be related to the field or problems being processed.

In grounded theory the code develops out of similarities/differences and degrees of consistency that the analyst reads in the data. By reading the data, the analyst 'generates an underlying uniformity' and this leads to a coded category. In this respect grounded theory was seen as being generated by looking at consistency and uniformity (Glaser 1978). The analyst was also to study variation, and, indeed, when differences emerged in the data these would eventually result in writing memos that recorded these differences and described how the theory could capture them. Once the analyst had at their hands a series of well-developed categories, they would have a good idea of the kind of theory they were looking at. At this stage they would take a decision to begin the process of selective coding.

Selective coding in grounded theory

While open coding is about establishing the fit of categories that might be relevant to the theory, the switch to selective coding involves a strategic decision to focus on key variables that can subsequently be used to delimit a 'parsimonious' theory. Selective coding involves focusing on the core variable, and those variables that are associated with it, including key relationships between the core variable and these variables. It involves delimiting the nature of the theory, what it is about, including the relationships that exist between the core variable and other key variables in the theory. It is at this point that the idea of theoretical coding becomes relevant to the process of doing grounded theory.

We are told repeatedly in *Theoretical Sensitivity* that substantive coding is concerned with capturing the empirical substance of the field under study. In this respect substantive codes conceptualise content; they are 'expressive' in Lazarsfeld's terms (Lazarsfeld 1959). If substantive codes are expressive, then theoretical codes are certainly more 'predictive'; they help the researcher delimit the relationship between the core variable and other variables. But before selective coding could happen, the grounded theorist had to select the core category.

Selecting the core category

The main considerations Glaser (1978) gave when deciding on the core category are summarised in Figure 5-3.

As you can see from this figure, there are quite a few things to think about when picking your core category. As you make your decision, try making that decision by looking through these points and writing memos on them. It is important to think about each point. It is also important to ask yourself in general terms what kind of category is your core category and what are its principal relationships. As we have seen, this also involves writing and reflecting on the

1. It must be central, and related to as many other categories as possible. It should be dominant and account for a large portion of the variation in a pattern of behaviour.
2. It must reoccur frequently. This leads to the perception that it is a stable pattern and can be related to the other variables.
3. It should take more time to saturate because of its relationship to the other variables.
4. It should be related easily with the other categories.
5. It may have 'grab' beyond the substantive field. This indicates its potential for formal theory.
6. The core category should enable the development of the theory rather than make it difficult.
7. It should be highly variable and ought to have frequent relations to other categories. It should also be readily modifiable through these dependent relationships with other variables.
8. The core category ought to be closely related to a dimension of the problem.
9. The core category can be typed through the use of any kind of theoretical code.

Figure 5-3   Selecting the core category

kind of theory you are developing, including its position in your field of study. The process of integrating your categories into a coherent theory is called theoretical coding.

In the same way open coding is a process with a specific outcome in mind, theoretical coding is also a process with an outcome. The process involves exploring the variables at the heart of the emerging theory, the core category and its major associated variables and specifying their relationships. Theoretical coding is primarily focused on *integrating* the theory and *delimiting* it. The major problem with this stage of coding in grounded theory is that the key variables might be related to each other in any number of ways. In *Theoretical Sensitivity*, Glaser (1978) outlined 18 different coding families to illustrate the myriad sets of relationships that might be 'discovered' between variables and used to help with the process of integrating your theory. A key feature of these coding families is the way in which they have copied into grounded theory the structure of many previous sociological theories (Gibson, Gregory et al. 2005). Rather than simply copying these back out, we urge you to explore *Theoretical Sensitivity* to see for yourself the myriad of relationships that can be developed in your grounded theory. The following illustration will suffice.

> 'This is the "bread and butter" theoretical code of sociology. It is the first general code to keep in mind when coding data. Most studies fit into either a causal model, a consequence model or a condition model. Causal has a sub-family called: sources, reasons, explanations, accountings or anticipated consequences. ... A sub-family of consequences is outcomes, efforts, functions, predictions and anticipated or unanticipated consequences. A causal–consequence model, depending on the focus, is the independent–dependent variable model. To focus on the former is to look for its consequence, the dependent variable, and the latter its cause, the independent variable. The causal–consequence model implies an ordering which is usually temporal.' (Glaser 1978: 74)

> One of the key coding families, we are told, is the 'Six Cs'. Glaser (1978) understood this theoretical code as a code that formed the core of much sociological theorising (please refer to the boxed quotation). If, during coding, the 'Six Cs'

becomes relevant, we ought to be thinking about how relationships between the core category and other key variables may be expressed in terms of 'anticipated consequences' or 'reasons'. Take the example of dying as an undesirable status passage. Glaser and Strauss (1971) stated that:

Often agents will not disclose to the passagee the direction of the passage, or even its existence, in order to forestall potential psychological consequences such as 'giving up,' suicide, or deep depression. (Glaser and Strauss 1971: 16)

Here the passagee is going through a passage related to dying. Others do not disclose the passage because of the potential negative consequences associated with revealing the nature of the passage to the passagee, in this case 'giving up', depression or even suicide. The substantive concept of 'dying passage' reveals the empirical content of the status passage being referred to. 'Giving up', suicide and depression are also the empirical content but they are related to dying passage as *negative consequences* of revealing such a passage (Glaser and Strauss 1971). In this example an undesirable state being revealed to the participant can result in negative consequences and in order to avoid such consequences the status passage is hidden from the passagee. The rest of the process of doing grounded theory is concerned with delimiting the theory by explaining how the core category relates to the other variables. This is achieved through the processes of sorting and writing (see Chapters 12–14 for more details).

QUESTION

Glaser specified 18 different coding families in *Theoretical Sensitivity*. Charmaz was critical of him because he did not include many other theoretical perspectives, including feminist theory. What does this tell us about theoretical coding?

Concluding comments

The issue of coding in grounded theory was clearly problematic from the outset. Glaser and Strauss (1967) specified a series of rules about coding that involved delimiting and specifying categories (see Figure 5-1) but made no reference to selective coding for or around a core category. It is clear that they were building a path between the work of Blumer (1940) and that of Lazarsfeld (1959) and that their solution broke with both of those writers in very important ways. After a decade of teaching grounded theory to graduate students, Glaser (1978) then went on to provide the details of a further set of rules and procedures that could be used in doing grounded theory. In this iteration of the method, we find an increasing specification of coding procedures that were designed to work from data to theory. Here coding was designed to generate categories and specify their relations, and then to look for expressive and predictive indicators. Glaser's (1978) specific innovation was to specify theoretical

coding as a way to delineate the range of relationships that we might find
between categories in a theory. Since then, however, there have been several
discontinuities in the method. We would argue that if there was ever a case that
illustrated better a 'loss of the name and the notion of things' it is the issue of
coding in grounded theory.

The process of forgetting has been accidental but it has also been purposeful
and planned. Charmaz (2000, 2006), in particular, went out of her way to produce a new version of grounded theory as a
result of what she saw as objectivist biases
creeping into the method post-Strauss and
Corbin (1990). If Charmaz's version of grounded
theory is a deliberate construction, it is also an
exercise in forgetting. Perhaps some degree of
forgetting is necessary for progress? Charmaz's
(2000) main objections appear to be directed at
Strauss and Corbin's (1990) insistence on fixed
procedures for coding. In this, we think Charmaz
(2000) has a point. Strauss and Corbin (1990)
produced a much more rigidly defined set of
procedures for coding and at the same time invented a whole new stage in
grounded theory (called axial coding). But they produced these additional processes in order to make grounded theory accessible to a wider audience.[10]
Indeed, as we can see, the increasing specification of procedures and rules was
in fact happening in the shift between *Discovery* and *Theoretical Sensitivity*. The
development of these rules and procedures are an important feature of the
disjuncture between grounded theory and the methodological environment in
which it was developed.[11]

In Chapter 4 we saw that grounded theory was proposed as an advance on
the work of Blumer (1940) and Lazarsfeld (1959). Glaser and Strauss (1967)
proposed to keep the sensitivity of Blumer's (1940) approach through the use
of more explicit coding procedures similar to, but quite different from, that of
Lazarsfeld (1959). In *Discovery*, there is an important relationship between the
dual function of categories and the techniques that you need to develop in
order to make sure you have the material to address those functions. In
Chapter 4 we discovered that categories in grounded theory must have two
major properties: they have to be sufficiently general and they have to be
related to the data. In *Discovery*, coding and analysis were the processes to be
employed to secure categories that fulfilled these criteria. The problem was
that the distinction between coding and analysis was in some senses too vague.
It appears that Glaser (1978) recognised this and so went on to generate a further set of procedures to clarify what we should do.

> The question of coding in grounded the-
> ory is really a question about how elabo-
> rate we think it should be and if it ought to
> contain certain stages or not. Over time,
> different writers with different intentions
> for grounded theory have provided differ-
> ent rules and procedures for coding. A
> key question to be addressed is if these
> elaborated procedures produce good
> grounded theory. The views of those
> working in grounded theory differ dra-
> matically in this respect.

In *Theoretical Sensitivity*, Glaser (1978) refined the processes of coding by proposing several 'rules' (see Figure 5-2). This increasing operationalism was justified because students had been struggling with the problem of understanding how to do grounded theory during the decade since the publication of *Discovery*. *Theoretical Sensitivity* takes as its point of departure from Lazarsfeld the distinction between expressive and predictive indicators. It does so by developing specific *procedures* designed to look for these elements of the developing theory. In this respect, Glaser (1978) talked about open and selective or theoretical coding as two different techniques of analysis. He also talked about a cutting point in the process of theory generation that involved selecting the core category and then coding around the core category to integrate the theory. In constructing these approaches Glaser (1978) seemed to be productively drawing on what Lazarsfeld (1959) was doing to clarify how to do grounded theory. In some respects he was successful. After all, *Theoretical Sensitivity* is widely regarded as a core text for those doing grounded theory.

QUESTION

Should we have elaborate procedures for coding in grounded theory, such as those proposed by Dey or should these be relatively simple?

Clearly, however, something went wrong in the forgetting process when it comes to theoretical coding. It seems unfortunate that Strauss and Corbin's (1990) goal to produce a generalised, easily accessible text for doing qualitative research would result in a fundamental discontinuity in grounded theory. The need to develop an easy-to-do manual appears to have produced too much operationalism and has resulted in some strong objections (Glaser 1992, 1998; Charmaz 2000; Glaser and Holton 2004; Charmaz 2006, 2009). Another consequence of the Strauss and Corbin (1990) text is that, in the need to make things simple, they presented the name of the things that made up grounded theory but changed the notion of what grounded theory was. They did so without carefully justifying their changes with reference to the original texts. It is, however, grounded theory, despite the protestations of others (Baker, Wuest et al. 1992; Glaser 1992).[12] What are we to make of this discontinuity?

In some respects it has been incredibly productive. It is not hard to see how Charmaz (2000) went on to suggest an alternative approach to grounded theory as a consequence of her rejection of the 'objectivist' tendencies in Strauss and

Corbin (1990). No one can deny that Glaser has also been productive as a result of his rejection of their approach (Glaser 1992, 2001, 2009; Glaser and Holton 2004). There is now an increasing range of innovations in relation to the blending of grounded theory with other traditions (Baker, Wuest et al. 1992; Wuest 1995; Gibson, Gregory et al. 2005; Gregory, Gibson et al. 2005). However, in other respects there is a risk that too many discontinuities may threaten to make the method incoherent and contradictory. This can cause problems when students try to use approaches to coding that are quite different. There is nothing congruent between Charmaz's (2000) approach to coding the meanings of what participants are saying and Strauss and Corbin's (1990) approach to coding phenomena. Yet, as we shall see,[13] alternative versions of grounded theory can be produced and the careful job of modification of the method to fit different theoretical contexts can be achieved.

So, in response to our questions earlier in this chapter, we feel that Dey's (1999) intuition about grounded theory is correct. Each of the approaches to grounded theory is part of the same tradition and in one sense we should welcome this pluralism. Unlike Dey (1999), however, our purpose is not to critique grounded theory but to clarify its meaning. What we have discovered is that one of the sources of discontinuity in the method is the tendency to specify how one should get on with coding. It is as though the lack of clarity that existed in *Discovery* was most acute and, as a result, Glaser (1978), and subsequently Strauss and Corbin (1990), went on to describe this process with increasing precision. It was in this process that discontinuities developed. What we have *discovered* by reading the background to the method and tracing the origins of the coding procedures is that the process of coding is effectively quite simple. The goal of grounded theory is to produce categories that perform two functions: they have to express what the theory is about and they have to express how they relate to each other. The real test of our approach of clarification, however, is to make doing grounded theory clearer, and it is to this task that we shall now turn.

Critical reflection 8

What is theoretical coding?

Now go back to your brief notes and respond by writing about how your perspective on theoretical coding in grounded theory has changed after reading this chapter. You might also want to make some notes on any further questions that have arisen while you have been reading this chapter. This could include notes concerning any further reading you might like to make.

Summary

This chapter has explored the range of perspectives on the mechanism of doing grounded theory – that of theoretical coding. The analysis has revealed that there is in fact a range of approaches to coding in grounded theory that are not always compatible. In revisiting the original texts, we have discovered new ways in which coding developed out of important continuities and discontinuities between grounded theory and the work of other writers, such as Lazarsfeld. We have noted that the distinction between open and selective coding in grounded theory bears some relationship between expressive and predictive indicators in the work of Lazarsfeld. We also explored in detail the meaning of coding in the original texts by careful analysis of the texts. We have observed that the process of elaborating coding in grounded theory continued to develop in the work of Strauss and Corbin where, it was argued, a new version of grounded theory was produced. The chapter considered if there was a problem of over-elaboration of rules and procedures in grounded theory when it comes to coding and explored the reasons why this may have occurred.

Further reading

Dey, I. (1999) 'Coding', Chapter 5 in I. Dey, *Grounding Grounded Theory: Guidelines for Qualitative Inquiry*. London: Academic Press.

Glaser, B. (1978) 'Theoretical coding', Chapter 4 in B. Glaser, *Theoretical Sensitivity: Advances in the Methodology of Grounded Theory*. Mill Valley, CA: Sociology Press.

Glaser, B. and Strauss, A. (1967) 'The constant comparative method of qualitative analysis', Chapter 5 in B. Glaser and A. Strauss, *The Discovery of Grounded Theory*. Chicago: Aldine.

Strauss, A. and Corbin, J. (1990) 'Part II: Coding procedures', in A. Strauss and J. Corbin, *Basics of Qualitative Research: Grounded Theory Procedures and Techniques*. Thousand Oaks, CA: Sage.

Notes

1   The truth, as we shall see, is a little bit more complicated. Some authors do not see the need to fully integrate their theory and are happy with a set of loosely related themes. We will leave it up to the reader to decide if this is appropriate or not.

2   The language used in this approach to grounded theory seems to be deliberately vague and imprecise. It might be because Charmaz seeks to resist the tendency towards 'operationalism' that you can see in certain parts of the literature. By 'operationalism', we are referring to the tendency to produce rigid rules of procedure for research that people feel they must follow to the letter. A consequence of

operationalism is that it can make the research process more deductive than inductive. Take the example of Strauss and Corbin's (1990) approach. This approach certainly gives the appearance of being more operational, with what appears to be a rigidly prescribed set of stages and analytical rules. But we don't think this would be an entirely accurate assessment of Strauss and Corbin (1990), who, after all, did say they were trying to clarify the method. It is an unfortunate side-effect of trying to clarify things that they resulted in producing a set of carefully worked-out stages and procedures that generated such a reaction within the literature. There is in fact a long history of resistance to 'operationalism' within grounded theory. As we have seen in the previous chapter, Blumer (1940) resisted operationalism. Indeed, a core aspect of Glaser's (1992) attack on Strauss and Corbin's approach could be seen as his own reaction against too much operationalism, captured by his desire to preserve the openness of grounded theory.

3   As we have said, there is something very valuable about Charmaz's approach to grounded theory. Charmaz has been careful to call her approach to grounded theory 'constructivist'. This change in nomenclature reflects the fact that she has modified the method. Innovations such as these should be welcomed and embraced because they allow grounded theory to be fitted to a range of research contexts and approaches. Our purpose is very different from that of Charmaz. Our purpose is to explore grounded theory by looking closely at the original texts and to explore those within the writing context of the time, as sociological artefacts if you like. We are not interested in reconstructing grounded theory as 'objectivist' (or, indeed, 'classic' for that matter) in order to justify changing it.

4   As you shall see, the answer to this question is less than clear.

5   On reading Charmaz (2000: 523–525), it is quite clear that she takes particular issue with operationalism and in particular the operationalism of Strauss and Corbin (1990). She talks of their increasing specification of rules for grounded theory as producing an objectivist grounded theory. We have a particular problem with her account because it is inconsistent when it comes to the original texts. At times she says grounded theory was objectivist, but then later in the text she states 'Guidelines turn into procedures and are reified into immutable rules, unlike Glaser and Strauss's (1967) original flexible strategies. By taking grounded theory methods as prescriptive scientific rules, proponents further the positivist cast to objectivist grounded theory' (Charmaz 2000: 524). So the original method was flexible but had somehow been corrupted by what we call operationalism. The key problem we have with her argument is that it is largely a reconstruction of grounded theory as objectivist in order to enable her to justify her constructivist approach. For us, this reconstruction is an exaggeration that goes too far beyond what was originally said. Despite our misgivings on this point, there remain important merits in her approach.

6   Glaser stated: 'My other purpose in presenting the constant comparative method may be stated by a direct quotation from Robert K. Merton – a statement he made in connection with his own qualitative analysis of locals and cosmopolitans as community influentials: "This part of our report, then, is a bid to the sociological fraternity for the practice of incorporating in publications a detailed account of the ways in which qualitative analyses actually developed. Only when a considerable body of such reports are available will it be possible to codify methods of qualitative analysis with something of the clarity with which quantitative methods have been articulate".' (Glaser 1965: 436–437).

7   This is, of course, why they went beyond Blumer (1940).

8   This is similar to the distinction Lazarsfeld made between expressive and predic-
    tive indicators, discussed above. What is crucial is that the search for explanations
    is articulated in *Discovery* to occur during the process of integration. As we shall
    see, this distinction becomes central to *Theoretical Sensitivity*.

9   A good way to see how this works is to look back at what Lazarsfeld was saying
    in the previous section.

10 They make it very clear in the introduction to their book that it was written in as
    accessible a way as possible to enable those who have never done qualitative
    research to get on with doing it. They also called their approach grounded theory.

11 See our discussion of the difference between the work of Glaser and Strauss in
    Discovery and the work of Blumer (1940) and Lazarsfeld (1959) in the previous chapter.

12 As we have already said in this respect, we are in agreement with Dey (1999) that
    all of these texts should be seen as part of the same tradition.

13 The work of Wuest (1995), we feel, is a clear example of a carefully developed
    alternative approach to doing grounded theory that retains enough of the original
    approach to be justified in retaining the label 'grounded theory'. Charmaz's (2000)
    approach is another example of an approach which is justified in using the label
    because her approach retains enough of the core principles to justify its use.

PART 2: DOING
GROUNDED
THEORY

6

How to Develop
Theoretical Sensitivity

Aim: To outline and explore the nature of theoretical sensitivity in grounded theory

Learning outcomes

After reading this chapter you should be able to:

- outline and explore the nature of theoretical sensitivity in grounded theory
- have an awareness of the concept of openness and its importance for grounded theory
- know about the problem of openness and how this relates to sampling in grounded theory and have a critical awareness of the implications of these for sampling
- develop skills for enhancing your theoretical sensitivity
- establish the centrality of prior interests and preconceptions to the development of grounded theory studies

The previous five chapters of this book have sought to clarify what grounded theory is through an exploration of the original texts and a critical evaluation of the ideas in those texts. Our remaining task is to take these ideas and explore how they can be used to do grounded theory well. Our project of rediscovery has taken us back through the original context and texts in order to explore the essence of what grounded theory was at the time it was developed. Our task is only half complete. In what follows we have continued our detailed study of the original texts. In this study, we have spent a lot of time teasing out the *positive statements of what grounded theory involves in a practical way*. In some senses this exploration will take you on a journey through something that risks becoming a lost craft. As grounded theory has been continually revised and updated, some of the procedures have lost their original emphasis. The style of this part of the book is practical and focused on *doing grounded theory*. We want to enable those new to grounded theory to be able to do it, hopefully, better. In this chapter, we will begin with a discussion of the important issue of theoretical sensitivity. We begin by asking the question 'What is theoretical sensitivity?' We seek to outline the main elements of theoretical sensitivity and explain why it is important. We then go on to discuss how you can develop theoretical sensitivity by providing some practical advice and tips. In order to provide this advice throughout this part of the book we will be drawing on what we have called exemplars of grounded theory. We will introduce these exemplars in the next section, before going on to outline the main elements of what theoretical sensitivity involves, including how to enhance it. After this, we will reflect on what the analysis in this chapter brings to current perspectives in grounded theory.

┐ Critical reflection 9 ┌

What is theoretical sensitivity?

Before reading any further in this chapter, take time to write down some brief notes on the following questions:

- What is your current understanding of the term 'theoretical sensitivity' in grounded theory?
- How might 'theoretical sensitivity' be enhanced?

What is theoretical sensitivity?

In 1978 Glaser stated that a secondary purpose of his book was to enable 'the development of the necessary *theoretical sensitivity* in analysts by which they can render theoretically their discovered substantive, grounded categories' (Glaser 1978: 1). Strauss and Corbin stated that theoretical sensitivity 'refers to a personal quality of the researcher', indicating 'an awareness of the subtleties of meaning of data' and that we all come to the research situation with different levels of sensitivity that result from our reading and experience with the area of study (Strauss and Corbin 1990: 41). Glaser went on to describe theoretical sensitivity as 'a must'; it was something that many researchers have but often do not recognise. The problem Glaser was attempting to confront was that often people doing grounded theory would struggle to 'set down theoretically' their findings. His book was aimed at presenting 'a fund of ideas and ways to systematically relate categories into theory' and this 'fund' was aimed at enabling researchers to 'render' their data and work with it (Glaser 1978: 1). Generating theory is not easy, we are told. Indeed, some people are just never able to develop this sensibility (Gilgun 2010).

Theoretical sensitivity is about being able to describe what theory is, know how to construct it and appreciate how it varies. As we shall see, it is enhanced by not only being steeped in literature, but also reading that literature in a particular way. By conceptualising these qualities of the researcher, Glaser (1978) was seeking to capture what should be the core concern of researchers doing grounded theory – being theoretically open and flexible. The 'sensitivity' of theoretical sensitivity, then, refers not only to the skill of being open, it also refers to a myriad of ways to conceptualise and integrate your theory. We have summarised the key elements of theoretical sensitivity in Box 6-1.

⎤ **Box 6-1** ⎡

The key elements of theoretical sensitivity

A quality of the researcher so that:
a. they can effectively ask and answer the following questions when doing grounded theory:

   i. What does the theory do?
   ii. How is it conceived?
   iii. What is its general position?

b. they have the attitude of being open to the fact that the theory might be constructed in a multitude of ways
c. they have an awareness of the various different coding families associated with grounded theory
d. they can analyse how a particular theory works and fits the problem being explained
e. they are aware of the importance of sampling and integrating diverse incidents of data into their theory
f. they know that anything that is observed can potentially modify the theory and are clear about how to do this

---

The importance of theoretical sensitivity is that it links the spirit of discovering theory from data to a series of attitudes and procedures that the researcher should develop. This concept also indicates that the researcher should know what a theory is before attempting to develop one and that a better understanding of how theories are constructed can only help someone doing grounded theory. The point can be pushed a bit further. There are many researchers who do not think or wish to think theoretically. Ethnomethodologists, for example, have good reasons for avoiding theory and instead value dense description. Indeed, grounded theory is littered with lots of examples of poorly developed theory. This problem is further compounded by the fact that a grounded theory might appear insightful to one person and trivial to another. Leonard Schatzman gives the example of a profound disagreement between himself, Strauss and Glaser over a student's work (Gilgun 2010). If Glaser, Strauss and Schatzman could not agree on the relative qualities of what appears to have been a 'mediocre' grounded theory, what chance do we have? Thankfully there is an answer to our dilemma, and in this sense we agree with Schatzman. Our selection of what we are going to call 'exemplars' has been developed for very similar reasons. They clearly stand out as examples of what a 'good' grounded theory should look like. They also cover several different substantive fields of research, are comparatively different and, as a consequence, can show how grounded theories can vary. We have selected two grounded theories from nursing research: the theory of 'precarious ordering' (Wuest 1995, 1997a, 1997b, 1998, 2000a, 2000b, 2001) and the theory of 'limiting intrusion' (Merritt-Gray and Wuest 1995; Wuest and Merritt-Gray 2001; Wuest, Ford-Gilboe et al. 2003; Wuest, Merritt-Gray et al. 2004; Ford-Gilboe, Wuest et al. 2005). From gender studies and sociology we have selected Richard Ekins' grounded theory of 'male femaling' (Ekins 1997). We will, of course, also be drawing from time to time on the work of Glaser and Strauss (Glaser and Strauss 1964, 1965, 1968, 1971).

> 'When you get a very good piece of work, it almost doesn't matter what method was used. I mean, you recognize excellence ... [A]s soon as you get papers that have other qualities that many people regard of lesser value, then the configuration within the analysis – and this is evaluative analysis, takes on this different set of dimensions.' (Schatzman, in Gilgun 2010: 362)

The use of exemplars does not stop there, however. It turns out that there are few detailed examples of how to do coding in the published literature and, as a consequence, we need to draw on examples where this detail is available. So in order to illustrate how to go about coding we will use three very different studies. Of particular note is the work of Helen Raphael (2008), who has very kindly given us permission to draw examples from her work on 'A grounded theory study of men's perceptions, understanding and experiences of osteoporosis'. We are very grateful to her for this. We also take a few examples from the PhD work of one of the authors, which was focused on the problems and concerns that dentists were confronted with when treating patients who presented to them a significant cross-infection risk involving infections such as Hepatitis 'B' and HIV (Gibson 1997). This study focused on dentists and their encounters with patients and involved observations and interviews with different dentists over a period of one year. It also involved follow-up interviews with patients. The third study is ongoing at the time of writing and involves looking at the problems associated with promoting lifestyle change in general dental practice.[1] This study involves observations of clinical encounters between dentists and patients which are occurring in general dental practices in the United Kingdom (UK). In this study, data will be collected from dentists, patients and service commissioners separately in interviews. The UK government wishes to try to change the direction of dental services in order to make them more health focused to promote lifestyle change. This study is one of quite a few studies exploring how this might be achieved and what the likely consequences might be for health.

The concept of theoretical sensitivity is often misunderstood. You may be confronted by bewildered colleagues who will say things like 'grounded theory, isn't that the method that starts with the idea that there are no a priori assumptions?' The reality could not be more different. What this concept tells us is that we should be aware of what a theory is, what possibilities there might be for a theory in any given area, and how a theory can be developed and applied. This concept is central to the openness of grounded theory. It is what makes grounded theory a general method.

Being open

A key feature of theoretical sensitivity is the attitude of being open. But what does this mean? *If you do grounded theory, you have to be open to the idea that the world you are studying, because it contains people, will be subject to immense variability.* Because of this variability, you will also need to be open to the myriad of ways that you might need to construct your theory in order to be able to:

a) describe the huge variety of concerns that your participants might be resolving
b) specify the way these concerns are related to each other.

While grounded theory originated in sociology, it has become a general method (Glaser 1978). In this respect, you will find all kinds of grounded theories in a huge variety of different areas, including sociology, business, marketing, nursing, education, architecture and psychology, among others. Given the huge variety of problems each of these fields will be processing, it is not surprising that a feature of grounded theory is its openness. Coupled with this openness is flexibility in the design and doing of a grounded theory.

Coding families and relations between categories

One of the key features of theoretical sensitivity developed and clarified by Glaser (1978) was that there are many ways to express the relationships between categories in a theory. Knowledge of the ways to express these relationships will enhance your theoretical sensitivity and enable you to produce a theory that better fits the area you are studying. We will cover this subject in more depth in Chapter 9. Needless to say, when you are reading grounded theory and thinking about the range of ways others have constructed their theories, it is particularly useful to see how others have developed the relationships between their categories.

Analysing how a theory fits (how it expresses the content of problems being studied) and works (how it explains the relationships between the problems being studied) is a good way to become more and more sensitive to how to do this in your own work. As we have seen in the Introduction, grounded theory departed from the work of the Columbian school of sociology in an important sense by favouring conceptual specification over conceptual definition. This means that a grounded theory grows and develops over time through the use of a set of processes that involve concurrent data collection and analysis. The theory is supposed to 'emerge' (Glaser 1992). Unfortunately, while the theory is supposed to 'emerge', this process is often not described when grounded theories are reported in the literature, although important exceptions do exist (Konecki 2008).

Diversity, sampling, integration and modifiability

Related to the attitude of openness is that grounded theory also involves being sensitive to the diversity of problems people experience and understanding that they experience them differently. This includes sensitivity to the variable ways in which these concerns are subsequently processed or resolved. Grounded theory studies not only sample a diverse range of participants, they are also based on the sensitivity that different types of data can express different things about the problems being resolved in an area. Glaser and Strauss (1967) put it as follows:

> No one kind of data on a category or technique for data collection is necessarily appropriate. Different kinds of data give the analyst different views or vantage points from which to understand a category and to develop its properties; these different views we have called slices of data. While the sociologist may use one technique of data collection primarily, theoretical sampling for saturation of a category allows a multi-faceted investigation, in which there are no limits to the techniques of data collection, the way they are used, or the types of data acquired. (Glaser and Strauss 1967: 65)

By understanding this you will begin to realise that the whole process and style of doing grounded theory is about sampling a huge range of viewpoints from which you will be attempting to build concepts and generate your theory. Take the example of Glaser and Strauss (1967), who discovered that the degree of attention given to patients when they were dying varied by the degree of loss that was attached to them. So, for example, patients of low social loss were given less attention than those who had a high social loss (Glaser and Strauss 1967). As a consequence, Glaser and Strauss (1967) paid close attention to comparing 'incidents' where patients who were dying would have had a low social loss to 'incidents' where a patient who was dying would have resulted in a high social loss. This involved listening to nurses' stories about the kind of social loss the patient would represent. Nurses' stories were treated in their own right as 'slices of data' and Glaser and Strauss (1967) actively sampled these. By sampling these stories from a range of settings, Glaser and Strauss (1967) were able to conceptualise that these stories had 'ingredients' and that they were related to 'the nurse's strategies for coping with the upsetting impact on her professional composure of, say, a dying patient with a high social loss' (Glaser and Strauss 1967: 109). In this process, 'social loss stories' as a category became related to 'professional composure'. Theoretical sensitivity is about being 'sensitive' to the development of such relationships as you collect and analyse your data. The quicker you are able to spot these relationships the better you will be able to specify and delimit your theory. This example demonstrates the importance of being able to modify your theory as you develop it.

The problem of 'prior interests' and 'preconceptions'

The final problem that relates to theoretical sensitivity is the distinction between prior interests and preconceptions and how these are to be handled during the research process. Strauss and Corbin (1990) discuss professional and personal sources of prior interests and preconceptions but do not make the distinction between them. For our purposes, we will define prior interests as the set of motivations that we bring to our research by virtue of being interested in doing research in the first place. They are easily recognised because they have a motivational component. Preconceptions, on the other hand, are the set of pre-existing concepts and ideas that we bring to the research process. These are especially problematic because they reflect a kind of selective blindness during the research process. What distinguishes preconceptions and prior interests is that we are often not aware of our preconceptions. Preconceptions can be much more difficult to detect and, as a consequence, special care needs to be taken in order to handle them effectively.

Wuest (1997a) articulated several prior interests in her research on 'fraying connections'. She used these interests to develop research that would primarily be of use to her participants, avoid oppression and reflect her feminist intellectual tradition. These interests were carefully integrated into her approach to grounded theory. So, for example, she was interested in avoiding a research process that was oppressive and which did not involve her participants. As a consequence, she went back to participants and discussed the relative merits of the different concepts as they were developing in her theory. Ekins (1997) described three prior interests for his grounded theory. First, he had an interest in sex, sexuality and gender. Second, because of his symbolic interactionist perspective, he was interested in how the problem of identity was situated and developed within the social worlds of his participants. Finally, he was interested in how three frames of reference about cross-dressing could mutually interact to affect the processes associated with male femaling.

The important point about these prior interests in our exemplars is that they were never allowed to drive conceptualisation but were used to enhance the situation of each of these grounded theories within professional and academic fields. We shall explore how this can be achieved in more depth in Chapter 9. Theoretical sensitivity, then, can be enhanced through the use of prior interests. Being aware of them means that they can be used positively when it comes to interpreting the status of your emerging theory.

Preconceptions are much more problematic and are something to be concerned with when doing grounded theory. If we fail to guard against our preconceptions, we can 'force' categories and interpretations on to the data. How we handle these is fundamental to grounded theory (Glaser 1992). Part of the answer to this problem has already been provided by, for example, asking what kind of theory is emerging and asking how it is conceived. We shall return to this problem throughout the rest of the book. For now, let us explore how prior interests and preconceptions combine to give complex effects in grounded theory.

Wuest (1997a, 1997b, 1998, 2000a, 2000b, 2001), in her theory of precarious ordering, was clear that she had a desire not only to observe the impact of foisting more and more care on to women, but also to show that there was something positive about women's responses to the increasing demands of caring. The desire to show that women's responses could be positive is obviously a prior interest that was used to try to make her findings relevant to nursing practice. This prior interest, however, carries with it several preconceptions that may have had an impact on her theory. By conceptualising her prior interest in terms of showing something positive about women's management of caring demands, there was a risk that the problem became 'individualised'. In her focus on individual women it is not clear if Wuest sampled data from different social units, for example, watching how the women in her study interacted with different professional groups. We know that she sampled women from different families but not much is said about the effects this had on her theory.

When it came to discussing her formal theory, Wuest (2001) recognised some of these consequences. She stated that a possible negative consequence of her theory – because of its focus on successful management and personal growth in precarious ordering – may have been to inadvertently justify government policies to foist more and more caring demands on to women. Likewise, throughout her work, Wuest was always at pains to recommend that nursing professionals had a responsibility to support women. This recommendation is hardly in keeping with the suggestion that there was a preconception that this problem was something individual women should cope with. The challenge to explore how precarious ordering would occur in different social units, along with showing how negative incidents might have consequences for this theory, remains. The beauty of grounded theory is that these challenges are something that can be used to enhance the theory through further modifications. They would in no way debunk or undermine it. Remember, despite our criticisms, the goal is to remain open and to imagine what the future might hold for Wuest's theory if it were to be further modified. In the next section we move on to explore how to enhance our theoretical sensitivity.

Developing theoretical sensitivity: learning to think theoretically

A key aspect of theoretical sensitivity is the ability to recognise theory and to think theoretically. The best way to develop these skills is to read theory. By 'reading theory' what we mean is that you should learn to recognise the key elements of what makes a theory compelling and understand how it has been constructed. *The novice researcher would be very unwise to begin doing grounded theory without some prior knowledge of what a grounded theory should look like.* Glaser and Strauss (1967) stated this as follows:

> The sociologist should also be sufficiently theoretically sensitive so that he can conceptualize and formulate a theory as it emerges from the data. Once started, theoretical sensitivity is forever in continual development. It is developed as over many years the sociologist thinks in theoretical terms about what he knows, and as he queries many different theories on such questions as 'What does the theory do? How is it conceived? What is its general position? What kinds of models does it use?' (Glaser and Strauss 1967: 46)

So, while doing a grounded theory, you should be constantly asking yourself 'what does this theory do? How is it conceived? What is its general position?' Take Richard Ekins' (1997) theory of male femaling. We can say that his theory seeks to explain how the problems associated with the typical career path of genetic males becoming female are processed. His theory is conceived as a basic social process composed of several sub-processes that occur to varying degrees in different stages of the ideal career path. It demonstrates how the worlds of male femalers clash with those of the medical profession and lay people. It also demonstrates how male femalers are confronted with the social structural problems of managing the awareness of others and gender, among other things.

Ekins' (1997) work contrasts with the work of Wuest (1997a, 1997b, 1998, 2000a, 2000b, 2001), whose theory of 'precarious ordering' reflects how women are often expected to be the main caregivers in society. When governments follow certain policies and withdraw state funding for caring, such decisions can have a negative impact primarily on women, who are expected to provide care. Wuest's theory describes how, as a consequence of these social changes, women move from dissonance and fraying connections towards consonance and growth. Her theory is conceived as a two-staged process – from fraying connections to precarious ordering – which is an outcome of the interdependent strategies of setting boundaries, negotiating and repatterning care. Wuest (2001) eventually proposes her theory as a formal theory of how women respond to caring demands and she successfully integrates feminist approaches with a grounded theory approach. We will be able to see how she achieved this as we come back to her theory again and again in this book.

If we are to be able to write grounded theory we need to be able to explain the general features of our theory and at the same time articulate how it fits existing theory. Glaser and Strauss (1967) clearly saw the development of these skills as an ongoing process. We would suggest that if Glaser and Strauss were obviously consciously engaged in developing their theoretical sensitivity, then perhaps you should make a conscious effort to do so yourself?

Reading the literature: skills and tips

As stated previously, one way to be able to develop this skill is to get into the habit of reading existing grounded theories, but how to do this? It should be pretty obvious that when reading existing grounded theories we should be looking for key things about the grounded theory we are reading. But what are these features?

In Chapter 1 we talked about what kind of theory grounded theory is. Having summarised the key features of grounded theory, it makes sense to evaluate the degree to which a particular paper enables us to assess the various features of a grounded theory. We have found it useful to read grounded theories while using two 'crib sheets'. The first crib sheet (see Box 6-2) is a general crib sheet and is designed to force us to assess the key elements of the theory.[2] The second (see Box 6-3) is designed to help you evaluate the methodology of the study. Rather than reading to describe the findings of a particular study, we seek to read for the elements of a study that make it grounded theory. This is especially useful because as you read the published literature and unpublished PhDs you will begin to see how they have put their theory together, why they did it the way they did, and what works particularly well and what works less well. By reading a range of grounded theories you will begin to appreciate the flexibility of the approach. This will hopefully help you become more and more open to integrating the variation of concerns people will express as you do your own study.

Box 6-2

Reading the structure of a grounded theory

Paper title:

1. What is the integrating idea or core category of the study? (Note the paper might present just part of the grounded theory being developed)

   - the theory should have a set of propositions organised around a core problem (core category)
   - there will be sub-core categories that are not directly related to the core concern but nonetheless modify it in some way

---

- the theory might have dimensions to the core and sub-core categories
- the theory might have propositions relating core category to sub-core categories; these propositions are achieved through theoretical coding

2. How well do the categories of the theory express the content? Is the content clearly linked to the categories?

   - Does it work?
   - Does it fit the problems being experienced by people in the area under question?
   - Does it seem relevant to people in the setting?

3. How were the categories arrived at?
4. How extensive is the description about decisions to go for focusing on the categories?
5. To what extent do the categories relate to each other in such a way as to either make predictions or specify relationships between them?

⌐ Box 6-3 ⌐

Evaluating adherence to the constant comparative method

1. Is there evidence that a clear logic of discovery has been followed?

   - Was the research question open? What unit of analysis did the study start with (setting, role or group of people)?
   - Was data collection neutral, and was there an open attitude towards exploring new areas?

2. To what degree is there an analysis of dominant preconceptions and how have these been guarded against?
3. Has there been a detailed description of any prior interests and has their role as starting points been explained?
4. Is there any consideration of how the theory sits within the field of relevant theories? Is this exhaustive?
5. Is there evidence of a focus on exploring new lines of enquiry in a process of building from substantive to formal theory?
6. Do the researchers show that different 'slices of data' were collected through theoretical sampling in different phases of the research? Is the logic for the selection of these clear?
7. Is there any indication of how 'deviant cases' might have challenged the theory and moved it in new directions?
8. Is there a good description of how the theory emerged from specific instances to general categories?

Exploring prior interests and preconceptions: skills and tips

We would like to suggest that it is important to spend time exploring our prior interests and preconceptions when we are doing research. Our purpose in doing so is not to 'bracket' them out, but to see if we can use them productively during the research process. The obvious starting point is to sit down and write out what interests you about the area you are investigating. Why are you doing the study? Are there particular outcomes you would like to see from your research? Are you motivated, as Wuest and Ekins were, to expose something hidden about the world? Do you have particularly strong views and professional insights into the field you wish to research? Take the time to write these down and to think about how these might impact on your research. Because they are linked to your motivations, prior interests are something that can be used to enhance our work. You need to use them appropriately, and this involves not allowing them to drive your conceptualisation of the problems being experienced by those in your study. We will come back to how to do this in more detail in Chapter 9.

Preconceptions are much more difficult to detect. As we stated previously, the key to guarding against these is to constantly ask yourself what is this theory about? What is its general status? A second tip is to avoid all professional and theoretical concepts when coding and conceptualising in your study (Glaser and Strauss 1965; Glaser 1978). This applies to the formulation of your research question. For example, if we were to ask the question, 'What coping strategies do smokers use when they are confronted with the stigma of social restrictions on smoking?', clearly this question preconceives the problem in terms of the psychological concept of 'coping strategies', the social psychological concept of 'stigma' and that the restrictions on smoking are of a social nature. It also preconceives that smoking is experienced as a problem. A more appropriate approach to developing a question around smoking might be to simply state that you would like to develop a grounded theory of smoking. In this respect, you do not preconceive smoking as inherently problematic, nor do you preconceive the problem as stigmatising or as something smokers need to cope with. Being open in this accrues a number of advantages. First, you are able to remain open to the conditions that make smoking both pleasurable and problematic. Second, you can sample around situations and social units where smoking is experienced differently and you can study what makes it both good and bad. If your interest is in trying to help people reduce smoking, surely it is as important to know what makes it such a pleasurable experience? The problem, of course, is that not all research can have the luxury of being so open and we are frequently required to deliver findings within a set time period (three years if you are doing a PhD). As a consequence, you may have to compromise the openness of your study. You might like to try Exercise 1 below to begin the process of becoming sensitive to the use of prior interests and preconceptions and to enable you to start becoming more sensitive to how these can impact on research.

████████████████████████ **EXERCISE** ████████████████████████

Prior interests and preconceptions – asking the right question

1. Take the time to write down why you are interested in doing your research. Make a note of what you would like to achieve and why. How can you use these interests to enhance your grounded theory? Can they make you more sensitive to certain things?
2. Take a look at a research paper published in the field in which you are working. Write out the research question and carefully read through it. Does the question conceive the problem through the use of professional concepts? How might the use of these concepts have restricted what the authors have found? Could the research have been explored in a more open way? If so, how?
3. Now think about the field in which you are looking to do your grounded theory. What would an open grounded theory research question look like? Write it out.
4. Now think about your question. Is it achievable in the time you have to do your study? Most open questions will not be. Can you rephrase your question by, for example, restricting your study to particular social units or groups? The selection of the units or groups to be studied should be carefully justified. You should also make some notes about the likely consequences of such restrictions.

Key points about theoretical sensitivity

In this chapter we have discovered that theoretical sensitivity is both a skill and an attitude of the researcher. It is also directed at the purpose of building a theory that fits and works. In this respect, your theory should fit and at the same time explain how problems are resolved by groups of people in different contexts. The problem is that the relationship between prior interests and pre-conceptions has become a hotly debated topic in grounded theory, most notably through the concept of *reflexivity*. We do not have time to do this issue full justice, but a few brief words will hopefully enable you to get the picture.

There is a complex debate about reflexivity in social science methods. It is defined in a myriad of different ways. For some, it is a concept that loosely refers to how the researcher's self-awareness affects the research process. For others, it takes on a much more detailed definition, becoming part of a process of reflection on the degree to which the researcher and the researched interact with each other to produce knowledge as co-constructed (Annells 1996; Charmaz 2000; Chiovitti and Piran 2003; Neill 2006; Denzin 2007; Mills, Chapman et al. 2007; Mruck and Mey 2007). Our analysis in this chapter confirms the assertion that a degree of reflection on the nature of the relationship between the researcher and those being researched is fundamental to grounded theory as it was developed. This point is relatively uncontroversial and has been recognised by many others (Charmaz 2000; Bryant 2003; Neill 2006; Denzin 2007; Mruck and Mey 2007). It forms part of the influence of symbolic interactionism on grounded theory (Neill 2006; Denzin 2007) and can be recognised as a central component of the method today. The *sensitivity* that there is a relationship and that this plays a part in the process of theory construction is fundamental to the openness and flexibility of the method. After all, the theory has to be grounded in something.

Where the differences develop is the degree to which this reflective process is to be developed and used as a formal part of the research process. In some versions the researcher may stand apart from participants; in other versions participants may be involved in the theory-building process. Reasons given for this are because, if the knowledge is to be useful, *it should first and foremost be useful for those who took part*. This takes us to the principal objection of those who argue for a more 'critical' or 'constructivist' turn in grounded theory. In this perspective, grounded theory does not problematise the relationship between the researcher and the researched enough (Wuest 1995; Charmaz 2000; Denzin 2007). These theorists often make this point by arguing that there is a version of grounded theory that is 'objectivist'[3] and, as such, claims some special neutral status for theory production (Charmaz 2000; Neill 2006). On one level, we might object that such a claim cannot be sustained. After all, we have discovered that some consideration of the relationship between the researcher and researched was part of the original method. The answer to this question appears to relate to the direction that grounded theory methodology took in Strauss and Corbin's (1990) iteration of the method.[4] If you look closely at the grounded theory literature, most of the criticisms of grounded theory as 'objectivist' usually refer to their book in sustaining this claim. But what are we to make of this?

This appears to suggest that you should take time to reflect on your prior interests and to try to explore your preconceptions as you develop your grounded theory. In order to do this, one of the questions you should ask yourself is 'What is the purpose of your theory?' As we have seen, this was in the method when it was conceived. *In asking this question, Glaser and Strauss (1967) were asking you to reflect on how your theory relates to other theories in your field of research.* What does it do? Is it something that can inform practices or is it just interesting? Others within the critical tradition in grounded theory often adopt a much more radical position on this question. Denzin (2007), for example, seeks to produce theory that disrupts 'hegemonic cultural and education practices' with the goal of promoting an increasingly democratic experience (Denzin 2007: 462). He is radically open about his preconceptions as well. In keeping with many in the critical tradition, he argues that knowledge is not neutral. It can be used to oppress different groups and so grounded theory that does not consider the ideological nature of knowledge may in fact reinforce negative power relationships (Gibson 2007). For researchers such as Denzin (2007) and Wuest (1995), 'critical' grounded theory is designed to attack the status quo. Reflexivity, where this refers to a co-operative relationship between participant and researcher, is central to developing a 'critical grounded theory'. But not everyone will be comfortable with this approach.[5] For some, there is a risk that the use of critical theory in grounded theory might end up preconceiving your theory, although there are ways to overcome this so as to reach an accommodation (Gibson 2007).[6] What if you are a professional seeking to develop a theory that can help you treat patients or that will enable you to develop better buildings? Clearly, the purpose of such a theory will be quite different from those from the critical tradition, and your prior interests and the associated sets of preconceptions will be different. Just because they are different, however, doesn't mean that they do not need to be considered carefully.

An important distinction between the approach of constructivist and critical grounded theorists and those from a more general grounded theory approach is clearly a difference in relation to the purpose of what the developing grounded theory should try to do. Denzin's (2007) perspective on grounded theory is that we should not be claiming that we are engaged in the production of 'middle range theory', but rather a critical pedagogy[7] designed to promote transformation. Yet from our analysis we can see that the work of Denzin (2007), Charmaz (2000, 2006) and Wuest (1995) reflect a new direction for grounded theory.[8] This takes us to perhaps the critical point that we think reveals something about this debate. Crucial to the development of your grounded theory is the question of what is *the purpose of grounded theory anyway?*

As we have seen, grounded theory was developed out of the embarrassing gap between theory and research in sociology (see Chapters 1 and 2). The goal of grounded theory was rather loosely described as producing theory that fitted and worked. Theory should have purpose. But what exactly this means is actually quite elusive. It takes a closer reading of the way in which Glaser and Strauss (1965) discussed the usefulness of their work to see that *usefulness had a dual purpose.* A particularly revealing aspect of their approach can be found in *Awareness of Dying* (Glaser and Strauss 1965). Here they state that 'most useful sociological accounts are precisely those which insiders recognize as sufficiently inside to be true but not so "inside" that they reveal only what is already known' (Glaser and Strauss 1967: 9). Grounded theories should be useful for those in the field, but they should also be sociologically interesting. The theory should be easy to use in the field, but at the same time say something that is *worthwhile.* This is quite different from the emancipatory purpose expressed by Charmaz (2000, 2006), Denzin (2007) and others (Wuest 1995; Neill 2006). Each of these authors, writing as they have been after a time when there has been a crisis of representation in social science, have developed different interests and preconceptions and subsequently brought these to their grounded theory. This contrasts with grounded theory when it was developed. At that time, the goal was simply to produce a theory that (a) fitted the concerns of those being studied and (b) worked in the sense that it explained (in sociological terms) how those concerns were being resolved. At that time, theoretical sensitivity involved establishing the sociological status of the theory. It is why we ended up with the distinction between substantive and formal theory in grounded theory.

Finally, one outcome of our analysis is that you can map your own path through these problems by reflecting on your prior interests, while also finding ways to explore the problematic preconceptions you might have. Each of the theorists covered in this chapter use their preconceptions and prior interests productively. All find a way out of the risks associated with preconceiving their grounded theory. The principal path by which they achieve this is through building a more reflexive relationship with their participants. The key points about theoretical sensitivity are that it involves:

- being able to describe what theory is, how to construct it, and how to appreciate its huge variability
- knowing what a grounded theory should look like
- being open to the idea that the world you are studying, because it contains people, will be subject to immense variability
- knowing the range of ways to specify the relationships that develop in producing a grounded theory
- being open to the variability of data and understanding that what counts as data can generate different things for your theory
- understanding that an important distinction in relation to theoretical sensitivity is the distinction between prior interests and preconceptions and how these are to be handled during the research process.
  - Prior interests are the set of motivations that we bring to our research by virtue of being interested in doing research in the first place.
  - Preconceptions are the set of pre-existing concepts and ideas that we bring to the research process. They are problematic because we are often not aware of them.

Critical reflection 10

What is theoretical sensitivity?

Now go back to your brief notes and respond by writing about how your perspective on 'theoretical sensitivity' in grounded theory has changed after reading this chapter. You might also want to make some notes on any further questions that have arisen while you have been reading this chapter. This could include notes concerning any further reading you might like to make.

Summary

The central problematic for this chapter has been rediscovering what was meant by theoretical sensitivity in grounded theory and then exploring how it can be enhanced. The chapter began with a critical reflection on the nature of theoretical sensitivity by highlighting its key elements. It noted the importance of openness and flexibility in grounded theory and explained why this was central to the method. It then explained the importance of being sensitive to diversity in the way the data will vary, both in the types of data we can get hold of and in the variety of ways the data can be used to enhance the theory as it develops. The chapter subsequently considered the importance of 'prior interests' and 'preconceptions', before considering how we might develop our ability to 'think theoretically' through reading grounded theory. The chapter finished with some exercises aimed at enhancing theoretical sensitivity.

Further reading

Denzin, N. (2007) 'Grounded theory and the politics of interpretation', in A. Bryant and K. Charmaz (eds), *The Sage Handbook of Grounded Theory*. London: Sage.

Glaser, B. (1978) 'Theoretical sensitivity', Chapter 1 in B. Glaser, *Theoretical Sensitivity: Advances in the Methodology of Grounded Theory*. Mill Valley, CA: Sociology Press.

Glaser, B. and Strauss, A. (1967) 'Theoretical sampling', Chapter 3 in B. Glaser and A. Strauss, *The Discovery of Grounded Theory*. Chicago: Aldine.

Wuest, J. (1997a) 'Fraying connections of caring women: an exemplar of including difference in the development of explanatory frameworks', *Canadian Journal of Nursing Research*, **29**(2): 99–116.

Notes

1 We would like to acknowledge that the research was funded by the National Institute for Health Research (NIHR) and the Collaboration for Leadership in Applied Health Research and Care (CLAHRC), based at the University of Leeds and the University of York, in collaboration with NHS Leeds and Leeds City Council Adult Social Services. The specific project was called 'Supporting lifestyle behaviour change in general dental practice' and those working on the project were Jenni Murray, Allan House, Barry Gibson, Melanie Hall, Peter G. Robinson, Gail Douglas, Rizwana Lala, Julia Csikar, Jan Hartman and Kate Hill.

2 This 'crib' sheet is obviously intended as an example. You can modify it to suit your own purposes by adding to it or taking away from it.

3 Glaser's reaction to the concept of reflexivity is often cited as evidence of his objectivism but if you read what he is saying, his objections are not epistemological; they are largely practical. Why? Because, for him, grounded theory is a method that has been developed to build theory from data. It is not a method that seeks to produce what he calls 'accurate descriptions' (2001: 47–49). In some respects they both appear to miss each other's point. We would suggest that one way to clarify the difference might be to explore in much more depth their views on what the purposes of theory are.

4 See especially our footnotes to Chapter 5 and our discussion of Strauss and Corbin's (1990) 'operationalism'.

5 See Gibson (2007) for a detailed discussion of the approaches of Adorno and Bourdieu in critical theory and how they might be related to grounded theory, including some of the compromises that might have to be made.

6 Reflexivity in the relationship between the researcher and the researched appears to be the most promising path to overcoming the 'scholasticism' of some forms of critical theory (Gibson 2007).

7 This term refers to the goal of promoting social change by engaging with power structures and forms of domination.

8 As we have said previously, at times within these debates there is a real risk that by writing 'constructivist' or 'critical' grounded theory in opposition to 'objectivist' grounded theory we are claiming that there is a form of 'objectivist' grounded theory that stands as a neutral aloof form of knowledge. This version might be attributed to the operationalism of Strauss and Corbin's (1990) text. As we have said previously (see Chapter 5), we don't think that the claim that the original method was objectivist can be sustained.

7

Rediscovering Skills for Theoretical Sampling

Aim: To evaluate and explore the issue of sampling in grounded theory

Learning outcomes

After reading this chapter you should be able to:

- explain how sampling is conducted in grounded theory
- apply your rediscovery of the techniques of data slicing and sampling in theory development
- describe and evaluate the relationship between theoretical sampling and coding
- understand what the key issues are in relation to theoretical sampling in' grounded theory

In the previous chapter we introduced you to the idea of theoretical sensitivity. In this chapter we will see how theoretical sensitivity can be utilised in a series of strategies for the collection of 'slices' of data for further analysis. This brings us to the problem of theoretical sampling. Theoretical sampling, as an approach to data collection, is clearly associated with comparative analysis in *Discovery*. There it is described as a strategy for the generation of theory through 'a multitude of carefully selected cases' (Glaser and Strauss 1967: 30). It is a strategy that was eventually specified in terms of the joint collection, coding and analysis of data, whereby the researcher decides 'what data to collect next and where to find them, in order to develop his [sic] theory as it emerges', a process of data collection 'controlled by the emerging theory, whether substantive or formal' (Glaser and Strauss 1967: 45). Theoretical sampling, we are also told, follows two logics: it is inductive and deductive. It is important to remember, as Schatzman and others have said, that grounded theory is a way of thinking as much as it entails a set of processes (Gilgun 2010). *What we take this to mean is that the thinking processes associated with grounded theory are to be considered relevant at any moment. You cannot separate these out and over-simplify doing grounded theory into separate phases of research where you only use one set of processes exclusively and ignore the others.* Grounded theory is not likely to work that way, or at least is not likely to work very well that way. In what follows we will describe how you can handle these multiple logics in a way that preserves your theoretical sensitivity but nonetheless enables you to move forward practically.

General principles of sampling in grounded theory

While grounded theory involves the dual logics of induction and deduction, when it comes to selecting further sources of data collection these logics each have different consequences for sampling. As we have seen in Chapter 6, grounded theory is all about finding out what the core concerns of people are in a field of research. Theoretical sensitivity entails being open to the fact that these concerns are likely to be highly variable and that there are *different kinds of data that will express different things about the problems and concerns of the people as they engage in action in the substantive field of research.* Your task, then, when it comes to sampling, is to make sure you secure a wide variety of concerns and a number of different perspectives from which to view these concerns.

Theoretical sampling follows on from theoretical sensitivity into a way of thinking that will enable sampling for the purposes of developing an appropriate theory. Sampling a variety of groups is fundamental to both Richard Ekins (1997) and Judith Wuest (1997a, 1998, 2000a, 2000b, 2001). Ekins (1997) focuses on male cross-dressers *and* male sex-changers in his study, clearly delineating these as being along a continuum of male femaling. He goes well beyond simply sampling along this continuum, however, to collect a huge amount of data for his theory. He describes his strategy as involving accessing the 'worlds of cross-dressers', which is clearly a reference to their total experience. He achieved his sampling through three different access points. He met individual cross-dressers and sex-changers, attended member support groups and frequented bars and attended drag balls. These points of access very quickly snowballed to the point where he was invited to parties in both private and public settings. He also observed speech therapy sessions, wig fitting, electrolysis and the purchase of clothes (Ekins 1997). His access to the worlds of his participants was extensive. If a participant was attending a psychiatric appointment, he would also attend the appointment and then meet the individual afterwards to chat about it. He obtained access to erotic networks, magazines and eventually became the Director of the Trans-Gender Archive. This in turn enabled him access to a huge collection of private correspondence of cross-dressers and sex-changers. As a member of the Trans-Gender Archive he had direct access to thousands of newspaper clippings and literature on Trans-Gender. His description clearly shows the immense range and detailed access to data that he had to enable him to develop this study (Ekins 1997).

Ekins' (1997) work was developed over a number of years. Indeed, his core category was not properly established until after a few years of research. Most people may not have the luxury of years of data collection; research is typically time-limited. So what do you do if you cannot be so extensive in your data collection? One way to proceed might be to vary data collection along a dimension you feel might be important at the outset of your study. It is here that the strategy and techniques of Wuest (1997a, 1997b, 1998, 2000a, 2000b, 2001) are especially pertinent. Wuest (1997a) began with an initial study of 'survivors of abusive conjugal relationships'. In this study the principal source of variation was the characteristics of the mothers, who were either employed or unemployed. *There is no way to predetermine if the characteristics that you have selected to yield variation in your sample will be the most relevant.* Nor can you be sure that these characteristics will yield the largest variation in the concerns of your participants. The selection of the characteristics of your initial participants is clearly going to be preconceived in some way. This is relatively unproblematic as long as you remain open and, if possible, enable yourself to engage in further sampling when this is required by your theory. The key thing to do is to seek to get some measure of variation in the characteristics of your participants from the outset, even if the criteria that you select to enable the sampling of a variety of concerns may not be the most efficient way to do so. The selection of a variety of characteristics that may be relevant to how core concerns within your substantive field might vary can be made on the basis of your prior knowledge of the field or on the basis of your pre-existing knowledge of the area you are studying. This form of sample selection is fine as long as you allow for other forms of data collection.

The characteristics of your participants are not the only dimension upon which you can base your initial data collection. You should consider collecting data from a range of different physical sources. These might include interviews, documents, observations, conversations, newspapers, books, magazines and videos, among other things (Glaser 2002). Data from these sources can then be used to develop your emerging theory by giving you more information on 'what is going on' in the area you are studying. Although the term 'what is going on' might strike you as a vague way to describe data analysis, it is important to understand that grounded theory is a way of thinking. How it is actually deployed in any specific set of circumstances will depend on the area being studied and the problems being processed. So, for example, you will frequently find reference to the dictum 'all is data' (Glaser 1998, 2001). While this dictum has been criticised by some for being too vague, others have claimed that it supports the idea that many sources of data can be used for data analysis (Bryant 2003; Birks and Mills 2011). The dictum points to a general orientation, a sense of openness in the researcher to the multiple ways they might investigate the area they are exploring.

The sources of data for analysis do not have to be restricted to different physical sources. *A far more imaginative, and indeed conceptually powerful, technique for sampling is to approach data collection through the myriad of social and social psychological units that are available to you.* One of the important sensitivities of grounded theory is that sampling can occur in a range of different types of social unit. It is impossible to give the full range. But follow the lead of Ekins (1997), who draws on a huge range of what we can call social and social psychological units of analysis. He did so arbitrarily at the start of his study by, for example, focusing on periods of life as social psychological slices of time, that is 'babyhood, infancy, childhood, adolescence and adulthood' (Ekins 1997: 61). He also used different social psychological units for his analysis. He focused on collecting data on the different stages of the process he was researching, such as beginning male femaling, fantasying male femaling, doing male femaling, and so on (see the section on 'From slices of data to theoretical sampling' on p. 128).

As we have seen in the Introduction to this book, a focus on different social units for the purpose of constant comparison is part of the heritage of grounded theory and can be linked to the comparative roots of the method in sociology. Over time, as grounded theory has become restated, there has been a tendency to erase this aspect of the method in favour of sampling other kinds of units, most usually individuals. *By rediscovering this aspect of grounded theory we can suggest that you explore the possibility of sampling in different social units.* Such sampling may produce useful points for theoretical comparison. The maxim in the early stages of research, however, should not be to force too many distinctions into your data but to bear in mind that any distinctions that you do use in your analysis may be less relevant as your theory begins to develop. So be careful to avoid forcing your initial preconceptions into your theory too much and allow more relevant distinctions and units for analysis to develop as your theory develops. Sampling for variation in data, for a wide variety of different perspectives on data and for different sources of data is only half the story when it comes to sampling in grounded theory. While these different approaches can be used to initiate data analysis, they only really become significant when they are combined with the purpose and goal of developing theory. This purpose can be combined with something Glaser and Strauss (1967) referred to as 'data slicing' or getting hold of 'slices of data'.

Slices of data: data analysis for the generation of theory

If the task of sampling in grounded theory is to sample as much variation in your data as possible, it is also to sample data from a range of perspectives, *but with the added purpose of developing your theory.* Glaser and Strauss called the collection of multiple perspectives on the problem getting hold of 'slices of data'. This approach is rooted in an extension of deviant case analysis and involves developing comparisons between incidents which are both positive and negative. While in the past the purpose of comparative sampling might have been developed to challenge an existing hypothesis (Lipset 1964), in grounded theory the purpose became to enable the discovery of further information about a category (Glaser and Strauss 1971). This kind of sampling can involve seeking out of 'slices of data' or it might involve something that Glaser and Strauss (1971) called 'anecdotal comparison'. Such forms of comparison involve thinking carefully about where else we might learn about the category – often in an unrelated area – to make quick comparisons that may subsequently enable the category to be developed (Glaser and Strauss 1971: 184). Data slices involve collecting data to reveal more information about the developing theory. In *Status Passage*, Glaser and Strauss (1971) used 'data slices' in an 'ideational' way in order 'to provide as broad and diverse a range of theoretical ideas on status passage as possible' (Glaser and Strauss 1971: 187). 'Slices of data' are characterised by the fact that they are primarily purposive and directed at the goal of developing as many categories, properties, hypotheses and problems on the subject being investigated as possible.

We feel it is very important to explain the open-ended and purposive use of selecting slices of data in grounded theory because understanding how Glaser and Strauss (1971) used this approach to develop their own theory may enhance the generation of theory for your own purposes. The use of this approach contrasts with the collection of data for the purpose of 'verification' and 'description'. In grounded theory, comparisons are made for conceptual reasons, not for the evaluation of evidence 'for its own sake' but for the generation of further dimensions of your emerging categories. In other words, you compare groups either because (a) they suggest the same category or (b) because a category that was developed through an analysis of the concerns of one group might be compared to how it is processed in another (Glaser and Strauss 1971: 184). In this way the comparison might suggest something about the nature of the category and therefore will help develop your theory.

In their discussion of developing and securing slices of data, Glaser and Strauss relax key criteria normally associated with comparative analysis. In comparative analysis, comparisons were only made between groups on the basis that they had sufficient features in common and key features that were different.[1] Likewise, in order to be excluded from comparisons in comparative analysis, a group must display fundamental differences (Glaser and Strauss 1971: 184). The complexity of trying to carefully control such comparisons often hampered theoretical analysis in *Sociologists at Work* (Hammond 1964). But the goal of comparative sociology is different from grounded theory. The goal of comparative sociological analysis was said to be to test hypotheses through carefully controlled analysis of similar cases. Glaser and Strauss (1967) did this to enable the development of theory rather than being tied to concerns about making tightly controlled and accurate comparisons in the service of verifying hypotheses.

The important thing about these comparisons is the effect that they might have on the conceptual level of your theory. For instance, the simplest comparisons might be between groups of 'the same substantive type' (Glaser and Strauss 1971: 185). So, for example, Wuest (1997) compared mothers with children who are disabled to mothers who have young children. Both groups are from the same substantive type because they are both confronting caring demands, albeit in different degrees (Wuest 1997a). More general comparisons might be developed by comparing different substantive groups from within other larger groups or, even further, to different regions and nations. *The key thing is to carefully develop the scope of your theory by working with different groups at different levels of generality.* Glaser and Strauss use the example of emergency wards and argue that you can compare 'emergency wards' to other kinds of wards in different types of hospital in different countries. It might be possible to compare emergency wards to different kinds of organisations that are focused on dealing with accidents or emergencies. Comparisons might include fire departments, police departments or plumbing companies (Glaser and Strauss 1971: 185–186). In the latter case, we are dealing with *comparisons of different substantive types of social unit as opposed to different substantive groups.*

Skills and tips 7-1

Data slicing

Hally has been collecting data on the subject of health promotion and behaviour change in general dental practices. A large section of her observations is about the manner and style of dental encounters. During her observations she notices that dentists tend to use the same sequence of conversation with different patients. She develops a category called 'scripting' to capture this aspect of the dental encounters.

1. Take other encounters between relative strangers in different social units, such as the encounter between hairdressers and their clients at the hairdressers, encounters on public transport between bus drivers and their passengers, and encounters in emergency hospital wards between nurses and patients. Make some notes reflecting on how likely we are to see 'scripting' in each of these encounters.
2. Make additional notes on the likely absence or presence of 'scripting' in each encounter. You should especially reflect on the potential for 'scripting' to develop into a general category in Hally's emerging theory.
3. How might 'scripting' vary in different kinds of encounters?
4. What are the implications of this variability for the next stages of Hally's grounded theory study?

From slices of data to theoretical sampling

As we can see, Glaser and Strauss (1967, 1971) move away from the tendency of comparative sociology to make careful and detailed comparisons towards a more relaxed approach that seeks to build comparisons with the purpose of generating theory. This is something so many of the commentators forget and it is something Glaser has continued to bemoan (Glaser 1992, 1998, 2001, 2002; Glaser and Holton 2004). But how do we use the mini logic of slicing data to build theory? We would like to make a distinction between data slicing and theoretical sampling. Data slicing, in keeping with Glaser and Strauss (1971), refers to the use of an individual comparison between different substantive groups or different social units for the purposes of developing theory, usually in the form of refining categories. Theoretical sampling refers to a process of combining several different slices of data for the purpose of developing theory. The work of Judith Wuest (1997a, 1997a, 1998, 2000a, 2000b, 2001) is an excellent example of how you can develop your research from one substantive study to a more formal theory through the use of different comparison groups. We would advise taking time to assemble her papers in sequence and carefully read through each of them, using the crib sheet we developed in Chapter 6. Of particular importance for our analysis in this chapter is her paper 'Precarious ordering: toward a formal theory of women's caring' (Wuest 2001). In this paper Wuest carefully details the successive stages of her constant comparative analysis.

The process that Wuest went through in her research is described as untidy and by no means linear. However, we can see the detail and logic of her approach (Wuest 2001). She began with a study of how women engaged in caring for young children. Her sample was composed of primarily middle-class women who were comparable in that they were employed and not employed (Wuest 1997a, 2001). She also wanted to begin her study by studying women who did 'all the right things'. As we can see, from the outset her work involved the comparison of two, more or less similar, substantive groups. In this initial study she discovered, among other things, that the women were trying to deal with competing demands between spouses and children, their self and others, parents and family. They also experienced dissonance in the form of dilemmas, changing job prospects and conflict with different professional groups. A consequence of this was the suggestion that she should sample:

a. women with increased demands
b. women with fewer demands
c. women experiencing poverty and therefore who had fewer resources.

By sampling women with increased demands, Wuest was able to add to her developing theory the fact that demands could have severe health consequences. They could also lead to conflict with different professional groups in relation to their own treatment and the education of their children (Wuest 1998). After discovering that caring demands could have negative consequences for women's health, Wuest went on to explore other demands that could result in heavy physical struggles and discovered that looking after a sick relative, an elderly relative and a disabled child could lead to such heavy demands that women became sick. They may even have to limit demands on themselves (Wuest 1998). Having discovered this, Wuest was then able to explore how women solved the demands placed on them. This resulted in a study looking at the processes and strategies associated with precarious ordering and how they repatterned care (Wuest 2000, 2001).

During her work Wuest developed an interest in the social context of caring. This interest was developed from her feminist perspective. By drawing on this interest, Wuest discovered the importance and centrality of resources both external and internal to each of these processes (Wuest 1998, 2000a, 2000b). As we can see, this prior interest was not used to force her data but to enhance her theory through the discovery that a few variables were salient, these being the nature of caring ideals, caring proximity, caring options and caring rewards (Wuest 1997a). Wuest also discovered that an unresolved problem for women remained. The problem was that there seemed to be an expectation in society that women were best placed to be involved in caring.[2] These expectations were being used to justify placing increasing demands on women. Each study suggested further questions. So, for example, she would ask what makes caring demands legitimate? What other demands can create physical struggles for women? These questions added an important critical dimension to the grounded theory. We will return to evaluate Wuest's sampling strategy in the next section. Before doing so, however, we would like to go through the various strategies used by Richard Ekins (1997).

As we stated previously, Ekins (1997) began with a comparative analysis of the worlds of cross-dressers and sex-changers who, from a common-sense perspective, might be placed on a continuum of male femaling. So cross-dressers vary in their male femaling by degree. However, Ekins very quickly discovered that one of the principal sources of variation in his study was in the interrelations between different group meanings when it comes to sex-changing and cross-dressing. His study evolved to the point where comparisons were being made between what he called 'the social worlds' of expert medical professionals, lay members, sex-changers and cross-dressers. The latter two groups were eventually conceptualised as male femalers. As we can see, his data slices were being developed with comparisons of a different order from those of Wuest (1997a, 1997b, 1998, 2000a, 2000b, 2001). Wuest's groups were from the same substantive area and varied by degree in relation to key variables that were discovered during the study. Ekins' (1997) main sensitivity was in relation to the clash of social worlds. This sensitivity came from the general theoretical approach of symbolic interactionism and resulted in general comparisons which dramatically increased the scope of his theory. His theory could now include the impact of clashes between these social worlds on male femalers. Ekins (1997) added several other units to the way he obtained his data slices. He analysed how the settings, interests and presuppositions of experts, lay members and male femalers varied. By selecting these different aspects of each of the three different social worlds, Ekins was able to show that medical professional definitions of sex-changing and cross-dressing were problematic. He was also able to expose the negative impacts these had on those who were male femaling. From the outset, then, his theoretical sampling involved comparisons that were of two kinds. One was a substantive comparison of different groups of male femalers who varied in the degree to which they were femaling (cross-dressers and sex-changers). The other comparison involved studying the clash of different worldviews on male femaling. These sets of comparisons had quite different consequences for the development of his theory. The first set of comparisons enabled the conceptualisation of male femaling as a matter of the degree to which a male females. The second set of comparisons dramatically increased the generality of his theory by bringing in the social worlds of others who were observing male femalers.

Ekins' (1997) approach to sampling did not end there. His work also included data slicing in comparison with the formal theory of 'awareness contexts'.[3] This enabled him to sample different units of awareness from open, to closed, to suspicion awareness and pretence awareness. By being able to sample these different 'units' of awareness, he was able to explore how male femaling could interact with social structure and also to study how male femalers were involved in 'masking' (Goffman 1959, 1961) their status as male femalers and how this process interacted with the different stages of male femaling.[4]

Ekins' (1997) theory is replete with examples of how the sheer variability of the experiences and combination of categories associated with male femaling resulted in a complex process of building relationships between categories. Take the example of beginning femaling. In this stage of male femaling, the typical pathway to male femaling is presented as a predominately private affair where the male who is femaling engages in experimenting with women's clothes, usually behind closed doors. These experiments are replete with guilt and unease and, as a consequence, the early stages of male femaling may take years for the male femaler to pass through. However, there were those who were propelled much more quickly through the early stages of male femaling. Ekins (1997) discovered this through the use of two very different slices of data. One related to Henry, who had already tried on women's clothes and who was asked to take the role of a woman in a school play. He was terrified of being found out and, as a consequence, tried to show less knowledge than he had of women's clothes. Also, by taking time to make sure his performance was not too convincing, he was hiding his status as a male femaler. After the play, however, he was propelled much more quickly into the process of male femaling because he enjoyed participating in the play so much. This case was used to theorise about how changes in awareness contexts could develop different pacing. The use of this case enabled Ekins to theorise that changes in the pacing of beginning male femaling could happen through temporary changes in awareness contexts. After all, Henry was able to perform as a female in an open awareness context, albeit in a temporary fashion, and this enabled him to develop his femaling more rapidly.

Ekins went on to challenge this finding with other, 'rarer' cases:

> where beginning male femaling initially takes place in the presence of another, male femaling is, of course, taking place within an open awareness context. Likely to arise, then, is fear that the interactant in the know will 'spill the beans' to others. This can give the knowing interactant considerable leverage over the beginning femaler. Horace, fearful that the knowledge would leak out to others, would bend over backwards to please his sister, who in turn capitalised on her hold over him for many years. Later she would insist that he continue with their 'girlie games' when he feared to do so. (Ekins 1997: 69)

This slice of data directly challenged his earlier finding but rather than reject this finding Ekins was able to add this to his conceptual scheme to help develop the variation in his theory. Not only can early experiences enhance the pacing of male femaling, they can block it from developing. Hopefully, you can see that theoretical sampling involves continually developing your theory through the conscious use of different data slices. Sampling is not aimed at verification, nor pure description, but the development of theory.

We have shown that a basic technique of theoretical sampling involves obtaining different slices of data and comparing them to generate theory. The trick is to pay close attention to the effects of this on your categories. As you can see, we have continued to develop this as a set of methodological principles rather than explain it as a sequence of techniques. Clearly, the process of obtaining slices of data is closely related to coding in grounded theory. We will make a few final comments on this before moving on to talking about theoretical pacing in Chapter 8.

Theoretical sampling and coding in grounded theory

If you remember, in Chapter 5 we discussed coding in grounded theory as a process that involved exploring the full range of types or continua of categories, delimiting the dimensions of a category, outlining the conditions under which it was either pronounced or minimised, exploring its major consequences and outlining its major relations to other categories. Clearly, getting hold of theory slices should happen in a way that enables you to help relate your categories to each other and also to delimit your theory. In *Theoretical Sensitivity* this developed into a two-stage process involving open and selective coding (Glaser 1978). Open coding involves a range of operations (see Figure 5-1, Coding in

Discovery, in Chapter 5) these are designed to expand the categories in your theory and relate your categories to your data. Selective coding involved making a decision on what the core category would be and then focusing on its core relationships (see Figure 5-3, Selecting the core category, in Chapter 5). As a consequence, then, *theoretical sampling should serve two general strategies: (1) to obtain slices of data to expand your categories and their relationships, and (2) to delimit and integrate your theory by specifying the core category and its major relationships.*

Our exemplars provide quite different ways to do this. Ekins (1997) sampled a huge variety of slices of data relating to very different units of analysis. The effect of this was to dramatically expand the *scope and generality* of his theory. Wuest (1997a, 1997b, 1998, 2000a, 2000b, 2001), in contrast, tended to gradually expand her use of slices of data to different groups of the same substantive type (i.e. women in caring relationships) and this had the effect of *expanding the scope of her theory*. The contrast between these two strategies indicates that you can do likewise. You can expand your sample by carefully expanding the scope of your theory to new groups, controlling your slices of data and the resulting comparisons, or you can engage in radical comparisons that utilise very different social units and groups to expand both the scope and generality of your theory. It is up to you. The important thing you need to do is to pay attention to the nature of the comparisons that result from sampling different theory slices and the consequences this has for your developing theory.

Skills and tips 7-2

Theoretical sampling

The study our intrepid explorer Hally is involved in involves dentists being paid to use a 'traffic light system' to rank patients in order to plan their pattern of care. A consequence of this is that after the dentist completes their examination of the patient's mouth the patient is given either a red, amber or green signal. A red signal means that they have significant disease and will need immediate treatment to stabilise the disease, an amber signal means they will need to be monitored closely and a green signal means they may not need to come back to the dentist for two years. Hally notices that this tool can in fact act on its own to trigger a 'script' that enables the dentist and patient to discuss changes to their health behaviours. So the use of observation tools can in fact open up directions for communication about health and behaviour change.

1) Make some notes on how Hally might confirm if this is the case or not? What kinds of encounters should she now theoretically sample in order to see if this is true or not?
2) Can Hally do anything else to check if her initial observations hold or not?

Key points about theoretical sampling

By carefully analysing the original grounded theory texts, we have been able to rediscover other aspects of the method that have become lost or, at the very least, neglected in the recent literature. There has been some application of different units in grounded theory so, for example, you will find authors using 'the situation' or individuals as the unit of analysis (Urquhart 1997; Clarke and Friese 2007). In other cases there is recognition that we can use different units of analysis but little reflection is developed beyond this (Kelle 1997). Understanding the fact that you can use different units of analysis and that these need not be just individuals was a fundamental aspect of grounded theory. This aspect can be seen as part of the legacy of grounded theory as a development out of comparative sociology. In such approaches, large-scale social units continue to be analysed (Lijphart 1971).[5] Comparisons through the use of different units of analysis, both organisational but also social structural, can enhance the scope and generality of your grounded theory.

The idea of getting slices of data or data slicing is never mentioned in the recent literature on grounded theory. In fact, the only person who mentions it is Barney Glaser in his introduction to *Gerund Grounded Theory* (Glaser 1996). Yet from what we can see, it is a fundamental technique that can be used to enable you to develop your theory.

If you use these rediscovered techniques for the development of your grounded theory you should note that they may have several effects. On the one hand, you need to pay attention to how they might enable you to expand the scope of your theory so that it might be applied to other groups in the same substantive field. On the other hand, they might enable you to expand the generality of your theory to cover other social phenomena. In order to achieve this it is suggested that you might want to sample other social units, for example organisations and situations, but also perhaps even social psychological units in the manner of Ekins (1997). The argument is that you should pay close attention to these two aspects of your theory development, which should be the focus of your notes and memos (see Chapter 10).

In summary, there are a number of key points about theoretical sampling:

- Different kinds of data will express different things about the problems and concerns of the people as they engage in action in the substantive field of research.
- There is no way to predetermine if the characteristics that you have selected to yield variation in your sample will be the most relevant.
- An imaginative and conceptually powerful technique for sampling is to approach data collection through the myriad of social and social psychological units that are available.
- Theoretical sampling involves the collection of 'slices of data' which are characterised by the fact that they are primarily purposive and directed at the goal of developing as many categories, properties, hypotheses and problems on the subject being investigated as possible.

- Slices of data can develop the scope of your theory by expanding its applicability to different groups in the field. It can also be used to expand the generality of the theory by making it applicable to different social units.
- Theoretical sampling should serve two general strategies within your study: (1) to obtain slices of data to expand your categories and their relationships, and (2) to delimit and integrate your theory by specifying the core category and its major relationships.

Summary

Having considered how to enhance theoretical sensitivity, in this chapter these sensitivities were then examined through a practical exploration of the consequences of theoretical sensitivity for theoretical sampling. A central aspect of the view being expressed about theoretical sampling in this book is that it is largely rediscovered and reconstituted as it was intended in the original method. In this chapter we sought to achieve this through an analysis of 'the lost skill' of 'data slicing' and an exploration of the consequences of this for sampling a wide variety of social and psychological units. By revisiting the idea of data slicing, we have discovered that sampling can be developed around a wide variety of *social units* of analysis, rather than simply by the views and perspectives of a sample of individual people or participants. The chapter then provided details of the sampling strategies of the exemplars being used in the book and explored how readers can sample slices of data from different social and psychological units in order to develop the scope and generality of their theory.

Further reading

Ekins, R. (1997) 'The social worlds of cross-dressing and sex-changing', Chapter 3 in R. Ekins, *Male Femaling: A Grounded Theory Approach to Cross-Dressing and Sex-Changing*. London: Routledge.

Ekins, R. (1997) 'Male femaling, masked awareness contexts and the methodology of grounded theory', Chapter 4 in R. Ekins, *Male Femaling: A Grounded Theory Approach to Cross-Dressing and Sex-Changing*. London: Routledge.

Glaser, B. and Strauss, A. (1971) 'Generating formal theory', Chapter 9 in B. Glaser and A. Strauss, *Status Passage*. Mill Valley, CA: Sociology Press.

Wuest, J. (2000a) 'Negotiating with helping systems: an example of grounded theory evolving through emergent fit', *Qualitative Health Research*, 10(1): 51–70.

Notes

1 Since the large-scale social world of nation states and large-scale groups are not subject to direct manipulation, comparative analysis developed to enable carefully controlled comparisons. In this respect comparisons were made between groups that were sufficiently similar but also different in certain key aspects. The carefully

controlled comparisons enabled comparative sociology to test hypotheses on large-scale groups. The problem for grounded theory was that this approach often did not generate enough despite all the efforts to generate such comparisons.

2   Wuest (1995, 2000) actually goes further. One of her prior interests is that the demands being placed on women in society to engage in more caring are a social structural phenomenon. It forms part of general social attitudes (Wuest 2000a).

3   The formal theory of awareness contexts was developed out of the substantive theory referred to in *Awareness of Dying* (Glaser and Strauss 1965). An 'Awareness Context' was defined by Glaser and Strauss (1964) as referring to 'who, in the dying situation, knows what about the probabilities of death for the dying patient.' They went on to state that it 'makes a great deal of difference who knows what, and the use of this scheme allows the organization of many events that otherwise might seem disconnected or paradoxical' (Glaser and Strauss 1964: ix).

4   In this respect Ekins was referring to the work of Goffman (1959, 1968). He stated that: 'Arguably, human beings are constantly "putting on fronts": adopting presentations of self which may have the simultaneous effect of expression and concealment (Goffman 1959, 1968) whether intentionally or unintentionally. ... In the area of male femaling, however, the masking is particularly fundamental. Male femalers seek to display as females while hiding aspects of their male identities.' (Ekins 1997: 51).

5   It might even be argued that perhaps we ought to explore more recent developments in comparative sociology to see what might be gleaned for grounded theory?

8

Theoretical Pacing and the Process of Doing Grounded Theory

Aim: To identify and outline the problem of theoretical pacing in grounded theory

Learning outcomes

After reading this chapter you should be able to:

- outline the difference between the pacing and processes of doing grounded theory
- summarise the basic techniques of doing grounded theory
- describe the place of the techniques of doing grounded theory within the process of doing grounded theory
- articulate the process of doing grounded theory in relation to starting out, open coding, selective coding and writing
- evaluate what the key issues are in relation to the rediscovery of theoretical pacing in grounded theory

By now we hope you will have a clear idea that there are two key features of grounded theory: flexibility and openness. While the end product might be to produce a theory that expresses and predicts how different groups of people process and deal with problems in specific settings or aspects of their lives, the approach that you will use to get to this end goal needs to be flexible and open. This brings us to a central feature of grounded theory, theoretical pacing.[1] Pacing in grounded theory refers to several things at once and this can make it very confusing for those new to the method. It is referred to as a 'social psychological process' (Glaser 1978). This means it should have a series of stages and should happen over time (see, for example, Glaser 1978: Chapter 6). What exactly these are in relation to doing grounded theory is hard to discern from the original texts. There are a number of ways to go through the various stages of doing grounded theory – probably as many ways as there are grounded theories. This of course means that you should vary your approach to how you go through the stages,[2] depending on the needs of your theory as it develops. In *Discovery*, Glaser and Strauss stated:

> We shall describe in four stages the constant comparative method: (1) comparing incidents applicable to each category, (2) integrating categories and their properties, (3) delimiting the theory, and (4) writing the theory. (Glaser and Strauss 1967: 105)

We have summarised these stages in Figure 8-1.

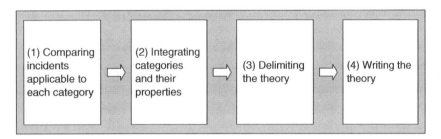

Figure 8-1   The stages of doing grounded theory derived from *Discovery*

Perhaps unsurprisingly, the situation became much more complicated after Glaser went on to develop the method. In *Theoretical Sensitivity*, Glaser (1978) elaborated a more complex process. According to him, the steps were related to the

> collection of research data, open coding of the data soon after, theoretical sampling, generating many memos with as much saturation as possible and emergence of core social psychological problems and processes, which then become the basis for more selective theoretical sampling, coding and memoing as the analyst focuses on the core. (Glaser 1978: 16)

He argued that the researcher would also need *to double back and collect more data* and conduct more coding, with an emphasis on developing memos both on data and on other memos (see Chapter 10). Eventually, as data collection and memoing continue, these 'processes' yield diminishing returns and 'the analyst turns to sorting', whereby memos are sorted into theoretical frameworks (Glaser 1978: 16; see also Chapter 11 in this volume). Sorting is conducted with writing-up in mind, where memos are placed into different chapters for the monograph. Finally, during writing, the analyst reworks and improves the integration of the theory. This elaborated process is summarised in Figure 8-2.

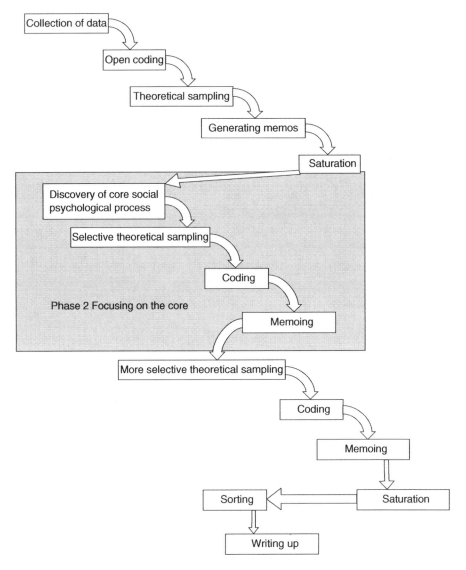

Figure 8-2 The elaborated process of doing grounded theory in *Theoretical Sensitivity*

The process was actually presented in another more simplified form later, in *Theoretical Sensitivity*, when Glaser (1978) discussed coding in grounded theory (see Chapter 9). In this respect, he indicated that there were two phases of the research process that gave greater emphasis to different forms of coding at different times. There was an open coding phase involving establishing as many categories as you can find that clearly articulate the content of the data. During this time you will also be looking for some relationships between categories and thinking about the main or dominant category. At the end of the open cod-ing phase of your research you decide to focus on your core category and then start to selectively develop this category through focused sampling and coding. This involves both coding and memoing around your core category and associ-ated categories, and includes the use of theoretical coding, which was effec-tively the use of a range of 'coding families' to help you integrate all of your categories (see Glaser 1978: 55–56). We have already covered these aspects of grounded theory but have yet to clarify what they actually involve.

In order to clarify this problem we would like to make a distinction between the 'pacing', 'process' and 'techniques'[3] *of doing grounded theory.* The pacing and the process are a series of logics that support how you will conduct your study. The techniques, on the other hand, are the things you will be doing when you do grounded theory. The use of these techniques will follow a particular pace in terms of how they are related and repeated in your study. The process of grounded theory refers to the stages you will enter over the course of doing your study. How this happens will be idiosyncratic and dependent on the prob-lem you are studying. Each stage in the process of doing grounded theory places more emphasis on certain techniques and less on others. Indeed, each stage will often yield a different combination of the basic techniques. Remem-ber, our purpose is to try to preserve the openness of grounded theory. We want to provide you with a way to do it that is in keeping with the spirit of what Glaser and Strauss (1967) intended. We do not wish to over-prescribe but to offer some advice on how to approach the process of doing grounded theory. In what follows we will outline the rationales behind the pacing and the pro-cess of doing grounded theory. In doing so, we will need to clarify the basic techniques of grounded theory. After outlining the building blocks of doing grounded theory, we will then discuss the variable ways in which the tech-niques might be combined and paced throughout your study. Having com-pleted this, we will discuss the overall process of doing grounded theory.

The pacing and process of doing grounded theory

It is because grounded theory is an open method that you need to pay close attention to how you ask your research question, the way in which you collect your data and the starting point for focusing on particular units for analysis. The way you combine the different techniques for the production of your grounded theory can have a significant impact on the scope of your theory and on your theory generally. It is very important to recognise that you will more than likely have limited time in which to finish your study, either for a PhD or for a funding body. If this is the case, you will need to pace the way you do grounded theory to enable the best possible outcome in the time you have available.

Pacing the techniques of grounded theory

Paying attention to the logic of pacing in your study will accrue two advantages: first, you will be prepared for the unexpected twists and turns of the study and, second, you will be able to provide a detailed account of how you arrived at your grounded theory. If you are doing a PhD, the latter point in particular could prove exceptionally useful since some form of explanation for how you arrive at your results is usually required.[4] From this you might be able to discern that pacing refers to the particular combination of techniques that you develop within your grounded theory. We can be more specific, however. *Pacing refers to how you engage in repeating the different techniques of generating theory as you move through the stages in doing grounded theory.* These techniques are described in Figure 8-3.

Now, remember the emphasis is on being open and flexible in this process. Your goal is to produce a good grounded theory. The best way to do this, as Glaser has often said, is to work flexibly in order to enable it to 'emerge'. How this will happen depends in large part on the problem you discover, the time you have available for your grounded theory and the kind of data you will need.

Our exemplars demonstrate very different pacing strategies. In one study we have a relatively slow, structured build-up towards a formal theory of 'precarious ordering' (Wuest 1997a, 1997b, 1998, 2000a, 2000b, 2001). This theory is focused on women as the unit of analysis and it was developed out of a series of different individual studies looking at specific aspects of the emerging theory,

---

- Sampling – the selection of cases, places or settings, subjects, documents and literatures from which to collect a wide variety of data
- Theoretical sampling (sampling variation and data slicing) – the selection of cases, places, subjects and literatures from which to collect data to enable comparisons with the purpose of generating theory
- Collecting data – the collection of information relevant to the generation of your theory. This can be through interviews, participant observation, non-participant observation, reading literature and different types of interviews, for example life history or semi-structured interviews
- Coding data – the grouping of data under codes
- Theoretical coding – the specification of the type of theory and elaboration of its key relationships
- Saturation – filling out categories with memos so they capture the major variations in the data and all of the ideas and observations of the researcher about their data so that as the study progresses further sampling and data collection will yield diminishing returns, eventually becoming redundant
- Reading the literature – the literature in grounded theory is treated as another source of comparisons to enable the development of the theory
- Sorting – the grouping of memos into the major categories of the theory while deciding on the order for writing up
- Writing – the final specification of the theory for the purpose of publication

Figure 8-3   The basic techniques of doing grounded theory

progressively expanding the scope of the theory to different groups of women. Wuest (1997a) began with sensitivity to the diversity of women's experiences and an interest in feminist theory. She states that this sensitivity guided her responses to the emerging theoretical concepts and helped her to direct her theoretical sampling (Wuest 1997a: 101). None of this information directly affected the pacing of her study. Wuest's (1997a) pacing strategy initially involved basic sampling, collecting and analysis of data from a convenience sample of middle-class women. Although we do not have a complete description of Wuest's (1997a) approach, we are told that she collected data through participant observation, initial interviews, repeat interviews and reading appropriate literature for integration into her study. She also conducted group interviews with two groups – one with two women and one with four women – to get a different kind of information which, we are told, 'triggered further thoughts' and resulted in rich data for the purposes of comparison (Wuest 1997a: 102). Clearly, here we have the use of a range of research techniques that resulted in a pacing strategy that was tied to her overall logic of sampling different groups of participants that varied in relation to each other in particular ways.

As we discussed in Chapter 6, Richard Ekins' study also began with pre-existing interests in sex, sexuality and gender, a symbolic interactionist perspective, the problem of identity within social worlds and how different frames of reference about cross-dressing could mutually interact to affect the processes associated with male femaling. These prior interests guided him, but in no way determined the logic of his pacing strategy. We are not given the full details of how he proceeded with his analysis, but we are told that his initial approach was to 'gain access' to the 'social worlds' of cross-dressers. He started with three 'access points'. He met 'individual cross-dressers and sex-changers; attended member support group meetings; and frequented drag bars and attended drag balls' (Ekins 1997: 42). His data collection also occurred in a range of different social worlds, from public to private. Eventually he secured entry to 'private parties, wine bar socials, drag balls and "transvestite" weekends held at various hotels' (Ekins 1997: 42). Clearly, he paced his study through a constant process of sampling, theoretical sampling, data analysis and coding.

From these accounts you can see that there is quite a difference in approach. Ekins' work took years to solidify into a coherent story whereas Wuest's work (Wuest 1997a, 1997b, 1998, 2000a, 2000b, 2001) shows a slow and deliberate build-up of complexity over years. You can also see that the units of analysis in the work of each of these authors have had a significant impact on how these works have been paced. In Ekins' work, a focus on social worlds led to an exploration of the many different kinds of settings within which male femaling took place. A consequence of this will have been a pacing structure of data collection and analysis shaped by the degree to which Ekins was able to negotiate access to such settings. Sampling and theoretical sampling will have been opportunistic and unstructured, with data collection, coding and analysis depending on when access could be negotiated. In contrast to this, Wuest's focus on individuals as the principle unit of analysis meant that she could sample and code in carefully planned batches.

So far we have discussed the pacing of your grounded theory largely with reference to the sampling, collection and coding of data. These tripartite processes are frequently found together. You will often find reference to the 'iterative' process of doing grounded theory in the literature, which frequently refers to these processes (Marsiglio 2004; Hesse-Biber and Leavy 2006; Weiner 2007; Charmaz 2009; Birks and Mills 2011). In each of these examples, writers refer to the combination of sampling, collection of data and coding of data. For example, Birks and Mills (2011) refer to the process of 'constantly comparing and collecting or generating data' (Birks and Mills 2011: 94). In terms of the pacing of grounded theory, this combination of operations will be most common. However, you may find it necessary to include other combinations within the pacing of your own study.

Another source of variation when it comes to the pacing structure of grounded theory techniques will be the emerging theoretical structure of your theory. By this, we are referring to the major variations and relationships that you may be exploring in order to develop your theory. Here we are referring to the coding families that Glaser elaborated in *Theoretical Sensitivity* (Glaser 1978). Let us say that you are working on a theory that is developing as a basic social process. During your data analysis it emerges that there is a critical point that people reach before moving on to the next stage. You might want to stop the analysis and chase up this lead by going back through your data and contacting some of your participants who have moved on to the next stage, to explore 'this cutting point' in more depth. You may also seek out a data slice from an unrelated field which might throw into sharper focus a key aspect of this cutting point. In this sense, the logic of pacing will need to change depending on how your theory develops. This brings us to the question of the process of grounded theory and how to pace this.

Pacing the process of grounded theory

While there are research techniques that you will use repeatedly throughout your study, these will be used with varying frequency as you progress through the different stages in producing your theory. In this respect, then, no matter how nuanced and varied the combination of ways in which you pace the use of your research techniques, you might find it helpful to expect to pass through several stages when developing your theory. The process refers to the manner in which you go through the series of stages involved in producing your grounded theory. How you pace this process will be important in ensuring that you have something to write about at the end of your study. In order to help you with planning the process we have suggested the following structure in Figure 8-4.[5]

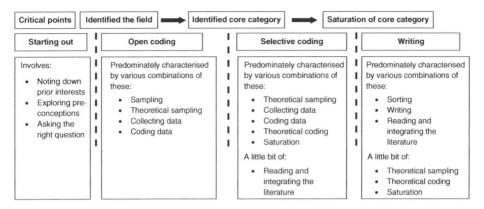

Figure 8-4   The process of doing grounded theory

The overall process we are presenting here moves beyond the original version of grounded theory for a number of reasons. First, it is quite clear that in *rediscovering the method we have found that the process of doing grounded theory has evolved significantly*. This evolution has been detrimental to understanding how to start doing grounded theory, then how to proceed and complete a grounded theory. As we have seen, in *Discovery* Glaser and Strauss (1967) described this as a process of four stages (see Figure 8-1). With the advent of *Theoretical Sensitivity* (Glaser 1978), this process appeared to disappear and several different routes to producing a grounded theory where proposed (see Figure 8-2). Second, we are attempting to clarify grounded theory. None of these suggestions should compromise the method. What we have done here is to attempt to separate out the techniques from the stages to enable you to plan the manner in which you will develop your theory. As you will see from Figure 8-4, we are proposing that you plan for four broad stages, which may or may not comprise the stages of your study: starting out, open coding, selective coding and writing. You do not have to follow these stages in the way they are specified; indeed, you should not expect this process to be tidy and linear!

Starting out

When it comes to starting out in grounded theory there are a number of things you might consider doing. First, make a note of any prior interests that you might have in the substantive field of study. These will relate to your motivations for doing the grounded theory. They might be personal interests or curiosities that have made you want to explore the field of interest. They are relevant not because they might be sources of bias (which they can be), but rather they will link with your interests for doing your study and can therefore continually motivate you. They can also enhance the final product *as long as they are not allowed to dominate the process.* As you have seen in Chapter 6, both Richard Ekins and Judith Wuest were able to really enhance their findings by linking what they discovered in doing their grounded theory to their motivations for studying the field.

A related set of problems that can affect your grounded theory might be your professional preconceptions about the field you are studying. As we have seen, Ekins and Wuest both had elaborate preconceptions. Ekins' preconceptions were derived from his interest in sex, sexuality, symbolic interactionism and a social worlds approach, among other things (Ekins 1997). Wuest developed her study from her interest in feminism. In each case preconceptions were used to enhance the interpretation of the theory as it emerged. This is all compatible with grounded theory. After all, you will have to integrate your findings into the relevant literatures. The important thing, however, is to ensure that these preconceptions do not dominate the process. If anything, you can use them to enhance your sensitivity to your emerging theory. But if you draw on the conceptual language of these preconceptions, you will risk forcing ideas into your theory which are just not relevant. This brings us to the research question.

The research question should be open (see Chapter 2). The rationale for this is that you cannot predetermine what are the most relevant issues to your participants. If your theory is to fit their concerns and explain how these are resolved, you need to be open to allowing these concerns to develop ready for coding into your theory. There should be a question. Don't just go out and collect data and expect your theory to develop. We have shown time and again throughout this book that most grounded theory begins with an area of interest but, more specifically, it asks a question that is open. Having prior interests does not mean that you cannot ask an open question. One small addendum: we suggest that starting with a unit of analysis (setting, role or group of people) is a useful way to enable you to generate categories for your theory (see Chapter 7). While this remains true, there is no need for you to specify the unit as part of your research question. Take the lead of Wuest (1997a) as a great example of how to simply focus on the problems and concerns of those you wish to work with when developing your theory.

Let us take a few examples. Richard Ekins (1997) began with a whole raft of questions that were derived from his symbolic interactionist background. His interest was in how his informants defined the situations in which they found themselves? Working within this framework meant that he did 'not approach the empirical social world as a tabula rasa' and avoided imposing his own version of reality on his subjects. He argued that researchers 'should enter the research setting with as few predetermined ideas as possible, and should be prepared to change those they already have, readily and frequently' (Ekins 1997: 37). Notice how he was focusing on a setting but remaining open to what his participants made of that setting. Wuest (1997a) was influenced by feminist theory when she began her study, which then focused on discovering what was 'problematic for women about caring', her goal being to generate a theory that explained how their central problem was resolved (Wuest 1997a: 100). As we have seen, the logic of Wuest's pacing followed her need to produce outputs throughout her career. Each time she developed her theory she identified an area that could do with further work and then focused specifically on the perspectives of those participating in that stage of her theory development.

The maxim is that while you may bring quite a bit of baggage to your study, this baggage is not something to be feared. Far from it! Just bring the baggage and constantly refer to it, but do so while guarding it from forcing you to only focus on certain issues. One way to do this is to ask a series of open-ended questions. We have provided a list of possible questions that are suitable for starting out when doing grounded theory in Box 8-1. In contrast to these, we have provided more modified versions of the same questions which are clearly not suitable for doing grounded theory. As you can see, the questions in Box 8-2 presuppose what is relevant; they use preconceptions about what the relevant theoretical issue is by presupposing that the risks of alcohol abuse are major concerns for people who drink in pubs. It might be, but we think that it might also be equally unlikely, much to the consternation of public health professionals. In Box 8-2 you can see that the second question also presupposes that coping patterns and strategies are relevant to the reintegration of servicemen into the civilian world. They might be, but these categories may also just be part of the overall picture and by forcing the study to explore the narrow band of categories associated with coping, we would be restricting the grounded theory approach and forcing psychological research ideas into the theory from the outset.

Box 8-1

Typical open questions suitable for doing grounded theory

1 What are the concerns of bartenders and their clients when they go to pubs? How are these resolved?
2. What are the concerns of servicemen as they re-enter the civilian world after being involved in conflict? How are these resolved?
3. What are the main concerns of dentists and patients in dental encounters? Do the funding arrangements for these encounters shape how those concerns are manifested or not?
4. What are the primary concerns of midwives and their clients when birthing happens in home settings? How do these concerns resolve themselves?

Box 8-2

Questions not suitable for doing grounded theory

1. What are the concerns of bartenders and their clients regarding the risks of alcohol abuse when they go to pubs? How do they resolve their concerns with this risk?
2. How do servicemen cope with re-entering the civilian world after being involved in conflict? Do they use problem-focused or avoidance-focused coping techniques?
3. How do dentists and patients handle dental anxiety in the dental clinic? Is the amount of funding of direct significance to the management of dental anxiety?
4. To what extent are midwives and their clients involved in a power game when birthing happens in home settings?

Staying open is a critical problem that you will have to confront when starting to do grounded theory. You can have prior interests and these will be relevant, but you must not allow them to dominate the early stages of your research. It is far more productive to focus on your participants and, as Ekins says, to get into their social worlds and explore these from their perspectives.

Skills and tips 8-1

Asking the right question

Take the time to try specifying the question you will address in your study. Refer to Boxes 8-1 and 8-2 when doing this. Take a note of how your question comes close to pre-existing concepts and ideas. Make a note of these under the heading 'preconceptions'. You can then reflect on these later. Try to make your question fit the general principle of openness we have discussed in this section. After this, look at your question and make some notes on what motivates you about this question. If the question does not motivate you, then you need to think carefully about another question that will motivate you more. You also need to describe what it is about different questions that motivate you so you can reflect on these motivations later in the study. Do you want to influence policy? Are you looking to promote the interests of a particular group?

You are noting these preconceptions and prior interests simply to be able to use them in your study productively. They should not drive what you do and should be modified to fit what you find as you collect and analyse your data.

Open coding

Having begun to ask the right questions, you are more or less ready to start collecting data. Grounded theory contrasts with most other research approaches because it does not place any direct guidelines or restrictions on the amount of data you will need. The only thing you can be sure about is that you will need a lot of data of different types (observations, interviews, documentary, literature). We will come to the details of how to do this in Chapter 9. All we want to say here is that when pacing at this stage in the process of doing grounded theory you need to move between sampling (see Chapter 7), collecting your data and coding it. The key thing at this stage is to code for as much variability and variety in your theory as possible. Glaser (1978) argued that it is important to move quickly and pay attention to the kinds of data you are collecting while also stopping to conduct data slicing to help you think conceptually. The pace should be quite fast. For Ekins, we have seen that conducting open coding took a period of time (equivalent to two years); for Wuest, this happened during the period of a PhD and so will have been anything between six months to three years.

The whole process is meant to lead you to discover what the main concern of your participants is. When you discover this you are ready to establish what kind of theory you will have and what kind of core category you will be developing. We will give more details about this decision in the next chapter. Deciding on a core category is a critical juncture in the process of building a grounded theory. Once you start to make this decision and begin to focus on *integrating your theory*, you are ready to begin the process of selective coding.

Selective coding

Once you have decided to code around what you think are the core concerns of your participants and how these concerns are resolved in the setting that you are studying, selective coding begins. As with open coding, we will go into more details about selective coding in Chapter 9. At this stage you will begin to theoretically sample much more (see Chapter 7). This will lead to a much more focused sampling strategy. The idea will be to check if the core category you have selected is really the core concern. *At this stage you will primarily be filling out your core category and focusing on how it helps to organise and integrate your theory. It is not unusual for people to make a false start and to have to go back to open coding and collecting more data.* This usually happens because not enough data has been collected in the open coding phase.

The pacing of this stage of grounded theory will be characterised by an increasing use of theoretical sampling and theoretical coding in the form of memoing. You should expect to return to the field to collect and code more data. As time passes, you will find yourself involved in more and more data slicing and going back through your notes and memos to explore and check your interpretations. The goal of this stage is to saturate your categories and to link them together into a fully *integrated* theory. At this stage you will also conduct more theoretical sampling by data slicing from the literature (for more details of this, see Chapter 12). The critical point about the selective coding stage of grounded theory is that you should be *thinking theoretically*. This means you should be thinking about your core category and finalising what kind of theory you have, including its major relationships. The pace of this stage of the process of grounded theory can be a lot slower because you are thinking carefully and making much more deliberately selected comparisons in order to enable you to specify the key relationships within your theory. This can take a lot of time. Once the theory has been developed to the point where data collection and data slicing is yielding very little new information and further data collection seems to be a waste of time, you are ready to begin writing up the theory.

Writing

When you are sure what your grounded theory is saying and you know what its main contribution to the field will be, you are ready to start writing up. By now the chances are that you will not be engaging in any further sampling. The chief techniques you will be cycling through will be sorting (see Chapter 11), further memoing, reading the literature and writing. Here the focus is on detailing your theory and preparing it for presentation to colleagues. When reading the literature, some good advice will be not only to look for more examples for your theory, but also to discover how others have presented their grounded theories. Here we feel the work of Ekins (1997) and Wuest (1997a, 1997b, 1998, 2000a, 2000b, 2001) can be especially helpful. Wuest, in particular, is an excellent example of how you can actually present different aspects of your overall grounded theory. Writing about the major conditions of the phenomena you have studied, on the one hand, or the major impacts of the phenomena on the people in your study, on the other, can make valuable contributions to the literature. Taking time to think through this stage of doing grounded theory is vital. Sadly, it is something a lot of people who have done grounded theory have not done sufficiently. Writing about grounded theory does not always involve presenting the whole theory. Writing about different aspects of your theory can be a valuable approach to ensuring that your theory contributes to the field. We will return to this problem in Chapter 13.

Key points about theoretical pacing

In this chapter what has become clear is that descriptions of the processes associated with doing grounded theory have developed over time as the method was gradually refined. The process is inherently complex and it seems that there has been a degree of both difficulty and reluctance to try to clarify how a grounded theory should be conducted over time. Few diagrams have been produced to provide an overview of the method, although some do exist (see Birks and Mills 2011). The risk of producing a guide (see Figure 8-4) is, of course, that it will be taken as a set of rules and procedures that must be followed rigidly. This is not our wish. In presenting the process we are seeking to prepare your expectations for doing grounded theory. If you read the original texts closely, there is a definite order to grounded theory, although this can be unclear. This order has been changed as the method has been increasingly refined so, for example, although Strauss and Corbin (1990) provide no illustrations of the actual process, it is quite clear that they were proposing a number of refinements to the process that did not exist previously. Another good example of the lack of clarity concerning the process of doing grounded theory is how Dey (1999) introduces grounded theory through the 'usual phases of the research process', involving 'how to initiate the research', 'how to select data', 'how to collect data', 'how to analyze data', and 'how to conclude the research' (Dey 1999: 3). In some respects, the different aspects of doing research don't quite communicate the process as it was expressed in *Discovery*. For the student who wants to know how to do grounded theory, what is needed is a clear sense of *what it might involve* well in advance of trying to do it. This is what we have attempted to do in this chapter. Our goal is to try to demonstrate that grounded theory can be portrayed as a process with a series of stages. These stages can be separated by a number of critical points.[6] Each stage will involve engaging with a multitude of techniques, for example sampling, theoretical sampling, collecting data and coding data. We have portrayed this as a building process because that is the way it is described in the original texts (Glaser and Strauss 1967; Glaser 1978). How these different techniques will be deployed will be highly variable and determined by the subject you are investigating. The key points about theoretical pacing in grounded theory are as follows:

- The definition and delineation of the structure and processes associated with doing grounded theory was refined and clarified over time. There are therefore several descriptions of this in the original texts.
- In order to clarify the problem, we have made the distinction between the 'the process' and the specific 'techniques' of doing grounded theory.
- The rationales of pacing and the process are a series of logics that support the particular style of theory development you adopt during your study.
- The techniques associated with doing grounded theory are the practical things you will be doing when you do grounded theory. These are summarised in Figure 8-3 (see page 140).
- Theoretical pacing in this chapter refers to the way in which you combine these different techniques in order to do your grounded theory. It also refers to how you engage in the repeating techniques of generating theory as you move through the stages in doing grounded theory.
- The stages we have proposed in order to clarify the method are starting out, open coding, selective coding and writing up.

Project planning

Having specified the question you will be using in your study, take time to work out the deadline for your study. When is it due for submission? Working back from the deadline, specify in a general sense when you will need to finish each phase of the research process. So when will you need to start writing? How long will you need to allow for selective coding? When should open coding be finished?

You might find it helpful to modify Figure 8-5 and plot this into a document with specific broad milestones.

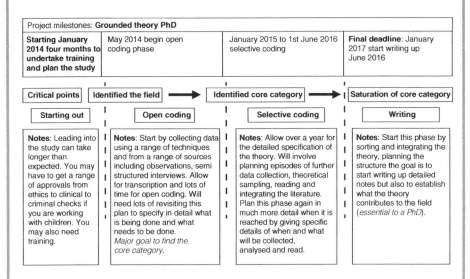

Figure 8-5   Example of a chart to aid project planning

This framework has to be constantly revised and updated as the study progresses. As time moves forward, it should become more and more focused on the specific details of your study. You may also find other approaches, such as a GANT chart, useful.

Summary

The process of doing grounded theory evolved over time although there are very few descriptions of what it actually involves. This chapter has attempted to provide an overview of the process by focusing on the various stages of doing grounded theory and mapping on to these stages the different techniques that will be used at each stage. The chapter proposed four stages for doing grounded theory: starting out, open coding, selective coding and writing. By mapping on to these stages the associated techniques, the chapter has sought to prepare you for what to expect when doing grounded theory. The chapter explored prior interests and preconceptions to enable you to prepare for doing a grounded theory. We also analysed how to ask the right research question. The chapter briefly outlined how each of the different techniques of doing grounded theory are to be used during the different stages. The chapter also discussed how you need to think about pacing the overall process and the techniques that will be used when doing grounded theory, including how this pacing structure might vary dramatically in different studies. By drawing on the exemplars, the chapter demonstrated how focusing on different units of analysis during the initial stages of a grounded theory study can in fact have different consequences for the subsequent process of doing grounded theory.

Further reading

Birks, M. and Mills, J. (2011) 'Planning a grounded theory study', Chapter 2 in M. Birks and J. Mills, *Grounded Theory: A Practical Guide*. London: Sage.

Ekins, R. (1997) 'The social worlds of cross-dressing and sex-changing', Chapter 3 in R. Ekins, *Male Femaling: A Grounded Theory Approach to Cross-Dressing and Sex-Changing*. London: Routledge.

Fernández, W.D. (2005) 'Issues and design', in D. Hart and S. Gregor (eds), *Information Systems Foundations: Constructing and Criticising*. Canberra: Australian National University ePress.

Wuest, J. (1997) 'Fraying connections of caring women: an exemplar of including difference in the development of explanatory frameworks', *Canadian Journal of Nursing Research*, **29**(2): 99–116.

Notes

1 Before defining this feature of grounded theory, we think it worthwhile to note that everything in grounded theory seems to be prefixed with the term 'theoretical'. We have theoretical sensitivity, theoretical sampling, theoretical pacing, theoretical coding, etc. In some respects the constant use of the term 'theoretical' in this way can be a bit irritating and might seem a bit excessive. So we will just use 'pacing' for the rest of this chapter to simplify the language.

2 In *Theoretical Sensitivity* Glaser referred to steps instead of stages. We will treat these as basically referring to the same thing.

3 Just to be clear, when we are referring to techniques here, we are using this term in the same way as it is used in any other approach to research. In this respect, grounded theory is really no different from any other approach to research. It has its methodology, it has associated techniques but it also draws on research techniques that you will find in many other studies, for example, participant observation, semi-structured interviewing and documentary analysis.

4   Glaser (2009) might complain that providing detailed information on the develop-
    ment of your theory is another form of 'worrisome accuracy'. While he has a point,
    we nonetheless think it is important that, if you are doing your PhD, you might need
    to remember that Glaser has his PhD (in fact he has two!) and that things might have
    changed since grounded theory was originally developed. PhD committees often
    require some element of justification when explaining how you analysed your data
    and arrived at your core findings. You would do well to remember this when con-
    ducting your grounded theory as a PhD student.

5   This diagram is presented to enable you to have an overview of the process of doing
    grounded theory from start to finish. Because it has a start and a finish, do not
    assume your pathway through the process will be simple or linear. On the contrary,
    you will engage in many different combinations of the techniques for grounded
    theory over the period in which you construct your study. We would also suggest
    that you review the diagram in Fernández (2005: 48), which provides a good depic-
    tion of how complex the process can be.

6   The technical term in grounded theory is 'cutting point'. Another way to put it is to
    call these 'critical junctures'. This is why you can find reference in the grounded
    theory literature to the fact that grounded theory is itself a basic social psychological
    process. The perceptive reader will realise that there is a hint here that we might
    discover a formal theory of the research process. Sadly, we don't have time to go
    into this any further here.

9

Rediscovering Coding in Grounded Theory

Aim: To explore the problem of coding in grounded theory

Learning outcomes

After reading this chapter you should be able to:

- describe the range of techniques and approaches to be used when open coding
- explore how to develop comparisons and engage in data slicing for the development of grounded theory
- establish when to cease open coding and how to do selective coding when you do grounded theory
- evaluate how our rediscovery of theoretical coding can enhance your techniques for doing grounded theory

In Chapter 5 we discussed the different views of coding that you will find in the literature on grounded theory. Many differences on this aspect of grounded theory exist. There is huge variability in the way different grounded theorists themselves approach coding, for example, some focus on coding meaning (Charmaz 2000, 2006) and others worry about their 'positionality' when it comes to coding (Lempert 2007). In this chapter we are going to look at the key issues to think about when you are coding in grounded theory. We will be discussing how to conduct open, selective and theoretical coding. After presenting our analysis of these techniques, we will then explore what, if anything, has been *rediscovered* about coding.

In Chapter 5 we discussed the fact that *coding appears to have two purposes: the first is to capture the substantive content of the area under study; the second is to articulate relationships that can be observed in the data.* While these are the goals of coding, these goals occur in two phases of grounded theory: open and selective coding. As we have also seen in Chapter 8, these forms of coding occur with different frequency at different times during the process of doing grounded theory.

Open coding

Open coding in grounded theory is a phase in the process that involves sampling, theoretical sampling, collecting and coding data (see Figure 8-4). As we have seen in Chapter 5, coding is aimed at 'capturing' what is going on in the area studied. But what does this mean? Open coding is essentially the phase where you primarily capture the content of the action and interactions that are happening in your field of study. As we have seen in Chapter 8, this phase ends after the culmination of coding results in the discovery of your core problem *and by capturing it in your core category*. This means that you read your data while asking a number of questions (see Figure 5-2 in Chapter 5). Before you begin coding, however, it is important to realise that you will need to put some time into thinking about where you can get the most relevant data for your study. As we said previously, you might have a preconception or some prior interests that lead you towards a particular source of information. But it is also necessary to think carefully about what might be *the best source of information and therefore data for your study*. Before we get into the mechanics of coding, it is very important to point out that this process is fundamentally dependent on what counts as data for your theory.

As we have seen in Chapter 6, there are different kinds of data, all of which will provide you with different types of information about your theory. This was the case in the specification of Wuest's (1997a, 1997b, 1998, 2000a, 2000b, 2001) theory, which began by focusing on the problems and concerns women had when being confronted with increasing caring demands. The relevant data for her study, then, related to different groups of women bringing different resources to the problem of caring demands. As a result, coding was primarily focused on the demands that were placed on women and how they dealt with these. You can see that it is when you start to code that you will be confronted with the question of what counts for coding and what doesn't. Your coding will very much depend on what you have written down in order to be coded. Every researcher has very different approaches to data collection and analysis, and frequently the focus of your study can determine the level and detail of the observations you might produce. Ekins (1997) was interested in the social worlds of his participants and, as such, collected data that was focused on encapsulating a wide variety of experiences and happenings in a huge range of settings. Wuest (1997a, 1997b, 1998, 2000a, 2000b, 2001), on the other hand, was focused on how different groups of women processed the problems associated with caring demands. Her data, which was collected in semi-structured interviews and focus groups, would have been quite different from that of

Ekins. It should be pretty obvious, then, that the position you occupy in relation to the direction of your study can and will have a significant impact on the types of data you identify as relevant. As you can probably see, for us, positionality in grounded theory is not something that was discovered by constructivists such as Charmaz.[1] It was there, albeit in a much more subtle form, at the beginning. Everything in the social world is always, in some way, socially constructed; this is one of the key findings of sociology as a discipline (Jenkins 2002).

As we have said previously (see Chapter 6 'How to develop theoretical sensitivity'), in order to be able to explore coding in detail we need to draw on examples where this detail is available. At this stage, we will begin to draw on the work of Raphael (2008), Gibson (1997) and our ongoing study into the problems associated with promoting lifestyle change in general dental practice.

What is data?

Each of these studies varies significantly in the way that they have focused on different kinds of data. One of the authors of this book (Barry Gibson) had a prior interest in the conditions and situations that led to decisions concerning whether or not dentists would treat patients who were diagnosed as being HIV positive. He took the time to observe dental practitioners working in a range of clinics. Some clinics specialised in treating HIV-positive patients. Here the decision to be involved in treating HIV-positive patients was taken as part of the condition of practising in the clinic. Other clinics he observed did not involve this condition and often the dentist was not aware of the patient's HIV status. His observations focused on the use of different infection control procedures and the dentists' decisions to either treat the patient or not. He was also interested in incidents that occurred in which the dentists' perceptions of risk varied from feelings that they were at relatively minor risk to feeling they were in real danger of acquiring an HIV infection. Data relating primarily to observations of risk in clinical practice, along with the perceptions of dentists and patients about risk, were relevant. You can see how these interests have acted to shape the observations that were subsequently analysed. In the following excerpt, the movement of 'dirty' instruments and the tracking of 'contamination' through the clinic during treatment were being watched:

> Whilst observing treatment in the clinic the dental team were using a zone system for the treatment of their high risk patients. From observing this regime what was apparent was that nothing could move back out of a dirty zone. Therefore as instruments were required from the dental nurse, they were passed onto the dentist's tray. They were never removed from this tray until they were ready to either be disposed of or cleaned. With respect to the dental team, if the phone in the clinic rang during a treatment session the dental nurse would get up and remove her external set of gloves before answering the phone. Therefore when the phone rang the new clinical regime was especially susceptible. (Gibson 1997: 176)

Observations in this study were clearly selective and focused on what the emerging theory is going to be about. This led to a focus on the concerns of the dental team with cross-infection. It is not hard to see that these were real concerns and that considerable effort was being made to organise the dental encounter to take account of the risk of cross-infection.

In contrast, Helen Raphael (2008), coming from a nursing background, was primarily interested in men's 'perceptions, understanding and experiences' of being diagnosed with osteoporosis. A typical slice of data from her notes is reported as follows:

> One such participant was James who had many health problems, including a life-long severe inflammatory lung condition. As a result of his lung disease he had been prescribed steroids for many years, which are now a known risk factor for secondary osteoporosis. As with many of the other participants, it was only by chance the way to osteoporosis was 'signposted'. Whilst attending a regular appointment for his lung disease, he saw a consultant who suggested that James should have a scan to check for osteoporosis. It was as an outcome of the scan that his osteoporosis was detected and treatments commenced.

> 'Well quite frankly, it [osteoporosis] had never even crossed my mind, until they sent me for a scan and the consultant said I had a problem.' (Raphael 2008: 135–136)

The relevance of what counted as data for her study was shaped by her professional interest as a nurse to enable men to come to terms with their diagnosis. It is not hard to see why groups of men with the condition were deemed the most relevant participants for her. Her strategy was to collect data from men who could provide as much information as possible about being diagnosed with osteoporosis and who were willing to take part. Clearly, this is quite different from the dental example in terms of its focus, not just because it is a different subject, but also because the data relate to a group's perceptions of a little known condition that can affect them. As you will see, Raphael (2008) had to confront the problem that her participants knew very little about the condition and often struggled to come to terms with it as she coded her data. This became especially relevant for her coding and presents quite a different problem for building theory from the conditions that might affect the management of risk and danger in dental practice.

Finally, in our contemporary study of health promotion in dental practice data is being collected from a range of observations of clinical encounters. Initial sampling contrasts encounters that have been taking place in dental practices which operate under the conditions of a traditional dental contract and encounters occurring in practices operating with a new contract designed to encourage a new type of dentistry aimed at health promotion as opposed to dental treatment. The observations are specifically aimed at whether or not health-related information is discussed and also at the cadence and sequence of the encounter.

Observation 8 This was a routine dental encounter with an appointment that lasted 10 minutes. The dentist screened for problems asking if there were 'Any problems?' 'Any changes to your medical history?'

To this the patient replied 'no'.

Dentist: 'Do you smoke?'

Patient replied 'yes'.

Dentist: 'How many?'

Patient replied 'depends on how stressful the day has been.'

Dentist: '15 or 20 a day?'

Patient replied 'yes'

Dentist: 'You know we offer a smoking cessation service?'

Patient replied 'don't even start... (patient laughs)'

At this point the dentist started the examination and informed the patient that they would be doing a scale and polish to remove 'plaque stains' and said 'if you want me to stop lift your hand up'. The dentist stated that they needed to take an x-ray as they had not taken one in a while and it was common practice to do one every two years now. The patient was happy with this and subsequently the dentist informed the patient that they would write to them if they 'find anything' on the x-ray. At this point the x-ray was conducted and they subsequently organised a 6-month follow-up appointment. At this point the patient asked for a 12-month check-up but the dentist said that they preferred to do a check-up in 6 months to check her gums. (Notes 07/08/12 4pm, Patient ID: SP8 Dentist ID: SD4 Centre code: 5)

The observations in this study are much more strategic and selective. The research team is not interested in everything that is being said in the encounter. So, for example, details of treatment planning are not relevant. When discussions about health-related lifestyle changes develop, the team pays particular interest to these and notes when these discussions don't happen. When such discussions do not happen, this is of interest because we are seeking to trace the conditions that affect where and when such information is discussed or omitted. Such comparisons will be especially valuable to our emerging theory. The goal, then, *is for you to collect as much strategically relevant data as possible over many encounters in different settings.*

As you can see, by virtue of asking a question you have already preconceived the kind of problem you might encounter. Preconceptions often lead to an interest in particular types of data and this can have quite an impact on what you observe as being relevant to your theory. However, despite all of these interests, *you need to try to remain open.* Of course this means that *you need to allow yourself to be corrected if necessary to the problem that is most relevant to your participants.* This will be especially important when you get data that suggests that what you think is central is in fact not so central. Helen Raphael discovered this in her PhD:

> It was by reflecting constantly on my own position in the research that I realised, with surprise, during the early stages of the analysis that my clinical experience was influencing my interpretation of the data. I had seen many people with severe osteoporosis who suffered terrible pain and for whom the slightest pressure resulted in a fracture, or fractures. As a result, when I analysed the first interviews with men with osteoporosis, when they appeared to disregard the problem, I had a code 'making light of the problem'. I was perplexed and at first found it difficult to understand when some of the men with osteoporosis reported that they 'ignored' osteoporosis on a daily basis. It soon became clear that considering osteoporosis a problem was my preconception but for the participants there may not be a problem. Once I was aware of this, I returned to the data and examined it afresh. This insight into my unrecognised preconceptions taught me that I needed to be extra vigilant when I interpreted the data since my position as a nurse and my ideas had been formed due to my clinical experience. (Raphael 2008: 75–76)

Thus, the very direction of your coding can be shaped by preconceptions. Helen Raphael (2008) was clearly confronted by this problem. Yet the process of doing grounded theory in some way corrected these preconceptions.

Techniques for open coding in grounded theory

Open coding in grounded theory is essentially the process of drawing boundaries around 'incidents' of data. These incidents might be observations, narratives and statements taken from semi-structured interviews, observations on documents or the literature, or they might be comments on data slices. When coding, you essentially call these incidents by the main feature of what you see happening in them. The words you use to encapsulate your observations of what you see happening in the incidents we will call the 'code'. The process of grouping data under these codes we will refer to as 'coding'. How this coding happens depends on what you count as an incident, but the dictum is that during open coding you should attempt to code everything 'line by line'. How far you carry the 'line by line' approach will be down to you. Sometimes it makes sense to take bigger sections of data. Why? Well, remember that the main aim

017 line 105	Codes
I've **_changed_** my um well **_I haven't changed_** my **_diet_** I've **_improved_** my diet and I eat lots of things with lots of calcium in now which perhaps **_I didn't do before._**	**Changing behaviour** **Changing diet** **Improving** **Now and then**

Figure 9-1 Example of line-by-line coding in grounded theory

of coding is to enable the development of the central categories that will become the main features of your theory. A good category can capture the variation in a range of data. We will now look at some examples.

As you can see in Figure 9-1, Raphael's (2008) strategy was to begin with line-by-line coding. Her codes, based on this strategy, were very descriptive. The problem she was faced with was to get these codes to eventually develop more generalised categories. Take the first example from our dental study above. This can be coded in a number of ways. One way is to focus on action, and in particular to highlight what is happening line by line (see Figure 9-2 below). In this set of codes you can see that important verbs are highlighted and the codes are directly related to what the dentist and patient are doing. But there is a problem. For a start, these codes are very descriptive – they simply redescribe what is happening. It is not very likely that they will enable us to reach a much more conceptual level unless we think beyond the specific codes to what the participants in the study are doing. A second problem is that they don't conceptualise what is going on in relation to the goal of the study. In addition, take a closer look at Figure 9-2.

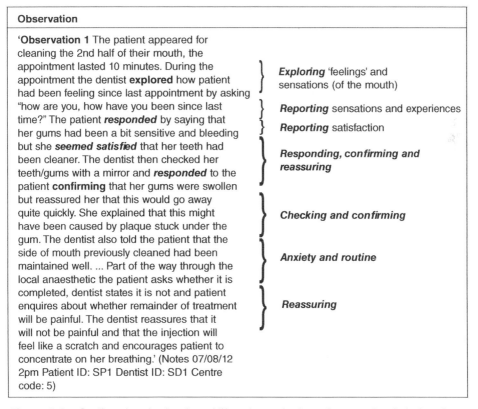

Observation

'**Observation 1** The patient appeared for cleaning the 2nd half of their mouth, the appointment lasted 10 minutes. During the appointment the dentist **explored** how patient had been feeling since last appointment by asking "how are you, how have you been since last time?" The patient **responded** by saying that her gums had been a bit sensitive and bleeding but she **seemed satisfied** that her teeth had been cleaner. The dentist then checked her teeth/gums with a mirror and **responded** to the patient **confirming** that her gums were swollen but reassured her that this would go away quite quickly. She explained that this might have been caused by plaque stuck under the gum. The dentist also told the patient that the side of mouth previously cleaned had been maintained well. ... Part of the way through the local anaesthetic the patient asks whether it is completed, dentist states it is not and patient enquires about whether remainder of treatment will be painful. The dentist reassures that it will not be painful and that the injection will feel like a scratch and encourages patient to concentrate on her breathing.' (Notes 07/08/12 2pm Patient ID: SP1 Dentist ID: SD1 Centre code: 5)

Exploring 'feelings' and sensations (of the mouth)

Reporting sensations and experiences

Reporting satisfaction

Responding, confirming and reassuring

Checking and confirming

Anxiety and routine

Reassuring

Figure 9-2 Coding data in the dental lifestyle study: focusing on what is being done

The section of the excerpt in Figure 9-2 that states: 'The patient **responded** by saying that her gums had been a bit sensitive and bleeding but she **seemed satisfied** that her teeth had been cleaner' is coded as two instances of 'reporting' and yet the term 'reporting' is not present. Clearly, there is a divergence between the code and the observations. Codes do not have to be directly tied to the actual terms and concepts that are in the data. *They will often have a degree of freedom from these.* Codes that are developed into categories that are directly related to the field under study are called *in-vivo* codes (Strauss and Corbin 1990; Glaser 1992; Ekins 1997; Birks and Mills 2011). Often, coding directly from what you write is not the best way to produce abstract codes that can be developed into meaningful theoretical categories. You have to think beyond the obvious and try to think about *what is going on behind the data in a more strategic sense.*

This produces a bit of a problem, of course. You want to be able to code your data and to develop categories that actually say something. But if coding what people are doing *moment to moment* is not necessarily the best way to do this, then what is? In Figure 9-3 we take exactly the same excerpt but slice the data into a bigger chunk and produce a very different code: that of **monitoring mouths**. This code is characterised by its focus on highlighting the purpose or goal of the interaction. Indeed, the whole series of actions that we coded in Figure 9-2 could all in fact be said to enable that goal to be developed strategically over time. By taking the larger strategic incident of data that is relatively unfractured, you can often develop more strategic codes that can in fact capture more variation and might even be able to incorporate the minor processes of exploring, reporting, checking and responding. With further coding it might even be possible to trace how the use of these processes varies in the field, including how they might be related to each other. So we might say that 'monitoring mouths' involves the processes of exploring, reporting, checking and responding. Each of these processes may vary in the way they are deployed in a routine encounter. They may be patterned in a stable way whereas in an encounter where a suspicious malignancy is discovered they may develop in a different way. It will all depend on how our data develops.

When coding, it is important to pay close attention to the extent and reach of the data you are coding. It is not enough to simply follow line-by-line coding by taking this to mean line by grammatical line. You can often fracture and recombine your data when coding. The goal is to get categories that have conceptual fit, grab and reach. If you only ever code what is obvious in your data, as we have done in Figure 9-2, you will struggle to get to the strategic nature of what you are observing. By paying attention to the reach of the data that you are coding, and by taking slightly larger slices, you can often improve the impact and scope of the codes in your developing theory. Yet *line-by-line coding is also crucial.* It keeps your theory tied to what is happening in the field of study and enables you to develop categories that describe what happens. You

Observation
'Observation 1 The patient appeared for cleaning the 2nd half of their mouth the appointment lasted 10 minutes. During the appointment the dentist explored how patient had been feeling since last appoint by asking "how are you, how have you been since last time?" The patient responded by saying that her gums had been a bit sensitive and bleeding but she seemed satisfied that her teeth had been cleaner. The dentist then checked her teeth/gums with a mirror and responded to the patient confirming that her gums were swollen but reassured her that this would go away quite quickly. She explained that this might have been caused by plaque stuck under the gum. The dentist also told the patient that the side of mouth previously cleaned had been maintained well .... Part of the way through the local aesthetic the patient asks whether it is completed dentist states it is not and patient enquires about whether remainder of treatment will be painful. The dentist reassures that it will not be painful and that the injection will feel like a scratch and encourages patient to concentrate on her breathing.' (Notes 07/08/12 2pm Patient ID: SP1 Dentist ID: SD1 Centre code: 5)

} Monitoring mouths

Figure 9-3 Alternative technique for coding data in the dental lifestyle study

need to be aware that there are different levels of analysis and to think about how you combine these in your coding.

The use of comparisons and data slicing

As we have already seen, another way to build categories and get conceptual pick-up is to conduct data slicing (see Chapters 7 and 8). Data slicing is a way of taking the incident you are observing and thinking, quite literally, where else might I see a similar incident? By doing this you are effectively exploring *the general relevance of your categories.* In some respects this will get you thinking about the potential of your theory to develop into a formal theory. However, it can have other less apparent and more direct consequences for your immediate theory-building exercise. Take the category 'monitoring mouths'. At first glance we might think that it would be unlikely that we will see mouths being monitored elsewhere in society other than in dental clinics. But by thinking more generally and reflecting on where else we might see similar things happening, we might, for example, consider that mouths are a sub-property of bodies and by generalising the object of study we can see if monitoring occurs at this different level. We can be sure that monitoring bodies does in fact happen in a range of settings: in the home, in front of the mirror, in the gym and in the doctor's surgery. By reflecting on this, you can see that monitoring bodies might be something everyone does in a range of contexts and that there might potentially be room for a formal theory on monitoring bodies. This kind of comparison can then also be reflected back into our developing theory. It suggests that we would perhaps be able to get more information about monitoring mouths by asking people if they look at their mouths in the mirror at home and, if so, why? We could also ask if they monitor their mouths in other ways; with their tongues, and so on. *By data slicing in this way we can reflect outwards towards a formal theory but then use the insights that have been gained in this way to reflect back into the developing theory.* Comparisons such as these can be very useful in enabling you to think more generally about your emerging codes. They can also suggest future directions for theoretical sampling.

Skills and tips 9-1

Open coding

Take some of the data you have collected. Analyse it line by line (see Figure 9-1) by making notes and creating a large margin to the right or left, whatever suits you. Code line by line by looking at what is happening in each meaningful section of your observations and summarising this in one or two words. Code several pages and each time you see more than one incident of a code stop and compare the two incidents for similarities and differences. Stop and write memos (see Skills and tips 10-1: Writing memos on page 180) as your ideas about what is going on in your data develop. In doing this, try to *write in the language of the code*. Try to specify what the code refers to and how it might vary in the way it manifests in the field.

Try 'data slicing' (see Skills and tips 7-1: Data slicing on page 127). Is the code you are looking at likely to recur in other settings? If so, make notes about any observations you have when you move the code from one place to another.

Go back over the same sets of data but this time code whole paragraphs. Can you see something else going on when you read larger incidents of your observations/interviews? Do the codes from your line-by-line coding fit with or relate to this broader code in some respect?

Stop and memo anything you notice when doing this. Remember you are meant to be thinking about your codes as concepts that might be related to your theory.

Finishing open coding

As we said previously, the goal of open coding is to capture the range of things that are happening in the data and to code as much variation as possible. A second goal for this phase is to select the core category. We have already covered the main features of the core category in Chapter 5, and rather than reiterating those here we would refer you to that chapter. The idea is that, after coding all of the variation of your theory, you should have a good idea of the main concern or main problem that is being processed in your setting. Once you have that, you should have a category that explains most of the behaviour in the field. Having selected what you think is your core category, you are now ready to move on to selective coding.

Selective coding

As we stated in Chapter 8, selective coding is the third major phase of grounded theory. In this phase you start to focus your analysis and coding to increasingly specify and develop the categories of your theory. In Chapter 5 we pointed out that the core category must be central, and related to as many other categories as possible. It should dominate the developing theory and you should be able to see how it links with all, or at least most, of the aspects of your theory. You should be able to account for a large portion of the variation in a pattern of behaviour.[2] Another criterion for the selection of the core category is that it should reoccur frequently in the data. This leads to the perception that it is a stable pattern and can be related to the other variables. Ekins (1997) says that he just found it easier to talk about what was happening in his study as 'males femaling' and this central process recurred in his observations time and again.

In some respects you should also find a similar thing happening. It should become easier to talk about your study and what is happening in it through the use of your core category. Your core category might have grab beyond the field you are working in. In this respect you might be able to data slice easily and think about other settings where a similar phenomenon might be observed. The core category should be highly variable and ought to have frequent relations to other categories. It should also be readily modifiable and you should be able to specify its dependent relationships with other variables. Finally, as we found out earlier, the core category will be related to many different kinds of theoretical code; it might be a process, a condition, it might have two dimensions, different consequences and so on (see also Glaser 1978: 95–96).

Helen Raphael (2008) gradually discovered that it was increasingly easier to talk about her study as 'a theory of gendered positioning'. Osteoporosis is largely seen, incorrectly, as a disease that affects women. This means that the disease is so gendered that men and health professionals frequently struggle to come to terms with the signs, symptoms and impacts that it has when it manifests in men. *As we can see, then, a key aspect of selective coding is establishing the centrality of your core category.* Another important task for selective coding *is establishing the generality of your core category.* Does it have the potential to go beyond the field you are studying? Can it be applied to a range of substantive groups?

Raphael (2008) settled on her theory of gendered positioning after reflecting on the fact that other illnesses also mask themselves in gender. For example, heart disease is largely attributed to men and breast cancer to women. Such theory slices enabled her to see how her theory could have general relevance beyond the substantive field she was working in (Raphael 2008: 181). She was able to show that such gendered illnesses could even have an impact on how advertising was targeted. As she developed her theory, she discovered that other researchers had highlighted how representations of other conditions were also masked in gender (Kempner 2006). In this respect Raphael (2008) was able to *selectively code for the generality of her theory.* A key thing that can enable you to generalise your theory is to selectively code for the applicability of the core category or core processes beyond the area you are studying. Glaser and Strauss (1967) not only discovered a general theory of *awareness contexts and social interaction* as a consequence of their study of dying, they also discovered a general theory of *status passage* (Glaser and Strauss 1964, 1971). We have summarised how you might select your core category below (see Skills and tips 9-2).

Skills and tips 9-2

Selecting the core category

Now you have collected a lot of data and you are starting to find that there is a lot of repetition in your incidents to the point where *you are not getting much* new *information for your developing theory.* You are close to the critical point at which you are ready to select your core category. Now is the time to look at Figure 5-3, Selecting the core category, and make further memos about your reflections on each of these statements. You may even want separate memos on the subject of 'selecting the core category'.

In addition to reflecting and memoing on these questions, you should also:

- make notes on the following question: What kind of theory will you have if you select this or that category as your core category? These memos will be preliminary but they are important. You will come back and modify them as you proceed. So perhaps consider opening up a memo with the title 'What kind of theory is [insert the name of your theory]?'
- revisit your notes on your preconceptions and prior interests (see Skills and tips 8-1: Asking the right question on page 145) and write about what you now think of your theory in relation to each of these in turn. This will enable you to go back to your motivations for doing the study. Note how these are changing, but also see if these have impacted on your theory development. You can also make notes on how your theory might challenge your preconceptions or, indeed, vindicate them in some respects.

Having reviewed the main features of what a core category should look like, it should be clear now that selective coding involves focusing on the core category and the other major categories of your theory and developing these to the point of saturation. Selective coding also involves specifying the major relationships between your categories. This brings us to the problem of theoretical coding in the selective coding phase.

Building theory: typologies and theoretical coding

Part of the process of integrating your categories into a coherent theory involves the techniques associated with theoretical coding. There are several approaches that you might adopt in this respect. You might construct typologies or you might use Glaser's (1978) theoretical coding families as a tool to enable you to think through the key relationships in your theory. The coding families are effectively types of relationship. By providing them as a general list that you can consult, Glaser was seeking to enable students to be able to think in terms of how categories can be related. His list remains highly innovative and if you consult it you will begin to realise that there is a huge variety of ways that relationships in data may be specified.

Building typologies is an old technique in sociology that goes back as far as the work of Max Weber. The construction of ideal types is therefore not peculiar to grounded theory. You should be aware that they are not a simple tool to be used in analysis and that they have been plagued with controversy in sociology. However, what you should note is that there is a link between Weber's use of ideal types and the way these were critiqued and developed by Lazarsfeld. For a detailed review of the history and debates behind ideal types in sociology please refer to Lindbekk (1992). Grounded theory adopts an empirical take on ideal types. This means that typologies are used to specify how categories are related. Glaser suggested that typologies could typically be built out of a distinction in your data. They could then be constructed through two basic operations. One was through reduction by moving from the criteria to the typology. The other was through a process of substruction, that is moving from the typology and then to generating the criteria. Substruction was described as something that could be done to construct a typology from something that had developed without you necessarily being fully aware that you had done so. How this is achieved is through the cross-tabulation of distinctions within your concepts.

In our study of what is going on in general dental practice when it comes to health promotion, we have been observing dental practitioners as they interact with their patients. We noticed that they have routine conversations and that these conversations often follow a pattern, discussing how the patient has been, the weather, and so on. We have decided to call this 'scripting', and you can see it in other settings too, for example, at hairdressers. By making this

Degree of Routine in the encounter

		Non-routine	Routine
		−	+
	Informal	Treatment of a well-known patient or a friend. With a filling or an extraction. Low degree of routine and formality in communication which will be focused on the knowledge patient and dentist have of each other. The dentist will take more time to communicate with the patient the kinds of reactions they might expect from their treatment.	Treatment of a well-known patient or friend for routine dental care. Typically light-hearted communication which will follow a routine that has a history in the relationship between the dentist and their patient. They might catch up and share information that is typically not shared between strangers, such as how a career change is going.
Degree of Formality in the encounter	**Formal**	Treatment of a patient for a life threatening or serious condition that carries a high risk. High degree of formality and the use of professional scripts to give information based on diagnosis and prognosis. Such scripts will contain standardised information and will follow a specific structure designed to minimise errors and the risk of misleading the patient.	Treatment of a stranger or new patient. Communication follows a friendly set routine used for all patients. This might include talking about the weather (if they live in the UK), something that has happened in the news. The encounter may also involve standardised friendly advice such as quitting smoking or brushing one's teeth more effectively.

Figure 9-4   Scripting and formality in dental clinics

comparison we can see that 'scripting' is a category that may be developed to have more *generality*. Figure 9-4 details how we might develop its dimensions.

In Figure 9-4 we have noticed how scripting occurs. At the early stages of our analysis we found it helpful to note that there is a relationship between the formality and routine nature of dental encounters and what is said. In highly routine and highly formal encounters communication tends to follow a routine script. This script will often be deployed in the same way with several patients. It may involve scripted topics for the conversations, such as the weather and routine jokes which bore the tears out of the dental nurse who has to listen to them over and over during the day. Such encounters are characterised by a high degree of formality and a high degree of routine. As you can see, this kind of encounter contrasts with other encounters which have differing degrees of routine and formality. The 2×2 table or grid format enables us to map the relationship and helps us begin the process of specifying the element of our theory relating to scripting in dental encounters. It also suggests further lines of enquiry. For a start, we can see that behind formality is another possible variable, that of intimacy. One suggestion we might then derive from this exercise is to explore if intimacy is important in dental encounters. Indeed, we may discover how it maps on to professionalism and friendship and how this can affect dental encounters.

Wuest (2001) used such typologies in her work. She articulated the relationship between the availability and suitability of resources and how these affected 'fraying connections'. The satisfied customer referred to women who had access to resources that they felt supported their caring. It was under such *conditions* that such women appeared to experience fewer fraying connections in caring. They were also more able to repattern care and take control of their situations. Such women contrasted with *comparison shoppers*, who were women who did have adequate resources but felt that these resources were not entirely suitable for their needs. Wuest (2001: 178) articulated these relationships in a typology which was effectively a 2×2 table specifying these relationships.

As you can see, a feature of theoretical coding as part of the selective coding phase in grounded theory is that we should specify how the core category has *frequent and dense relationships to other categories*. When you selectively code you need to be thinking about what the main relationships are in your theory. This will enable you to answer the question 'what kind of theory is emerging here?' You might find it helpful to consciously think about how to specify the key relationships in your theory through the use of various coding families (see Chapter 5). Helen Raphael (2008) found it very useful to think of the main relationships in her theory in terms of the six Cs (causes, contexts, contingencies, consequences, conditions and covariances) and also in terms of the strategy family. In contrast, Ekins (1997) discovered that his theory is best characterised as a set of processes occurring in a series of social psychological stages throughout the career of the male femaler. *Specifying the key relationships of your theory, including the kinds of theoretical codes it uses, is a core component of selective coding in grounded theory.*

Now look back at Figure 9-2 on page 159. We have already discussed how to code through the use of line-by-line coding and larger chunks of data. In Figure 9-2 you can see a series of processes. How might these be related to the category 'monitoring mouths' which was coded in Figure 9-3? In Figure 9-2 there is a degree of synchronisation between checking and responding. The patient reports something and the dentist checks it and responds to that information with more information taken from observations of the patient's mouth. Now if we check Glaser's (1978) list of coding families, we discover that there are a large number of ways that categories might be related. One such coding family is the strategy family, which, we are told, involves strategies, tactics, mechanisms, manipulation, manoeuvrings, and so on. From the data in our observations, the statement from the patient and the response of the dentist doesn't seem to involve any kind of manipulation or tactic. So this family doesn't seem to fit the data we have. We can then search for another coding family. We discover that there is a coding family called the interactive family, which is used to describe a series of mutual effects, reciprocity, dependency and interdependence. This code suits relationships where we need to capture the interacting patterns of two variables, especially when the order of the variables doesn't matter. This seems to fit our data. So we can now write a memo detailing that 'monitoring mouths' involves reciprocal interaction between checking and responding on the part of the patient and the dentist. In the encounter we can note more things. The checking and responding is relatively well synchronised, but not every encounter may be like this. Some encounters involving monitoring mouths may involve an asynchronous process of checking and responding, especially when the encounter is non-routine and when the discussion involves something which has a high stake, such as a diagnosis of oral cancer. So the patient and dentist might miscommunicate. They might not understand each other and they may even disagree. In such instances we might then suggest that checking and responding can be asynchronous.

What we are suggesting is that coding involves building up a detailed study of each of the main relationships in your study. It is important to monitor how new information from sampling can modify your relationships. What if we discover that there is manipulation behind checking and responding? This might challenge us to modify our earlier findings to include situations where the dentist and patient are involved in manipulating the interaction. As you can see, coding families can be used to help you to think beyond describing your data to articulating relationships between your categories. They enable you to begin to think more theoretically about your study. We would suggest you experiment with fitting theoretical codes from the list in *Theoretical Sensitivity* (Glaser 1978) to your data. Make notes on how these change the way you look at your categories and data. Bear in mind that multiple theoretical codes will be useful at different times and it is very important to be flexible and open in the way in which you apply them.

Key points about theoretical coding

As grounded theory has become more and more decontextualised and developed into a general method, some techniques for coding have been forgotten. Others have been refined and added. With Strauss and Corbin's (1990) book coding became increasingly operationalised. As a consequence, there has been some debate about coding in grounded theory (Glaser 1992). Rather than getting bogged down in this debate, our approach in this chapter has been to attempt to connect the practical aspects of coding back to the purposes for which we code – to generate categories.

We have discovered that categories have to perform two functions – they have to *fit and work*. The problem you have to overcome in your study is that in your coding you have to make sure your categories fit the data. However, in so far as they have to fit the data, they are not synonymous with it. You also have to be able to explain how the data varies. Coding therefore also involves looking at incidents of data while summarising and grouping similar incidents and describing how they vary. One way that you will need to code will be to take incidents of data 'line by line'. But we have seen that it is also useful to contrast this kind of coding by increasing the size of the incidents to paragraphs and, beyond, to look at what such larger incidents might indicate about your data. In doing this you should look to see how the codes generated from looking at these larger incidents might incorporate codes generated on a line-by-line basis. Coding is not just about capturing the content of your theory, it is about trying to account for variation. This might also involve 'data slicing'. Such explorations can be used to expand your analysis in more general directions and they can then be reflected back into your theory to enable you to develop new directions for sampling and coding.

What counts as data for coding varies and often what we think is data needs to be modified as we engage in coding. Finally, there are several different points to consider when we think about coding in grounded theory:

- Coding in general has two purposes: the first is to capture the substantive content of the area under study, and the second is to articulate relationships that can be observed in the data.
- There are two phases of coding in grounded theory: the open and selective phases.
- In the open coding phase, coding primarily involves thinking carefully about what might be the best source of information and therefore data for your study.
- Open coding involves coding as many 'incidents' of data as possible, where the term 'incidents' refers to relevant chunks of information. These chunks can be observed line by line or taken in larger discrete sections.
- When open coding, a good technique for generating more general categories is to switch between line-by-line coding and coding larger chunks of data. When doing this, check to see if the codes that summarise smaller line-by-line incidents might form part of the more general category.
- Coding can also involve 'data slicing'. Data slicing involves taking a code and reflecting on whether or not it might be observed in another area. This kind of comparison can yield information about the potential for the theory to be developed into a formal theory. The information gained from these kinds of coding can then be reflected back into the theory to suggest new directions for theoretical sampling and coding.
- A critical end to open coding occurs when you settle your attention around your core category. The core category must:

  o be central, and related to as many other categories as possible
  o account for a large portion of the variation in the pattern of behaviour
  o reoccur frequently in the data
  o become easier to talk about when developing your theory
  o be related to different theoretical codes

- The selective coding phase focuses on developing the core category. Such coding should involve the specification of the core category's key relationships. This involves:

  o establishing the centrality and generality of your core category specifying the key relationships of your theory, including the kinds of theoretical codes it uses.

Summary

The primary focus of this chapter was on coding techniques in grounded theory. Here we have seen that coding involves the grouping of similar 'chunks' of data under 'codes' that summarise their content. The chapter started with a discussion of the different types of data that could exist in a study and highlighted that an awareness of this is important when it comes to coding. The chapter then explored how to open code in detail by looking at the implication of coding different chunks of data. Here we illustrated how line-by-line coding, combined with coding broader 'slices' of data, might generate different kinds of categories, all of which could be integrated. We discussed how open coding primarily focuses on capturing the content of the field under study, including how this varies. In contrast to this, selective coding was said to primarily focus on the core category and delineating the theory. The technique of data slicing to explore the general properties of a code by taking it and placing it into a different substantive context was also discussed in some depth. The chapter then discussed the switch from open coding to selective coding and the decision to focus on the core category. The problem of selective coding for key relationships between categories in your grounded theory was also discussed before focusing on enabling the development of skills for choosing the right core category.

Further reading

Charmaz, K. (2006) 'Coding in grounded theory practice', Chapter 3 in K. Charmaz, *Constructing Grounded Theory: A Practical Guide through Qualitative Analysis*. London: Sage.

Glaser, B. (1978) 'Theoretical coding', Chapter 4 in B. Glaser, *Theoretical Sensitivity: Advances in the Methodology of Grounded Theory*. Mill Valley, CA: Sociology Press.

Glaser, B. and Strauss, A. (1971) 'Generating formal theory', Chapter 9 in B. Glaser and A. Strauss, *Status Passage*. Mill Valley, CA: Sociology Press.

Strauss, A. and Corbin, J. (1990) 'Open coding', Chapter 5 in A. Strauss and J. Corbin, *Basics of Qualitative Research: Grounded Theory Procedures and Techniques*. Thousand Oaks, CA: Sage.

Notes

1 The recognition that the social world is socially constructed was in grounded theory when it was first discovered and in all likelihood was forgotten as the method was increasingly operationalised. This is especially the case with Strauss and Corbin's (1990) *Basics of Qualitative Research* text. We certainly feel that Charmaz was justified in being critical of that text. We do not, however, accept in any way that the criticism can stretch back to the origins of the method.

2 Charmaz (2006) doesn't code behaviour at all but chooses to focus on meaning.

10

Thinking Theoretically and Writing Memos in Grounded Theory

Aim: To explore when to and how to write theoretical memos in grounded theory

After reading this chapter you should be able to:

- know when to memo in your grounded theory
- know what to memo your grounded theory
- know how to develop memos for grounded theory
- evaluate how to memo in grounded theory

As we have seen from our earlier chapters (see Chapters 8 and 9), one of the key operations associated with doing grounded theory is writing theoretical memos. It is here that we return to grounded theory as another version of the constant comparative method (Chapter 1). Within *Discovery* (Glaser and Strauss 1967), memo writing appears as perhaps the central operation in doing grounded theory. In fact, if you look through *Discovery* it is not hard to see that memoing is used in many different ways in *Discovery*. Unfortunately, however, there are no direct definitions of what memos involve. The closest thing we get is that memo writing on your field notes will provide you with 'an immediate illustration for an idea' (Glaser and Strauss 1967: 108). In *Theoretical Sensitivity*, however, you will find the following very helpful statement at the start of the chapter on 'theoretical memos'.

> The core stage in the process of generating theory, the bedrock of theory genera-
> tion, its true product is the writing of theoretical memos. If the analyst skips this
> stage by going directly from coding to sorting or to writing – he is not doing

grounded theory. Memos are the theorizing write-up of ideas about codes and their relationships as they strike the analyst while coding. Memos lead, naturally to abstraction or ideation, Memoing is a constant process that begins when first coding data, and continues through reading memos or literature, sorting and writing papers or monographs to the very end. Memo-writing continually captures the 'frontier of the analyst's thinking' as he goes through either his data, codes, sorts or writes. (Glaser 1978: 83)

So while coding is aimed at 'capturing' 'what is going on in the area studied' (Glaser and Strauss 1967: 23; see also Chapters 5 and 9), when you are writing your theoretical memos, here you will be writing up your ideas about the codes you are developing, including writing about how these are related to each other. Memos are where the creative spark of grounded theory comes into its own. They help you to build on the process of abstraction and are aimed at building categories that have grab and which fit your data. Like everything else in grounded theory, there is more to this technique than meets the eye. A great way to grasp what you are supposed to be doing when you write your memos is to look closely at the example Glaser and Strauss (1967) gave in *Discovery* (see Box 10-1).

Box 10-1

An example of a memo from *Discovery*

Visits to the various medical services were scheduled as follows: I wished first to look at services that minimized patient awareness (and so first looked at a premature baby service and then at a neurosurgical service where patients were frequently comatose). I wished next to look at dying in a situation where expectancy of staff and often of patients was great and dying was quick, so I observed on an Intensive Care Unit. Then I wished to observe on a service where staff expectations of terminality were great but where the patient's might or might not be, and where dying tended to be slow. So I looked next at a cancer service. I wished then to look at conditions where death was unexpected and rapid, and so looked at an emergency service. While we were looking at some different types of services, we also observed the above types of service at other types of hospitals. So our scheduling of types of service was directed by a general conceptual scheme – which included hypotheses about awareness, expectedness and rate of dying – as well as by a developing conceptual structure including matters not at first envisioned. Sometimes we returned to services after the initial two or three or four weeks of continuous observation, in order to check upon items which needed checking or had been missed in the initial period. (Glaser and Strauss 1967: 59)

You can see from the example in Box 10-1 that memos can contain notes about the process of data collection. Glaser and Strauss (1967) noted down the way their sampling was conducted *in order to develop their theory*. The memo describes how they sampled for variation *in awareness* of staff and patients about dying. It describes how they selected the setting where they might be able to see if this variability was happening. The memo contains the logic of their sampling but if you read it closely you can see that *they were thinking in terms of the categories of their emerging theory*. This is what Glaser means by 'thinking theoretically' (Glaser 2005, 2007). In their next example of a memo, Glaser and Strauss showed that they sampled around even bigger units of comparison – the nation state. They talked in the memo of going to compare dying in wards in Japan versus the United States. In this memo they also noted that their unit of analysis could also be the *type of unit*, which closely related to the form of how people died. Memoing in this case involved discussing *their units of comparison and their sampling strategy*, but memoing *also involved writing them theoretically*. By this we mean that *they were thinking in terms of their theory as they wrote the memo and the memo reflected this theoretical thinking*. This is why it is called theoretical memo writing. You are supposed to *think and write theoretically* throughout doing grounded theory. Theoretical memos are the principal way of doing this.

In what follows we will provide you with some guidelines on when to memo. We discuss the timing of memoing and explore what you should be memoing. Finally, we look at how to memo, before giving you examples of various types of memo. Our goal is to strip away some of the mysticism of the method and hopefully to help you build better quality grounded theory.

When to memo

Grounded theory is described as a 'constant comparative method'; this is important when memoing. As you code your data, you will be coding incidents of data (see Chapter 9) that are basically the same or very similar. The idea is to stop and compare similar incidents. When making these comparisons, if you notice anything about the comparison that in turn suggests something about your emerging category, then you should stop and write about that in a memo. As you can guess, *memoing in the early stages of doing grounded theory will be characterised primarily by noting down differences* in incidents. Early memos, then, may well be characterised by their descriptive content – *they may well tend to focus on how categories vary*. You can see how Helen Raphael approached this in Box 10-2. We will come back to the kinds of memos you may need to develop in the last section of this chapter. In reality, memoing occurs throughout the grounded theory process and because of this you need to be completely flexible and write them when you observe developments in your theory. You might need to memo when you are in the bath, when an apple hits your head, on the toilet, when you are shopping or even in the middle of a conversation with a partner. As you can see, doing grounded theory might lead to the development of some quirky personality characteristics.

Box 10-2

The experience of memoing in grounded theory

Since the early memos seemed to only be slightly more detailed than the open coding it was important to build on them. As the study progressed, the ideas about the data began to be more and more revealing and exciting. This helped to make memo writing easier as the thoughts regarding the suggested theory flowed. Glaser (1978) urges the researcher not to re-write memos but to move forward through continually writing and adding to memos by coding and comparing. Therefore, the initial memos were not discarded but worked with. Consequently, each time a memo was read it became more detailed as new thoughts, ideas and questions about a category were raised and incorporated. Accordingly, the memos became more theoretical, conceptual and dense. (Raphael 2008: 85)

Although this might seem a bit strange, it is crucial to memo as much as possible throughout the grounded theory process. Glaser and Strauss warned that without memoing in grounded theory you may well fall into the trap of collecting too much data that would be of 'dubious relevance' (Glaser and Strauss 1967: 72). The fact you need to be flexible when you memo is important, but this also means you need to make time for memoing and generate the space to think carefully through your data and your comparisons of incidents. It takes time to build theory and failure to allow enough time to think while developing memos will leave you struggling. So make the time and create the space to enable this to happen. It can take hours to develop really well thought through memos that help you to saturate categories, develop new categories and design further sampling (see Glaser and Strauss 1967: 107). Memos perform a very important function for you and the way you do them will have significant consequences for the development of your theory. They are effectively your memory. You will need them because you will produce many categories, all of which will have relationships to other categories. The better you memo, the more dense and integrated your theory will become. Your memos will perform the function of saturating your theory. They help you 'get out of the data' and enable you to think theoretically (Glaser 1978: 56). This process, Glaser (1978) argued, was the key process that would enable abstraction.

What to memo

Before reading the rest of this chapter you should take a close look at Box 10-1 and then compare it to Box 10-3. You might like to make a few notes on some of the principal differences that you can see. Box 10-3 is a memo from Helen Raphael's (2008) study of 'gendered positioning'. As we go through this chapter, we will refer to both boxes as illustrations of our key points.

Box 10-3

Memo example

Is seeking a reason a basic social psychological process?

17.2.02 020 line 129 'I was never told what the reason was, ummm, I know it somewhat idiopathic in the way they don't know any cause of it.' For him the cause is unknown – there is no known reason why he has this problem, no explanation. Hence does this mean if the cause was unknown there was nothing he could have done to prevent it? Is this about control or responsibility? 'They don't know' is he saying it is nothing to do with me it is not my problem – is it them that do not know. This could be about responsibility.

017 line 139 'I never quite know what brings it on. Another one that's bad is flying long distance on a plane sitting in the same position.' Here he is trying to find a reason or cause for the pain. It may also be the compelling nature of pain makes searching for a reason necessary to avoid, become warned or aware of risk.

Seeking an explanation/rejecting responsibility 017 line 269 24.2.05 I might have done I might have questioned it more if I had known that there is probably a family history here as well because they have investigated all my brothers and my children as well and they found what I think that my son has got a tendency towards it and one of my daughters has had one of my brothers has in Australia. Had I known that I would have done something about it years (heavily emphasised) ago.

Does he do this in order to reject any responsibility – being able to blame an outside event or person? Regretting the past and resisting responsibility 'if I had known', this is not his fault it is beyond his control, someone should have informed him and had they done so he could have taken action. By searching for, and finding, a hereditary explanation he is able to resist any feeling of responsibility or blame as it becomes something that was beyond his control. Why is he searching for a reason?

These quotes encompass many different concepts as there is the issue of not being in control, selecting blame, lack of knowledge, seeking an explanation

(Continued)

(Continued)

and rejecting responsibility. He seems to be trying to understand when he did not know. He is also comparing himself to his other family members who have now been diagnosed as having osteoporosis or at risk of developing it. Is this similar to the comparisons that were being made during the interviews with Leslie and Gordon who were also comparing themselves with others? Why is there a need to compare themselves with others? There is an impression that by comparing they can convince themselves that they were doing the right thing so they should not have any problems. By comparing himself to the others in his family he can resist any blame himself but as they have the information they would not have the same problem as they will be in a position to take action based on prior knowledge. Could this lead to a potential category gaining knowledge which includes concepts such as looking for reasons for the problem, trying to rationalise why they have it, this often appears to lead to rejecting any idea that their osteoporosis or its symptoms is like the osteoporosis that women have – rejecting the feminine side. Justifying and explaining why knowledge about osteoporosis was lacking. This also links closely with selecting information and gendered surprise as some of the reasons for not taking notice earlier were due to the disease being associated with women.

009 line 400 I have seen men who doubled over and walk like this but I'd assume that was caused by some problem but it hadn't struck me that that man got osteoporosis I just thought the poor chap he's got something wrong with his back, so no I mean certainly I'm only aware it affected ladies. And I possibly did know that ummm it did could happen in men but I didn't know to what extent. (Raphael 2008: 86)

When constructing memos it is very important to explore your emergent categories. You should be writing notes that constantly adjust and increasingly specify what your categories are about. Your focus should be on developing the best fitting category. Memoing is about developing 'creative theoretical forays' (Glaser 1978: 20) into the data which means you should write about the terms that fit your data. Raphael's (2008) memo (Box 10-3) is a particularly good example of an early memo. As you can see, it records her search for the right terminology as her thinking is grounded in direct observations of her data. She is trying to find an adequate description of what the men are doing with the problem of becoming aware of having osteoporosis. She clearly entertains several ideas, such as taking responsibility or resisting osteoporosis, but settles on 'seeking a reason', which seems to fit what the men describe. Another important thing to note is how the memo uses several different incidents and links her category of 'seeking a reason' with other categories such as 'gendered surprise'. The memo has several dates on it and has clearly been modified in keeping with her description of how she approaches building her theory. Memoing will involve you in a constant process of specifying your categories and developing their dimensions. You might write about a feature of your category such as where it can be seen, what its conditions and consequences are. Obviously these kinds of notes should not be forced into your theory, especially if these kinds of aspects of your categories are not really clear. *Instead you should write about the evident features of your incidents as they present themselves in your data.* We would also suggest that you remember what we exposed about coding in Chapter 9. Try using comparisons between different incidents of different sizes and explore the effect this has on what you can see and say about your data. Where you use an incident from a larger chunk of data, note how this might suggest ways to group other codes that have been developed from smaller scale incidents. Use your small scale codes to correct broader comparisons. In this way your notes might trace how you have *collapsed and added to your list of categories.*

Of critical importance to the development of your grounded theory will also be notes about *how you decided on your core category*, including how this category came to occupy a central position in your theory. Study *how it became related to other categories*, including modifications in your core category, as you gradually specify its nature and shape as your core problem. *As you engage in writing memos about the specification of your core category you should find that you are now writing about your theory in terms of its key concepts.* As you do this you will also find yourself writing memos that articulate themselves in terms of the concepts and their key relationships. They will therefore be less descriptive and much more focused on the developing concepts in your theory. Clearly, how your core category has emerged is critical. Notes about how you developed your sampling strategy in order to specify your theory can also be useful (see Box 10-1 on page 172). If you compare this memo to that of Raphael (see Box 10-3) you can see the direction you will want to develop your thinking and writing in your memos. Box 10-1 clearly shows not only how theoretical sampling was developed in the theory, but also demonstrates that Glaser and Strauss (1965) *were thinking theoretically at this stage in their analysis.* Raphael (2008) went through a similar process from a very descriptive beginning towards more theoretical insights as she continued to write her memos (see Box 10-2). The key thing to remember is not to be too anxious in the early stages. It is a very common occurrence for those new to grounded theory to struggle to develop thinking theoretically.

Glaser and Strauss (1967) also discuss the use of memos to compare substantive areas. This is an important strategy that can really enable you to develop your categories. As we have said previously, make notes on what your unit of analysis is, try to go beyond thinking purely in terms of individuals and try focusing on different social units where you might observe the phenomenon you are investigating. We have seen how Ekins (1997) was able to move around the social worlds of his participants. We would suggest you write memos on similar issues. Perform data slicing (see Chapter 7) and make notes on which categories might have greater conceptual reach beyond your substantive problem.

You will also want to write memos on the theoretical coding families that emerged as relevant to your theory. When doing so, your writing might articulate the general nature of your theory, and connect it to existing theories that are in the literature and which may have something to say about your study and its position in relation to these theories. All of these notes will become important when it comes to writing up (see Chapter 13). In short, you should be writing memos on all aspects of your grounded theory. The subjects that ought to become important for your memos are summarised in Box 10-4.

Box 10-4

What to write memos on in grounded theory

When developing your memos you might want to write about:

- how you are developing your emerging categories
- the best fitting nominalisation to develop your category. This means that you have to choose the best words to describe your category. These words have to be able to directly link to the idea and image your category is supposed to convey to your readers
- how your categories have been reformulated
- how they have been specified
- how you have collapsed and added to your list of categories
- your reasons for selecting your core category
- specifying hypotheses as relationships between categories
- relating the main categories of your theory to the core category (i.e. integrating the theory)
- describing how you developed your theoretical sampling
- discussing new directions for the emerging theory
- comparing substantive areas
- recording ideas about your data
- integrating theoretical ideas from the literature and other theories
- making notes on data slicing and experimenting with your emerging categories to check if they might be more general and therefore worthy of more attention towards formal theory
- outlining which combinations of theoretical coding families you are using
- discussing the general nature of your theory
- checking and correcting impressions that might not fit and may not become core problems

How to write memos in grounded theory

Having discussed the kinds of subjects you will have in your memos it is important to briefly outline what you need to consider when memoing in grounded theory. The first thing you need to know is that you need an approach to memoing that involves flexibility, modifiability and a degree of freedom. You will also need to be able to edit and update old memos, to be able to duplicate them and, most of all, they need to be held in such a way as to be able to sort them (see Chapter 11). Your memos will also need to be separate from your field notes but at the same time clearly indicate where they link directly to these. As you can see from Raphael's (2008) memo (Box 10-3), there is a clear indication of where the incidents came from that generated her comparisons. Her memo clearly links the incident with the category and one assumes that this heading meant she placed it under that emerging category. Likewise, she has produced dates when her memo was developed and so can reflect on how her ideas have developed.

It is very important that you interrupt coding to memo. Indeed, Glaser (1978) suggests forcing yourself to write descriptions and to modify your early codes through memoing. As we have seen, an important aspect of grounded theory is to describe what is happening, so descriptive memos are fine. Where you do have them you might like to pause and engage in data slicing with your codes, while noting down the results of these comparisons. It is very important to be writing memos and not to be coding blindly without thinking. Remember, the goal is to move from description to generate theory so your memos need to contain sentences that cover not simply how your data varies but also how your categories might be related. Glaser (1978) clearly indicates that it is important to think theoretically in terms of your categories, to look at your substantive field through the categories you have developed. Then, of course, this kind of thinking should be reflected in your memos as you write about your theory (Box 10-1).

The goal of this process is to produce a memo fund that you will be using for the next stage of grounded theory: sorting. If this is your goal, then obviously your memos need to be sortable. You should be able to move them around and place them in different piles. There is then a kind of mechanics to memo writing. One way to achieve this is to write your memos on large index cards and file them in a box to be used for the sorting process later. Often there is disagreement in grounded theory about, for example, the use of computer software. The rule of thumb is that if you cannot take your memos and look at them one by one while moving them around in the next phase of doing grounded theory, then your system for writing memos will not work for you.

Skills and tips 10-1

Writing memos

Take time to consult Box 10-4, 'What to write memos on in grounded theory'. Try developing a memo by reflecting on several incidents that appear very similar in your data. Develop a heading for a memo that reflects what the memo is about. Make sure you refer directly to each incident of data to which the memo refers. You may wish to quote the observations or statements that you are linking to and then discuss them. Each reference to data should be detailed carefully so you can locate the quotation and observation later in the context from which it has been taken. You might need to do this to double-check your interpretation.

Make sure you *write about your concepts.* Try not to redescribe the incidents but think carefully in terms of your concepts, about your concepts and how they are developing. What theoretical codes do your concepts reflect? How might they be related to other concepts in your theory? Do you need more data on the concepts and their relationships and, if so, where might you find that information?

While coding involves developing codes that summarise your data, memos are focused on developing those codes and then reflecting back to the data. The direction of thinking is no longer inductive but theoretical. You should practise thinking theoretically by writing about your codes and their dimensions as they develop.

Remember to be flexible and open – preserve your memos in a *modifiable form.*

A brief note on the use of computers

Since the goal of this book is to revisit grounded theory as it was originally intended, discussing the use of computer-aided analysis will take us well beyond that goal. Not only this, but the topic is actually more complex than it seems. It is not a case of simply buying some software and then starting to play with it. It needs time and preparation to think through the likely consequences of adopting all of the processes associated with software and then reflecting on how those may or may not improve or negatively impact on the grounded theory process. There just is not enough room for such a discussion in this book and, as such, it will have to remain something we should revisit.

There are several software programs that can be used to help in doing qualitative data analysis. These include ATLAS.ti, QSR NVivo, Ethnograph, Nudist, MAXqda and Kwalitan. While there are quite a few packages out there, you will find that there is a debate about the use of computer software as an aid in the process of doing grounded theory. In the past purists have argued that the approach can force you to organise your theory in particular ways, for example, by prioritising hierarchical theoretical designs. These criticisms are not without merit. After all, in the early days computer software packages often forced researchers to adopt hierarchical relationships between categories in their research. This is something that would clearly not be suitable for grounded theory. Times have changed, however, and so have the software packages. More and more people are now using the new packages which are becoming increasingly flexible and powerful. The authors have experience of supervising several students who found the use of computer software such as ATLAS.ti and QSR NVivo (NVivo) very useful for conducting grounded theory.

There is a growing literature on the use of computer software in qualitative data analysis (Richards and Richards 1995; Bazeley and Richards 2000; Bazeley 2002). There is a lot less in the literature on grounded theory and the use of computer software. Bringer et al. (2007) discuss the use of NVivo in their study, providing a detailed description of the way NVivo supported their study. This description clearly demonstrates that NVivo can enable you to organise your grounded theory. In their paper you can clearly see software as an aid rather than a substitute for thinking theoretically. It is quite clear that Bringer et al. (2007) had a good awareness of how to go about doing grounded theory, and consequently a good sense of how the software might be used. So, for example, they used it to help them group together similar incidents of data and then link codes (which become nodes in the software) with each other in different kinds of relationships that were clearly not hierarchical. Of particular interest is the fact that you can also generate groups of memos. Bringer et al. (2007) grouped their memos into code note memos, theoretical memos, operational memos, diagrams, news and contextual memos, NVivo memos and Executive meetings. A particular advantage of the software is the ability to print out code definitions and, of course, to modify them as needed. Clearly, you might arrange your memos differently and it is for this reason that we would suggest you need to consider the adoption of software in grounded theory carefully. As you can see in this book, the procedures and techniques of grounded theory have changed over time. Indeed, there are different types of grounded theory out there. How each of the specific techniques we have discussed here will interact with the software to produce a good grounded theory needs to be considered carefully. So despite the positive contribution of Bringer et al. (2007), we would suggest a word of caution.

Others also discuss the use of grounded theory but here it is not as clear how the software helped them to organise their theory any better than they would have done without it. It is unclear to what extent they were doing grounded theory (Peters and Wester 2007). In fact, we would volunteer a caveat in relation to use of software in grounded theory. We feel it is basically fine as long as you are clear what you want from the software and are able to see that the strategy you adopt for grounded theory has to *interact* with the software. Otherwise we would suggest carefully reading the relevant texts on the subject before engaging in this process (Richards and Richards 1995; Bazeley and Richards 2000; Bazeley 2002).

Key points about memoing

Memoing has become perhaps the most operational aspect of grounded theory. There are lots of examples on how to do this in the literature. In this chapter we have focused our account of memoing on the purpose of theory generation and to challenge you to think theoretically in this process. While we feel that description has become a feature of some approaches to grounded theory, not enough authors discuss theoretical thinking and theory generation. Strauss and Corbin (1990) place memos into the third section of their book, entitled 'Adjunctive Procedures'.[1] This is unfortunate. As we have seen, there is in fact nothing adjunctive or secondary about memo writing in grounded theory. Memo writing is central to the process of building theory. The purpose of memos is to enable you to 'think theoretically' and this key principle should not to be buried as a mere adjunctive feature of memos.

Thankfully this downplaying of memos and their purpose is not a feature of other grounded theory texts. Birks and Mills (2011) describe memo writing as an essential process. Their approach becomes somewhat elaborate, including arguing that you should produce an audit trail of decisions that you have taken during your study, but their main purpose for memoing appears to be to secure the 'quality' of your study. Little is said about the purpose of memoing to enable you to build categories and think theoretically. So while they clearly see this technique as central to grounded theory, they do nonetheless risk losing a key thrust of the purpose of grounded theory – to build theory from data.[2] This is, however, something that is also covered in some detail in the work of Charmaz (2006). We would refer you to her chapter for more excellent examples of how to 'think theoretically' through your memos.

Although the memo-writing process will vary dramatically from study to study and from researcher to researcher, we would like to summarise that it involves writing about:

- how your theory has developed
- how you have been thinking and writing theoretically. By this we mean it involves documenting how you can think about the phenomena you are studying in terms of the categories you have generated
- your units of comparison and how you have sampled around these
- memoing in the early stages of coding, which will more than likely be short and descriptive. By this we mean it is likely to describe how the phenomena you are studying vary
- how memoing involved exploring, how you discovered the core category and then how you specified it
- aspects of your theory as it develops but being flexible in how you do this (see Box 10-4 on p.178).

Summary

This chapter has outlined the practical details of a key technique for doing grounded theory: memo writing. Here we have found that memo writing in grounded theory involves more than simply writing down notes during the coding and analysis of data. Memo writing has been shown to be a core process in grounded theory because it primarily involves 'thinking theoretically'. We have outlined what this might mean when writing memos – where the researcher learns to think in terms of his or her categories and to apply these to the area being investigated. We have shown that memo writing should happen throughout the process of doing grounded theory. In keeping with the method's openness, it is vital to enable a flexible approach to memoing. Memos should be readily modifiable. The chapter has sought to reassure you that while early memos might tend to be quite descriptive, the goal of memoing should eventually be to enable theoretical thinking and writing. The chapter has made suggestions for different topics for memos in grounded theory and provided some exercises to enable the reader to develop their memo writing skills.

Skills and tips 10-2

Writing conceptually

The following memo has been developed out of Figure 9-2, 'Coding data in the dental lifestyle study'. It has been written in a very descriptive way. There are a lot of descriptive comments that appear to redescribe the data. Now try to rewrite this paragraph *by reversing the order of the language and bringing the concepts forward* (see the note 3 for an example of how this can be done).

Monitoring mouths (Notes 07/08/12 2pm Patient ID: SP1 Dentist ID: SD1 Centre code: 5 page 20 paragraph 2)

Dentists and patients seem to be involved in routine interactions that appear to repeat themselves over different periods of time. A characteristic of these encounters is 'Exploring "feelings" and sensations (of the mouth)' where the patient is involved in 'Reporting sensations and experiences'. For example, in our notes, one patient appeared for cleaning. The dentist explored how the patient had been feeling with pretty routine questions, such as asking 'how are you?, how have you been since last time?' In these encounters you will often see patients responding and discussing how well they think they have been doing. In so doing they are 'Reporting satisfaction'. Then there will be a time when the dentist checks their mouths and in so doing they are 'Responding, confirming and reassuring'. In this example the dentist confirmed that the patient's gums were swollen but then

(Continued)

(Continued)

reassured her that this would go away quite quickly. She explained that this might have been caused by plaque stuck under the gum. The dentist also told the patient that the side of mouth previously cleaned had been maintained well, which is 'Checking and confirming'. ... Part of the way through the local anaesthetic the patient asks whether it is completed. The dentist states it is not and the patient enquires about whether the remainder of treatment will be painful and, as you can see, this involves 'Anxiety and routine'. The dentist then did some 'reassuring' that it 'will not be painful and that the injection will feel like a scratch' and encourages patient to concentrate on her breathing.

Note that the overall category is 'Monitoring mouths' and that there are several processes happening within the category. Now try writing about the category and its dimensions.[3]

Further reading

Birks, M. and Mills, J. (2011) 'Quality processes in grounded theory research', Chapter 3 in M. Birks and J. Mills, *Grounded Theory: A Practical Guide*. London: Sage.

Charmaz, K. (2006) 'Memo-writing', Chapter 4 in K. Charmaz, *Constructing Grounded Theory: A Practical Guide through Qualitative Analysis*. London: Sage.

Glaser, B. and Strauss, A. (1967) 'Theoretical sampling', Chapter 3 in B. Glaser, and A. Strauss, *The Discovery of Grounded Theory*. Chicago: Aldine.

Strauss, A. and Corbin, J. (1990) 'Memos and diagrams', Chapter 12 in A. Strauss and J. Corbin, *Basics of Qualitative Research: Grounded Theory Procedures and Techniques*. Thousand Oaks, CA: Sage.

Notes

1 Dey (1999) barely mentions memoing, although he clearly acknowledges its importance to the process of building theory.

2 We do think that writing memos as an audit trail may be important for grounded theory studies conducted in some areas of enquiry, for example, nursing. As such, the relevance of Birks and Mills (2011) advice to use memoing to enhance the quality of your grounded theory study by tracing aspects of how you developed your theory should be considered carefully. However, our purpose in this text is to clarify how to do grounded theory and therefore we feel strongly you should place priority on memo writing to develop your theory.

3 An example of how this might be achieved is as follows: Monitoring mouths involves several interactive processes that may or may not occur in each face-to-face

encounter. These are 'Exploring "feelings" and sensations (of the mouth)', 'Reporting sensations and experiences', 'Reporting satisfaction', 'Responding, confirming and reassuring', 'Checking and confirming', 'Resolving anxiety and routine' and, where necessary, 'Reassuring'. Each process is characterised by turn-taking where dentist and patient seem to follow interactive rules and a kind of scripting where the order of these processes can have routine characteristics from the point of view of both parties. See Notes 07/08/12 2pm Patient ID: SP1 Dentist ID: SD1 Centre code: 5, Page 20, Paragraph 2. Satisfaction seems to be related to how expectations are being met in relation to positive changes in the physical state of the mouth. Likewise, reporting satisfaction may also be conditioned by how the dentist confirms, checks and reassures the patient. In this respect, checking and confirming seems to map closely to changes in patient expectations. Can we be sure of this? From these data it is hard to tell. We don't know anything about how salient each of these features is for the patient. Did they notice these things? After all, they were lying down with their mouth open and were clearly anxious about the procedure they were experiencing. In this way, anxiety may condition how aware the patient is in the encounter. Another important thing to note here is that there is a congruence between the patient and the dentist's goals in this encounter, which is to improve the physical properties of the mouth. There is no mention or little interest in general health-related behaviour and lifestyle changes. Is this lack of focus because the encounter is dominated by a physical examination? Hypothesis: Does the physical nature of dental examinations result in an interaction dominated by physical goals? Need to check this against other encounters where lifestyle change becomes a feature of the encounter to check how this is conditioned.

11

Theoretical Integration and Sorting in Grounded Theory

Aim: To evaluate the importance of integration and sorting in grounded theory and establish how this can be achieved for a range of formats

Learning outcomes

After reading this chapter you should be able to:

- evaluate and manage the problem of integration in grounded theory
- evaluate the critical issues you will be faced with when sorting for a range of presentation formats in grounded theory
- appreciate the importance of rediscovering the lost skills of integration and sorting in grounded theory

Once you have been selectively coding for some time, involving different combinations of sampling, data collection, coding, and memoing, you may find that you have marked most, if not all, of your categories as saturated. Saturation means that it is increasingly unlikely that collecting more data will help you develop your grounded theory any further. You are now ready to enter the writing-up phase of doing grounded theory and to begin sorting. Glaser (1978) detailed theoretical sorting as a stage in the grounded theory process in *Theoretical Sensitivity*. There is no mention of sorting in *Discovery* (Glaser and Strauss 1967).

As a technique, sorting involves taking your memos, reading them and thinking carefully where they should be placed. Its goal is to enable you to present your grounded theory to others. Such presentations might involve lectures, seminars, books and, of course, journal articles. As a key technique, sorting can therefore help you to further integrate your theory. We place sorting as a key technique associated with the writing-up phase of doing grounded theory (see Chapter 8). As sorting relates to the sorting of memos, it is therefore primarily a conceptual enterprise.

There are several advantages to sorting. It helps you to produce a fully integrated model that is both general and conceptual. It enables you to carefully consider the connections between your categories and therefore contributes to helping you build a dense theory that has a sense of being complete. As you become more and more engaged in your theory, you might discover that more memoing is required, but these memos will almost entirely be focused on the conceptualisation of your theory. They will focus on the overall status of your theory, specifying its key relationships and at the same time integrating relevant literatures.

Sorting will effectively produce the first draft of your presentation or manuscript. You should be thinking in terms of what it is you are trying to achieve in the presentation of your theory. Glaser advised that each sorting process should be conducted with only one presentation in mind (Glaser 1978: 117). In what follows, we will explore sorting for presentations and lectures and contrast this with sorting for the purposes of writing a book or a paper. We hope that by reading this chapter you will also get a much greater sense of the central importance of sorting to theoretical integration.

Theoretical integration and sorting

The key thing about sorting is that it is guided by the specific purpose of the presentation of your theory. The sorting process, we are told, involves looking at memos and sorting them in relation to their 'similarities, connections and conceptual ordering' (Glaser 1978: 117). Glaser (1978) suggested that for a lecture or presentation you will sort into sections and maybe sub-sections, but for a book you will be sorting into chapters, sections and sub-sections. We are not told much more, but obviously, apart from the density of presentation, there might be other things to think about in presenting your theory.

The core thing about sorting, the way it is presented in *Theoretical Sensitivity* at least, is that it is conducted to provide an integrated picture of how your categories are related. It then involves laying out the order in which you will present your categories. But all of this occurs in relation to the overall goal of your presentation and it is this particular issue that can complicate things. If you look at the exemplars we have been using here, first we have a PhD (Raphael 2008), then we have a book (Ekins 1997), and finally a whole series of papers (Baker, Wuest et al. 1992; Merritt-Gray and Wuest 1995; Wuest 1995, 1997a, 1997b, 1998, 2000a, 2000b, 2001; Wuest and Merritt-Gray 2001; Wuest, Ford-Gilboe et al. 2003; Wuest, Merritt-Gray et al. 2004; Ford-Gilboe, Wuest et al. 2005). Sadly, there are virtually no details in any of these presentations concerning how these authors conducted their sorting.

The analytic 'rules' of sorting and grounded theory

Glaser (1978) outlined several 'rules' or guidelines for sorting in grounded theory. He presented these rules as rules for the integration of your theory. They are therefore not directed at sorting for presenting your theory in a lecture or scholarly article. Knowing about these guidelines can help you prepare fully for this part of the writing process.

1. **Starting to sort**: The first guideline is to start sorting and to do so with characteristic freedom, such as beginning with any place in your memos. Basically, you start with your memos and just sort. Now clearly Glaser (1978) has in mind sorting *to present your theory as a whole, most likely in a book*.
2. **Core variable**: While you may start anywhere, it is important to remember the integrating idea or principle of your theory. You should sort in relation to your core variable. You sort your other categories *as they relate to your core category*. In this respect, then, you are thinking about categories and their relationships, but also their relationships to the central tendency of your theory. As you sort, if you discover that you have a category that isn't related to your core category, then you should leave this out and perhaps follow up this category at a later date. Glaser (1978) argued that by doing this you are becoming selective and you are also setting out the boundaries of your theory at the same time. You should be focusing on writing out the details of the kind of theory you have by characterising the core category, including the kinds of theoretical codes and relationships it involves. A key approach during sorting is to ask yourself *how does the core category vary*? By asking this question you will be able to specify the way the core variable varies, perhaps by specifying how it relates to another category (see Chapter 9).
3. **Promotion-demotion of core variables**: Glaser (1978) argued that you might confront problems if there are more than two central variables in your theory. In this instance, it is important to remember that once again you are not trying to write a theory about everything. Your goal is to produce a theory that explains some variation in the way people organise their solutions to a problem they are dealing with. Glaser's (1978) advice was to demote one core and promote the other, and at the same time drop any unrelated memos and use those at a later date for integrating into a new paper. You can make your decision what to drop often on the basis of what empirical material you have (Glaser 1978).
4. **Continue memoing**: Once you start to sort around your core variable the goal is to start writing memos about your theory as it starts to integrate. As we suggested in the last chapter, you should be thinking and seeing your substantive area in terms of your categories. On top of this, you will get further ideas about how to integrate your theory.
5. **Sorting for 'carry-forward'**: Glaser (1978) suggests that you make sure as you sort that you think carefully about how to allow for the build-up of your theory. It is important to think about which categories should be presented first, in what order and how they will gradually relate to each other. Nothing could be more important than thinking carefully about the way you will be presenting your theory. You might find this difficult to do. If so, stop and read a grounded theory study such as Ekins (1997). As you read it, look for structure. Note how the grounded theory is developed, how the author defines each category as it is presented. When a new category is presented, explore what happens next in the text. For example, often an author will outline how the category varies and then will explain how its main relationships lead to this

variation (see Chapter 13). The important thing is to make more memos on how each category will be presented and why you are placing it where you are. You also need to pay attention to the density of the theory and to ensure that you do not present too many categories simultaneously.

6. **Sorting for integrative fit**: When it comes to integrative fit Glaser (1978) seems to indicate that while you are sorting you should be developing an outline of your theory. The main categories must fit into the outline in some way. So, during sorting not only are you placing your memos in different order you are also building up a proposed outline of what your theory should look like in your presentation or in your thesis. This will involve drawing up your writing plan by outlining what the table of contents might look like. Glaser (1978) indicates that once more you will switch your observations between your developing outline and your memos. In this process you will be changing levels of observation which in turn helps you to develop your theory. Another interesting aspect of Glaser's (1978) writing on integrative fit is that there is an assumption in grounded theory that the social world is organised in some way and that your task is to attempt to provide an account of how this organisation occurs.

7. **Sorting levels**: As we stated above, Glaser (1978) indicated that sorting needs to consider your overall goal for the presentation of your theory. If you are going to be presenting it in a seminar, then the complexity of the sorting will be relatively simple compared to what it will be if you are writing it up for a book. When writing for a book, you might find that you can sort into higher order sections, chapters and sub-sections.

8. **Problems of order**: One of the problems of theoretical integration is often deciding on where best to present your ideas. In the case where you have conflicts of presentation, you are advised to place a note on the memo to 'pass it forward' through your outline (Glaser 1978). The important thing about this rule is that you should be seeking to control the repetition of categories in your presentation. This will enable you to carefully trace how you define and then elaborate on a particular theme of your theory in your presentation. You need to pay attention to when the idea first appears, to define it and then to trace its development through your paper or book. A sign of a poorly developed presentation is when ideas appear out of nowhere without any contextualisation for the person reading or listening to the presentation.

9. **Stopping sorting**: The main reason to stop sorting and to start thinking about writing is of course that you might have run out of memos. You may have enough saturation in your core variable to the point where adding any more complexity might be excessive and produce too much of a burden for the presentation of your theory. On top of these reasons, you may well run out of time and money. According to Glaser (1978), the main reason for stopping sorting is theoretical completeness. By this he means that your theory 'explains with the fewest possible concepts, and with the greatest possible scope, as much variation as possible in the behaviour and problem under study'. (Glaser 1978: 125)

Clearly, then, there are quite a few things to consider when sorting. All of these guidelines mean that you will be moving your memos around, placing notes on them, writing further memos, writing what Glaser (1978) calls 'pass on notes' and developing a theoretical outline. The suggestion is that you will need a large table or space on which to do this. It can be hard to achieve all of this level of integration and the degree of engagement that you will need on a computer screen, so we do suggest that these operations would be better achieved physically. All these rules are summarised in Box 11-1.

Box 11-1

A summary of the analytic 'rules' for sorting in grounded theory

1. **Starting to sort**: it is important to just start and to do so with characteristic freedom by beginning with any place in your piles of memos.
2. **Sorting for the core variable** is designed to fill out and delimit the core variable.
3. **Promotion-demotion of core variables** involves making decisions on which major variable to focus on in a presentation.
4. **Continue memoing** involves writing memos about the theory as it starts to integrate.
5. **Sorting for 'carry-forward'** refers to sorting memos *into an order for a presentation*. Here you think about how your theory will build up for those you are presenting to. In other words, you are thinking about how best to present the ideas without confusing the audience.
6. **Sorting for integrative fit** involves dropping categories that do not relate to the core category that is being sorted around. It also involves switching between the developing outline and the memos while changing the levels of observation, which in turn develop the theory.
7. **Sorting levels** involves focusing on the overall goal of the presentation of your theory and varying the density of the sort to suit this presentation.
8. **Problems of order** can mean that you might need to move memos up and down the order of the presentation.
9. **Stopping sorting** typically happens when memos run out, or where it makes little sense to continue to make the presentation of the material more complicated than is necessary, or when time runs out. But the key factor is that by putting more and more into the presentation of the theory you might reduce the parsimony of the theory.

Obviously, a major source of variation for sorting is the purpose to which you are sorting. In this sense, we have identified four major modes of presentation which we will briefly talk about below. There are very few places where sorting is discussed in the scholarly literature and when it is discussed it is often not considered in real depth.

Skills and tips 11-1

Planning for sorting

Before sorting you should be prepared to be able to answer all of the following questions succinctly and clearly:

- What is your theory about?
- What is its general position both with respect to the literature and with respect to either practical or policy-related outcomes?

> - What is the core category?
> - What is the purpose of your write-up or presentation?
> - Will you be presenting the whole theory or just parts of it?

Sorting for your PhD

Sorting for a PhD in grounded theory can be quite complicated and frequently leads to consternation in students. If you are in a science or medical faculty there is more or less a set routine for presenting a PhD, but this can vary dramatically from faculty to faculty and university to university. A PhD presented to a humanities faculty may look very different from one presented in a science or medical faculty. This can cause all sorts of problems for students. Our advice is to be very clear about what is expected of you. One thing you can be pretty sure of is that the usual maxim for a PhD is to demonstrate some sort of addition to knowledge. Find out if this is the case. If it is the case, then you will need to be able to clearly demonstrate how your findings produce a new form of knowledge. This might mean that when you are sorting that, you will need to explicitly write into your theory not only uses of the literature as examples for expanding your theory, but also what your theory adds to the literature. Of course this is not something Glaser (1978) talked about. In his later writings he often said that a grounded theory will produce self-evident knowledge and there will be no need for any form of justification. Assuming this for a PhD is a very high-risk strategy. The following suggestions might be useful for you to consider integrating into sorting.

Be aware that the literature can clearly be used in several different ways, so sorting and memoing may need to take account of this. A source of frustration for students using grounded theory (this can be true of qualitative methods as a whole) for their PhD is that often the standard approach to a PhD can involve writing a literature review, then a methodology, then a materials and method section, a results section and then a discussion followed by some conclusions. Grounded theory doesn't fit this format particularly well, so, for example, some element of discussion will often be needed with findings and therefore the division is often not so easily maintained. Helen Raphael (2008) was returning her thesis to the School of Nursing and Midwifery at the University of Southampton. Part of the process of supervision involved a long discussion of what would be expected within this context. It was agreed that some sort of compromise would be necessary and, as a consequence, she conducted a very brief review of the literature in advance of undertaking her study. In this review she stated openly that this was not the sort of thing to do in grounded theory but because she was doing a PhD some kind of review was justified.

You might also be faced with making some compromises when you are undertaking your study and it would be wise to seek advice early in the process and to explore your options. Even if you are allowed to undertake a grounded theory in its purest form, you will still have to prove that what you have is an addition to knowledge and often this means guiding your reader to this contribution. *You might want to consider this during the sorting process.* In addition to the guidelines above, you might need to ask yourself at key points during the sorting process questions concerning what this or that finding or category might add to the relevant field? *It is a very high-risk strategy to assume that the contribution to knowledge is self-evident and often your examiners will challenge you if it is not clear.*

An additional problem associated with conducting a grounded theory for a PhD is that a PhD may well require some form of justification for the status of your claim to knowledge. This is something that can often sit very uneasily with grounded theory, as it was developed. Nonetheless, it is important when you do a PhD that you should be able to justify your interpretations. You might find yourself having to provide more justification for the development of your theory and the claims you make for its status as knowledge. This can be unusual for a grounded theory study, but it might be essential for a PhD in the faculty in which you are based. One suggestion would be to ask yourself to provide some form of justification for your categories when you are sorting. You can do so by asking yourself: Why have I chosen this category? How did it develop from my data? Why was it justified?

Finally, if you find yourself having to compromise the way in which you present your grounded theory, we would suggest that this may have important consequences for the way in which you carry forward your categories. When sorting your findings, you may have to carry forward additional memos into a discussion section, flagging up where important discussion needs to take place that will document how your findings might be discussed in relation to the literature. Memos that relate to the literature might need to be carefully separated from findings and sorted into a discussion section. Then they might need to be modified with additional notes to indicate how you think they should be discussed in contrast to your findings. The beautiful thing about grounded theory is that because of its flexibility this is entirely possible. The only caveat we would add is to try to make sure that you do not force your study to take new directions; these notes *are purely for the purposes of demonstrating what the theory brings to the literature.*

Other ways to handle this can often be to maintain the integration of your theory but then to have a short concluding section that outlines what the theory adds to knowledge. For those conducting grounded theory in professional disciplines, such as architecture, nursing, dentistry, medicine and education, it can often be wise to ask yourself if there are any practical consequences of particular findings and to memo on these into an 'Implications for practice' section for your conclusions. You may also have to write out some policy implications. If so, make sure you consider this while sorting and then carry forward your memos into the relevant section as you go. Just remember that such sections are frequently essential in some departments.

Another great way to enhance your findings during sorting is to consider how your categories might have general implications. As we have said throughout this book, data slicing is a great way to reach beyond your findings and so such memos can often have direct relevance to your discussion. You might find it beneficial to sort your findings forward into a section in your discussion or conclusions on 'The formal implications of this theory'. By establishing the relevance of your findings to other substantive fields, not only will you be able to provide a further justification for your findings, but you will enable your examiners to see the general relevance of your theory. If you have carefully worked such questions and answers into your sorting process, you will find your thesis becomes much more convincing.

Another great technique when developing your grounded theory for a PhD is to consider if your thesis relates in some way to a common-sense understanding of your problem. What does that look like? Take Ekins' (1997) lead and ask yourself, while sorting, if your category relates to some sort of public understanding or controversy. What does your theory have to say to this? How might your theory enhance our understanding of such controversies? Finally, if you look at the work of Glaser and Strauss, the work of Ekins, Wuest and Raphael, they all expose something hidden about the world that just was not considered before. *This is perhaps the most dramatic way of showing that your grounded theory adds to knowledge.* So perhaps feed into your sorting processes by asking yourself if this or that category answers or tells us something that previously was not obvious. All of these questions have been added to Box 11-2.

Box 11-2

Additional questions to consider asking when sorting for a PhD thesis

1 What does this category or dimensions of a category add to the field of research?
2. Why have I chosen this category?
3. How did it develop from my data?
4. Why was this category justified?
5. What are the implications for practice?
6. What are the likely implications for policy in this field?
7. What are the formal implications of this theory?
8. How does the theory relate to a public understanding of the subject area? Is it related to a public controversy or not?
9. Does the theory answer some questions that are not directly obvious?

It is important to remember that these questions may only be relevant because there are additional things you need to consider when attempting to secure a PhD, and often these things can carry with them an additional set of burdens that are not covered in the original method. *We in no way consider these essential or required for doing grounded theory. The important thing is to integrate such questions into your sorting stage and use the flexibility of the methodology to make additional notes and memos that can then be carried forward to the relevant sections later in the thesis.*

Sorting for books in grounded theory

When it comes to writing a book you can be sure that you will be seeking to utilise the fullest range of guidelines that have been outlined in Box 11-1 above. There are, however, a number of additional requirements that you might need to think about when sorting for writing a book. The most basic question you need to address is who is this book for? Thinking about your audience is a key element of putting together a book proposal and most publishers will want a good answer regarding the extent of the audience. Will it be a small, technical audience or a broad, interdisciplinary audience? Obviously, publishers usually prefer to present to as broad an audience as possible, in which case having a clear focus with a well thought through and integrated core category will make communicating your theory much easier. You should also seek to bring as much of your theory together as you can, ensure that the integrative fit is good and, most importantly, as you prepare each chapter, that the concepts you use are clearly defined and easy to follow. It will also be important to make sure that your reader can follow those developments as they are developed in the book. Obviously, writing a book is a significant task and you can potentially have a lot of scope to specify your theory at several different levels. The biggest problem will be on deciding when too many concepts will dilute your writing and make it difficult for your reader to follow your main arguments.

You can deduce the outline of Ekins' (1997) sorting in *Male Femaling* by looking closely at his table of contents and exploring the structure of the book. The book itself begins with an exposé of the worlds of male cross-dressers by showing how male femaling appears alongside the apparently mundane, everyday world. Ekins (1997), therefore, is introducing the problem of his theory by exposing that there are different social worlds and that they treat the subject matter of his book in very different ways. In this introduction he compares and contrasts the different worlds of his analysis along the dimensions of insider and outsider perspectives. He then goes on to introduce his perspective and shows how grounded theory handles the literature (see Chapter 12 in this book). He discusses the social science of what he has been doing in the next section of the book, with a final section dedicated to the findings. This final section has been structured to have broader appeal, including perhaps those who are interested in the subculture of male femaling. In some respects, some of the additional questions in Box 11-2 can also be of relevance to this process. It all depends on what you want to achieve and who you envisage is your audience, there are any number of ways to sort your memos.

Sorting for papers in grounded theory

Most academic careers will require you to provide some level of research outputs in the form of papers in scholarly journals. Once again, there is huge variability in the way that journals accept papers. It is unlikely that you will be able to simply write up your grounded theory in its purest form without having to modify your sorting processes in some way. As a consequence, you will need to look carefully at your target journal, make notes on how papers are presented and then fit your sorting processes around your target journal. Another important step might be to look at your target journal and see if any grounded theory studies have been published in this journal and then consider carefully how you might wish to sort your memos for publication. We have included the work of Wuest (1997a, 1997b, 1998, 2000a, 2000b, 2001) in this book because she has been so prolific and successful at sorting her memos and grounded theory process to demonstrate incremental developments in her theory.

If you take her approach, you will see that she has clearly gone for segmented discussions of the various aspects of her overall theory. The theory itself appears to have been outlined in her PhD and then she has gone on to elaborate on each of the key aspects of her theory by selecting categories that are worthy of discussion and will contribute to the literature, each in its own way. Her first two papers (Wuest 1997a, 1997b) focus on improving our understanding of the perspectives and experiences of women who are being asked to take on the burdens of caring. In these papers, Wuest has taken out a section of her original theory, sorted her memos for the purpose of the paper and then written her paper around the specific contribution these findings provide to the literature. In her first paper she adds to the literature by expanding on the diverse realities of women's caring. She explores in detail the various experience of her main category for this paper – 'fraying connections' – which was identified as women's initial response to competing and changing caring demands. She then documents the dimensions of fraying connections and how these relate to key topics in the literature on gender, culture, age, ability, class, and sexual orientation (Wuest 1997a).

In her next paper Wuest (1997b) goes on to explore the conditions that influence women's caring, since it appears that little is known about what influences women's caring. The contribution to the literature is to highlight that health care reform seems to be conducted with the assumption that women are 'natural' carers. As such, policy makers seem happy to dump caring on to families and it is women in particular who are left to carry the burden of care. This part of her theory, then, was able to show that little was known about the process of women's caring or the effects of caring on women, and demonstrated how women managed caring. Her paper then focused on the ways that environmental influences had an impact on women's responses to their caring demands. The big contribution of her theory was to establish how social structure could intensify the problems for women's caring. Her work goes on to discuss the policy-related impacts and implications of her findings. As you can see in each of the examples, Wuest (1997a, 1997b, 1998, 2000a, 2000b, 2001) sticks to the empirical methods of the journals she is writing for and presents *slices of the theory*. These slices are then placed in the context and format for the relevant journal. They are often just a key category or an overview of the basic social process that she is researching. You can, of course, do likewise. Try not to think that because you produced a complete theory that it needs to be disseminated in its completed form. In many ways getting more than one paper out of your theory is a sign of just how productive grounded theory can be.

Sorting for a lecture or seminar

Presentations such as lectures or seminars are frequently a lot of fun but can also be very tricky. A common mistake is to try to present too much information, and this can be a real problem for those doing grounded theory, especially since grounded theories are dense and multidimensional. As with the papers above, we would suggest that you slice your theory into relevant sections. Try sorting out an important aspect of your theory and then carefully sort the key aspects of this part of your theory. A very important aspect of preparing a presentation for a seminar, a lecture or a conference presentation are the well-established guidelines that, at best, you will manage to speak 60 words a minute. So allow 480 words for an eight-minute conference presentation.

It is here that perhaps you should try to go for a great degree of detail in your sorting, breaking it right down to line-by-line sorting. As you can tell, you will need to be able to have a duplicate copy of your memos in order to be able to cut them into small chunks for your presentation. Then you will need to consider what the purpose of the presentation is. Is it to provoke discussion? Is it a lecture or an overview? Obviously, it might prove really difficult to get across the complexity of your theory and so you might need to focus on a general overview, only giving examples to illustrate your findings here and there. Alternatively, you might want to present one aspect of your theory in a lot of detail. When it comes to short presentations you are more than likely going to have to be very careful what you sort into the presentation and what you leave out.

┌───┐
Skills and tips 11-2

Memoing while sorting

Please refer to Box 11-1, 'A summary of the analytic "rules" for sorting in grounded theory'. Having consulted these rules, prepare to sort by making sure you can answer the questions in Skills and tips 11-1: Planning for sorting on page 190. Try sorting and write a memo that refers to one of the analytic rules in Box 11-1. You might write about how you start to see the limits and extent of your core category. This might involve writing about any decisions to promote or demote particular core variables. Particularly useful will be to start memoing on the structure of the presentation by making memos to note which ideas should be introduced where and why. In developing these memos, remember you are slowly developing the outline of your book, paper or thesis.
└───┘

Key points about sorting

Sorting is a technique that will also further enable you to think conceptually about your theory. In fact, Glaser (1978) said it was essential to the grounded theory methodology. Yet when it is discussed in the literature the emphasis tends to be on sorting as the specific technique for putting the theory back together again (Strauss and Corbin 1990; Dey 1999; Charmaz 2006; Birks and Mills 2011). Sorting is not very well discussed in the grounded theory literature. For example, Birks and Mills (2011) devote two pages to sorting, describing it as one of the techniques for integrating the theory. This is in keeping with the interpretation of Charmaz (2006), who describes it as both a technique for integration but also as a way to refine your theory. Strauss and Corbin (1990) also present sorting in terms of the way in which it relates to theoretical integration of the theory. They later present it as part of the writing-up process in relation to developing the outline of your book or paper, but do not give us much to go on when it comes to how to do this. The failure to link sorting to writing is a significant deficiency in the literature. If you are to think of it as the first stage in the process of presenting your theory, then it is likely that you will be able to integrate your theory in a range of ways *for the purpose of presentation*. This flexibility can give you significant advantages for the development and presentation of your grounded theory. It might be that because there is considerable overlap between sorting and writing-up that many authors have underplayed its significance. But as you can see (Figure 8-4), we place sorting into the same phase of research as writing-up and we hope that by expanding on the ways you might consider doing this that we have widened the range of approaches to writing grounded theory.[1] We feel this is in keeping with Glaser's (1978) approach, which is aimed at the integration of the theory *but also the purpose of the presentation of the theory*.

If understanding sorting is a common problem in the literature, it is also a problem in the empirical literature. It is very difficult to locate details of sorting in empirical studies. In many respects this aspect of the method remains its least discussed aspect. There is very little in the way of scholarly debate concerning sorting. Indeed, it might be that sorting has become one of those lost skills of grounded theory. Yet, as we can see, it is potentially very useful to think openly about it, to plan the kind of sorting process and even to develop your own approach to sorting.

We have sought to outline how some of the guidelines of sorting that Glaser (1978) developed can be carefully modified to support different presentation styles. We have focused on modifications that might be used to help you think about how to sort for a PhD, using guidelines such as carrying forward observations that can highlight the contribution of your theory to existing knowledge. Some of what we say here takes us away from the original method slightly, but we hope it does so with sensitivity to the project that Glaser and Strauss (1967) were developing.

The key points about sorting are that:

- it is associated with Glaser's elaboration of the method and became a key stage in the method after *Discovery*.
- it is guided by the specific purpose of the presentation of your theory, for example in lectures, seminars, books, research papers or as a PhD.
- it is guided by several analytic rules (see Box 11-1).
- consideration needs to be given to the purpose of your sorting. So, for example, if you are presenting your theory as a PhD you need to consider the regulations for a PhD and to address those. We have offered some ideas on how this might be achieved (see Box 11-2).

Summary

In this chapter the poorly and often unelaborated technique of sorting has been explored in some depth. As we have seen, the primary focus of sorting has been to enable the full integration of the theory around a core category. Sorting is primarily associated with Glaser's (1978) elaboration of grounded theory and is not often included or developed in any real depth in the secondary literature. We have seen that sorting involves preparing the theory for different forms of presentation. The chapter has provided a summary of the various different 'analytic rules' that were developed for sorting by Glaser (1978) and has tried to outline how to conduct sorting for various different purposes, including the PhD, books, seminars and papers. We have discussed the importance of paying attention to the density of the integration that is required for the presentation of the theory. So, for example, for a book the theory will be presented in quite a dense form, whereas for a seminar the level of density of the presentation will be relatively light. Another aspect of sorting that we have discussed is to pay attention to when key ideas are presented, making sure they are adequately defined and illustrated and that their meaning is 'carried forward' in the particular presentation.

Further reading

Birks, M. and Mills, J. (2011) 'Theoretical integration', Chapter 7 in M. Birks and J. Mills, *Grounded Theory: A Practical Guide*. London: Sage.

Charmaz, K. (2006) 'Reconstructing theory in grounded theory studies', Chapter 6 in K. Charmaz, *Constructing Grounded Theory: A Practical Guide through Qualitative Analysis*. London: Sage.

Glaser, B. (1978) 'Theoretical sorting', Chapter 7 in B. Glaser, *Theoretical Sensitivity: Advances in the Methodology of Grounded Theory*. Mill Valley, CA: Sociology Press.

Strauss, A. and Corbin, J. (1990) 'Selective coding', Chapter 8 in A. Strauss and J. Corbin, *Basics of Qualitative Research: Grounded Theory Procedures and Techniques*. Thousand Oaks, CA: Sage.

Note

1   We are in agreement with Dey (1999), who also commented on the failure to expand analytical rules or guidelines for sorting. The elaboration we make in this chapter is designed as a flexible aid to enable readers to do this aspect of the method better. We also hope that it might stimulate further debate in grounded theory methodology.

12

Integrating, Challenging and Contributing to the Literature

Aim: To explore the debate about the use of the literature in grounded theory

Learning outcomes

After reading this chapter you should be able to:

- be aware of the debate about the use of the literature in grounded theory
- develop skills to enable you to integrate the literature in your grounded theory
- articulate how you can develop memos on the nature of the relationship between your theory and various different literatures
- explain the key debates about the use of the literature in grounded theory

Now we come to one of the most controversial and often misunderstood aspects of grounded theory – the literature. By now, we have already covered the underlying issues that relate to this controversy in some depth. What we will do here is briefly explore some of the remaining issues before going on to discuss writing and formal theory. As you can see from most of what we have written so far in this book, for us there is nothing that is really shocking or problematic about grounded theory. We find it full of an elegant simplicity; indeed, in places it is ingenious. Sometimes we think that people have over-complicated grounded theory. As we have seen in the introduction to this book, *a central reaction within grounded theory was to research that has been derived from preconceived questions*, usually in addition to and partly in response to the professional sociological literature (Hammond 1964).

Glaser and Strauss (1967) were careful to prioritise reaching a theory that fitted and worked to explain the area that was being studied. They argued that there was no guarantee that categories taken from existing theory could fit and work. Borrowing categories and using them would turn the exercise of doing research into just another form of data collection. In addition, it was argued that by drawing on existing categories the researcher was often confronted with trying to find the right indicators that would fit the categories. In contrast, if you simply generate categories from your data, the problem of getting them to fit was more or less solved. It was for these reasons that Glaser and Strauss claimed that 'our focus on the development of categories solves the problems of fit, relevance, forcing, and richness' (Glaser and Strauss 1967: 37). It was from this point that the notorious suggestion to 'literally ignore the literature of theory and fact on the area under study' was made. This, however, in no way implied that doing grounded theory involved ignoring the literature completely. In almost the next sentence, Glaser and Strauss (1967) talked about establishing similarities and differences after the core category had emerged. The goal of a grounded theory, then, was to establish as much variety as possible in concep-tualisations that could enable the development of a fully relevant theory. Draw-ing on existing grand theories, they argued, would often lead to a few categories that were not particularly well applied to the field.

These discussions form the backdrop to the development of the debate in *Discovery* about how to handle existing literature. Studies that often started out doing one thing ended up having to focus on something else. Avoiding the lit-erature in the initial stages can be seen as an entirely rational response. It is one thing to see this as a response to improve sensitivity and to enable the better generation of theory from data, and it is entirely another to claim that grounded theory avoids the literature.

Reading *Discovery*, one of the most valuable assertions concerning the literature appears to be the key lesson taken from the debate in *Sociologists at Work* (Hammond 1964). It is to promote researchers as 'highly sensitized and systematic' agents (Glaser and Strauss 1967: 251). Grounded theory was written in response to these particular forms of research. It has embedded within it a learned sensitiv-ity to the fact that research questions derived from the literature might not be relevant to the field of research. In many respects there is nothing more elegant than simply getting on with the study and going to the literature when you need to. None of this means you have an empty head to begin with, that you have an excuse not to read the literature, or that it will remain irrelevant. You need to take the literature very seriously indeed. Before getting into the practical details of this let us briefly explore how the literature is discussed in grounded theory.

As we have already seen, *Discovery* discusses the literature in response to the debates that were going on at the time. The principal debate seems to be to hold back on reading the literature until the main categories of your theory have fully emerged. This would be our selective coding phase, discussed in Chapter 8. If you already have a good knowledge of the literature, the key thing to do would be to hold back on using any of the categories in this literature until this stage. So avoid drawing on pre-existing theory until you are sure you have the right core problem and the right set of categories to explain how this problem is resolved. The majority of the discussion in *Discovery* concerns pre-serving the sensitivity of the observer (see Glaser and Strauss 1967: 251–253).

A joke of Glaser's is that libraries will still be there after you have collected some of your data and you really ought not to panic.

In *Theoretical Sensitivity*, Glaser (1978) went on to discuss some more principles of theory development. Here he talked about where ideas in the literature had an 'emergent fit' they should be linked to your theory (Glaser 1978: 4). 'Emergent fit' refers to the fact that if they add something to your interpretation, they should be used in your theory. It is in these passages that we find Glaser's (1978) most controversial statements. He talked about 'All is data *at some level*'. In other words, the literature was to be treated in the same way as the data, compared and contrasted to your emerging theory and, where it fitted, to be worked into your theory. After integrating the idea into your theory you should avoid getting bogged down discussing the theorist from whom you borrowed the idea, but merely footnote that source and move on. The grounded theory researcher 'does not deify another sociologist'; rather, 'he de-deifies "great men" to their rightly portion of recognition and does not lose his own valuable contribution. His analysis is preserved as his own and not attributed with excessive reverence to someone, who did not do it. The analyst need not constantly refer to a Weber, Durkheim, Merton, Becker and so forth, and interrupt the flow of his theory. He merely footnotes' (Glaser 1978: 9). So there you go. Your job is to reduce Weber, Durkheim, Marx and Merton to footnotes in history. You are to work in the ideas of others after you have secured your main categories and after your first draft has been prepared.

Strauss and Corbin (1990) developed further ideas on how to integrate the literature into grounded theory. First, they talk about how you will bring knowledge of literature to your study. They argued that this 'technical' knowledge can actually get in the way of doing your grounded theory because, as we have seen above, it can block the development of categories that are based on what is going on in the area under study. Likewise, when you have developed some categories your goal will be to go back to the literature and explore if the same category has been developed in the literature. If so, what can existing knowledge add to your study? In turn, the literature can also be used as another source of data and for further stimulation of questions, and it can help you direct your theoretical sampling by suggesting other locations to collect data. Finally, they argued that it can also act as another source of validation of key aspects of your theory, although they do suggest that you will not want to validate everything in your theory (Strauss and Corbin 1990).

Why is there a debate about the literature in grounded theory?

There is an extensive and serious debate about the literature in grounded theory. The problem seems to be that closely tied with the question of the literature is the problem of preconceptions. Authors do not make this very clear. Charmaz (2006) places Dey (1999) as critical of grounded theory in this respect. However, when you look at Dey (1999) he clearly shows that having a little knowledge of the literature is not really problematic. His main criticisms of grounded theory are reserved for Glaser and Strauss's (1967) handling of the problem of preconceptions. For Dey (1999), preconceptions are part of the process of doing good social research. In fact, he claims that often an in-depth understanding of one's discipline can enhance rather than undermine good research (Dey 1999). Yet, as we have shown throughout this book in our exemplars, those who do grounded theory do use their prior preconceptions and interests to enhance their grounded theory.

You should by now have a good sense that we don't think this claim can be sustained. It cannot be sustained in the great examples of grounded theory that we have presented and it cannot be sustained by a careful reading of the original texts. We agree with Charmaz (2006), following Karen Henwood and Nick Pidgeon (2003), that the term 'theoretical agnosticism', at least in the early stages of the research process, seems to fit the methodology pretty well. What we can say, however, is that the debate about the literature is also a debate about how preconceptions and prior interests are handled in the research process (see Chapter 6). What, then, remains to be said about this topic? In what follows we will briefly show you how our exemplars have handled the literature before we go on to explore some practical issues.

How to handle the literature in grounded theory

As we have said, the issue of the literature is closely related to the issue of handling preconceptions and prior interests. You should be able to handle the problem with relative ease. Raphael (2008) carefully drew on the ideas of Chenitz and Swanson (1986) when discussing her approach. She was also aware that she could not begin her study without any preconceptions. She explained her rationale for including a very brief literature review as follows:

> In this study, I had some prior knowledge of the research area through my previous clinical practice and research experience, which had included fracture prevention in primary care. Hence, I had previously accessed the literature concerned with osteoporosis and gained some knowledge of the proposed research area. As well as this prior knowledge, ... a preliminary literature review was necessary as the requirements of the funding institutions that I approached for support for this study required sufficient literature to be presented to provide background and justification for the study. Supporting information from the literature was also needed when I was developing the application to seek ethical approval to conduct the study. As a result, there was a requirement to establish what, if any, research had already been conducted in the substantive area of men's osteoporosis. (Raphael 2008: 7–8)

Raphael (2008) then went on to outline how her search was conducted and subsequently reported on her findings. The details she provided in the text established general information about osteoporosis, its definition and widespread impact, which established it as an important public health problem in older people. She then discussed the costs of osteoporosis-related treatments, including how it might be prevented. In the rest of her review she very briefly demonstrated that men had not been included in many studies on the impact of osteoporosis. In doing so, she provided information that demonstrated that her study was needed and justified. Overall, her review was short and to the point and did not include any theoretical or conceptual details from the literature. The brief review of the literature enhanced her study by highlighting that her question was urgent and significant.

Ekins (1997) took a very different approach to the literature, critically evaluating it from the standpoint of grounded theory. In his approach, there were three 'worldviews' on cross-dressing: a lay worldview, a medical worldview and a subcultural worldview. Each of these worldviews had generated its own literature and each was critiqued from the perspective of grounded theory (Ekins 1997). The medical model is critiqued thus:

> The definitions of the situation of cross-dressers and sex-changers themselves (member definitions) are never explored as social constructions of reality with their own legitimacy. In particular, the focus on doctor–patient encounters precludes systematic exploration of the social worlds of cross-dressers and sex-changers outside the clinic and consulting room. (Ekins 1997: 28)

Ekins (1997) went on to critique the medical literature for taking for granted sex role stereotypes and reinforcing the oppression of cross-dressers. For him, the advantage of grounded theory was that these perspectives could in fact be used as 'data'. Clearly, the perspectives contained in the medical literature could be used for his very productive analysis. Ekins (1997) effectively creates a space and generates three worlds against which his grounded theory can be contrasted. The main thrust of his critique of the existing medical literature is that it is taken from an outsider's perspective and, as such, is a framework with which his subjects clash. Likewise, when he compares and contrasts the frameworks that have been used from a sociological viewpoint, he discovers that similar problems exist. These perspectives do not fully ground themselves in the worlds of cross-dressers and transsexuals. So in one sense Ekins (1997) draws on the findings of other research *to set his own theory against these perspectives* and in another *he uses these perspectives as data, as part of the context against which his participants have to live. He therefore integrates the literature both into his theory and against his theory.*

A similar approach is adopted by Wuest (1997a, 1997b), who argues that there are gaps in the literature which take too much for granted when it comes to women's caring. Her grounded theory closes this gap and challenges the way in which social structure assumes that women are naturally the best placed to engage in caring. The literature is also a source of findings in the sense that much of the professional literature on caring *props up* a neo-liberal approach to women's caring. This literature, then, is not just something to be contrasted with their work; *it is also part of the problem against which they are writing*. It serves to prop up an ideology that places more and more burdens on women despite the fact that these burdens are often not well received, and can, in fact, have severe health consequences for women. She discusses her use of literature in some detail:

> The final issue for me in my struggle with emergent fit is the issue of theoretical sensitivity and knowledge of the literature. ... Although Glaser cautions the investigator to gain such sensitivity by entering 'the research setting with as few predetermined ideas as possible' ... he also acknowledges that 'sensitivity is necessarily increased by being steeped in the literature' ([Glaser 1978] p. 3) and understanding how variables are constructed in diverse fields. 'Disciplinary or professional knowledge as well as both research and professional experiences, that the author brings to his or her inquiry' enhances theoretical sensitivity (Strauss & Corbin 1994, p. 280). I found it difficult to reconcile these apparently contradictory positions. ... I ceased to worry that extensive knowledge of the field of study would drive the analysis. ... I have learned to remain close to the data in my initial open coding, to avoid language that is theory laden, and to keep asking, 'What category does this incident indicate?' and 'What is actually happening in the data?' (Glaser 1978, p. 57). These strategies ensure that the initial coding and category development is grounded in the data. (Wuest 2000: 55–56)

Here we can see that there is a tension in grounded theory between increasing your theoretical sensitivity by being 'steeped' in the literature in your field and avoiding preconceptions and prioritising concepts and categories that develop from the data. Wuest (2000a) was clearly able to overcome these problems. Indeed, the grounded theory process enabled her to do so by simply avoiding using professional concepts and terms and sticking to the data. As long as you realise that you are supposed to prioritise the data and then bring the literature in after you have developed your theory, you will be fine. What practical steps, then, can you take towards the use of literature in your study?

Practical ways to use the literature in grounded theory

In many respects, grounded theory is not really any different from other research approaches. There is a need to be just as systematic and critical with the literature. There are, however, some very important differences when you use the literature in a grounded theory. Grounded theory research often results in findings that can cut across numerous intellectual fields. Glaser (1978, 2005) makes this point when he discusses the 'integrative fit' of grounded theory.

This means that you may discover that the relevance of literature from many different substantive fields can be of use to you, and that your grounded theory study can help tie together many disparate findings. This is also true of the general relevance of your theory, which can often reach beyond your substantive field (see Chapter 14). In addition, since you are involved in developing a grounded theory, you will perhaps discover that your theory is closely related to the perspectives of your participants as they attempt to resolve their main concerns. You may have accrued an important advantage in opposition to other approaches and you might need to show how problems of fit and workability might exist in transposing certain theoretical ideas from one place to another. As you can see, your task is slightly more complex than simply doing a descriptive review of the evidence in a field of study. The most obvious thing that we need to consider is when and how to engage with the literature.

When to start

As we have said previously, you usually start searching the literature for *integrative fit* after you have a decent bank of memos and categories. In many ways you should have a good idea what your theory does and what its core problems are. You may have prior knowledge of the field of research because you are steeped in it or you may be a novice researcher. Once you are pretty sure what your theory is about, you are ready to start reviewing the literature to explore what the position of your theory is in relation to that literature. The best place to start will be to map out your major concepts and then begin by asking yourself where you will find research on the topics suggested by your categories. As we have seen, Raphael (2008) knew from her findings that the nature of gender and illness would be the general area that would be relevant to her. It is obvious that the feminist literature in the sociology of health and illness would be relevant. Ekins (1997) talks of three social worlds and explored the medical and sociological literature on cross-dressing and transsexualism. Once you have your categories, you might wish to do a literature search using the relevant databases, such as PubMed, IBSS, Web of Knowledge, Google Scholar and Medline. You might want to map out where the significant literatures are. Your problem, however, will be setting limits on this process since your study may touch on a multitude of different literatures. You might want to look for key literature in each of the relevant fields while also checking out the studies that are recognised as central to the field. You can do this by analysing citations. You can help yourself by drawing an outline of your theory and mapping out the various literatures to which the theory relates. But this is searching for literature that is directly relevant to your study. What about research that covers a similar set of problems but in a different field? Obviously, deciding to go beyond your particular substantive field can lead you towards the generation of a formal theory and so engagements with a more general literature will need to be carefully controlled. As we have seen, these explorations can also be quite valuable and can increase the scope and generality of your theory.

How to engage with the literature

There are several things you can do to integrate the literature into your study (see Box 12-1). As Glaser stated, it is important to see the literature as a source of ideas that can be used to enhance your theory. By reading the relevant literature, you might be able to further specify an important concept or category. The most basic operation, then, is to read the relevant literature and continue to engage in processes of constant comparison. Make memos on similarities and differences between your findings and those of the field. You can then code into your theory important points of connection and important disjunctures between your study and those that are embedded in the literature. Where you find connections you might draw on the findings of another study to enable you to extend the categories in your own theory. If you are doing a PhD, it will be necessary to code what your theory brings to the field of research and what its contribution is. This will be a central task in making sure you clearly demonstrate a contribution to knowledge.

Box 12-1

Suggestions for the critical use of the literature in grounded theory

- Compare and contrast the literature for ideas that can be integrated into your theory and to further modify your categories.
- Look through the literature for findings that can be used to extend your categories.
- Are there any gaps in the literature that your study can fill?
- Does the literature reinforce categories of classification that can replicate particular power relationships in your field of study? How do your participants encounter these relationships?
- Can the literature suggest other places to sample theoretically?

But there is another important aspect to engaging with the literature. Your task when doing grounded theory, just like any other study, is to be critical. We have shown throughout this book that each of our exemplars clearly expose the fact that the literature is often partial. It can act to oppress those in your field by producing categories that then become the basis for negative stereotyping. The work of Raphael (2008), Ekins (1997) and Wuest (1997a, 1997b, 1998, 2000a, 2000b, 2001) all show that the literature is as much part of the social fabric of the field and frequently generates problems with which those in your study might struggle. Is this the case? Don't simply read the literature in a neutral fashion. *Ask yourself to what extent the literature contributes to the social environment of the groups you are studying?*

Another important task for you to consider when reading the literature will be to write memos about the degree to which your findings might expose gaps in the literature. Raphael (2008) demonstrated that men were virtually excluded from research on osteoporosis and, as a consequence, the professional medical literature had served to marginalise men from this condition. This marginalisation further reinforced their position on the outside of direct concerns and served to hamper diagnosis of osteoporosis in men. This was and is something which could be life-threatening. Her analysis of the literature focused on this finding and sought to expose how illness can be the subject of feminisation processes. Finally, as Strauss and Corbin (1990) have pointed out, you can draw on the literature to access other worlds and settings that you may not have direct access to. In this sense, then, it can enable you to target your theoretical sampling by sensitising you to some of the key concepts and variables that you might find in other settings. You will, of course, have to be cautious about how you treat these literatures. Take the approach of Ekins (1997), who was able to treat several different literatures as having something to say about male femaling. These literatures were then used to fashion different contexts that the people in his study might encounter as they male femaled.

Skills and tips 12-1

Suggestions for the critical use of the literature in grounded theory

- Take a core idea in your theory and search the literature in your field by looking at research that has been written on any terms that can be associated with your theory. Your search should be systematic and should use all of the standard databases.
- Compare and contrast the literature for ideas that can be integrated into your theory and to further modify your categories.
- Look through the literature for findings that can be used to extend your categories.
- Are there any gaps in the literature that your study can fill?
- Does the literature reinforce categories of classification that can replicate particular power relationships in your field of study? How do your participants encounter these relationships?
- Can the literature suggest other places to sample theoretically?
- Google Ngrams can in fact be very useful for finding additional data slices for comparison and integration of further examples around your key terms.

Key points about integrating the literature

The position we have adopted on the literature in this chapter and in the book as a whole is in keeping with the position that others have outlined (Strauss and Corbin 1990; Dey 1999; Henwood and Pidgeon 2003; Charmaz 2006; Birks and Mills 2011). The finer point of this debate is the underlying issue of how you handle preconceptions and prior interests. In this chapter we have gone on to extend our analysis and have shown through the use of our exemplars that your use of the literature should go beyond a simple synthesis of prior evidence. We have shown that not only is the literature a source of further observations that can be used to extend your theory, but that it can also act as a system of classification that can act against those you are studying. This final point is critical.

In many respects, one of the most valuable aspects of grounded theory is that it can uncover the ways in which existing research can act as a source of categorisation and constraint in various substantive areas. We have seen in each of our exemplars that existing literature formed a component of different 'worldviews' and, as such, acted to reinforce prejudice and bias. Existing literatures were therefore not neutral and could potentially support a selective blindness which in turn could increase the risk of harm.[1] Charmaz (2006) uses the term *ideological* in her description of the research act. Here 'ideology' refers to the fact that researchers, including grounded theorists, will defend their position. This is akin to our view of prior interests. In Charmaz's view, all of these views are in some senses ideological. This is one sense of 'ideology'. In contrast to Charmaz, however, we would also contend that 'ideology' can often act *without us knowing, through our preconceptions*. It is this more problematic aspect of ideology that we would say potentially poses especially difficult problems for you when you are doing grounded theory.

One way researchers have attempted to deal with the problem that the production of grounded theory is not neutral is by involving participants more in the process of theory building. The idea is that their involvement will enable a more fit theory (see Chapter 6). Others, such as Denzin (2007), have acknowledged that knowledge is not open and it can act as a form of oppression. But then the problem becomes the degree to which this knowledge acts to change your purpose. Do you wish to avoid producing theory altogether? Is your goal directed at generating theory that can be used to inform practice? The answer to each question implies a set of presumptions. Perhaps the only answer we can have to the problem of preconceptions acting as ideology is that we have to just trust in the method and acknowledge that these factors may play a part in the production of the theory. So while we may integrate the literature and seek to modify it into our theory, we also have to acknowledge that our grounded theory may need to be modified at a later date. While it might fit and work to explain what is going on in the area in question, it remains partial and open to modification. The key points about integrating the literature are as follows:

- A central reaction within grounded theory was to research that has been derived from preconceived questions.
- Avoiding using the literature in the initial stages of your study can improve sensitivity and enable a better generation of theory from data.
- Avoiding the literature does not mean you have an empty head to begin with or that you should ignore the literature. You need to take the literature very seriously indeed.
- The problem with the literature is closely related to the problems associated with handling preconceptions and prior interests (see also Chapter 6).
- The literature can be used both against your theory and for your theory. It can be used to:
  - o establish the importance of your study as a new set of findings
  - o critique and extend the literature
  - o help you develop your categories as a fund of ideas
  - o demonstrate that the existing literature can act against your participants, as ideology and sources of classification
  - o suggest further areas for theoretical sampling.

Summary

In this chapter we have discussed the literature as a topic in grounded theory that has caused unwarranted debate and tension. We have argued that many of the main reasons for this relates to the way grounded theory handles preconceptions and prior interests. Thinking about prior interests and preconceptions is a core aspect of grounded theory and in some respects has already been covered elsewhere in the book. The purpose of this chapter was to explain why the literature is handled in the way that it is and to go beyond a simplistic view of the literature as a source of facts. The chapter followed other writers by illustrating that the literature can not only act as a source of data, but it can also be seen as a source of assumptions and systems of classification. We have advised that the literature should not be considered as a neutral phenomenon; it can often be problematic for those acting in the area under question. The chapter has attempted to illustrate how the literature has been used in each of the exemplars and provided practical advice and tips on how to position a grounded theory against and within the literature.

Skills and tips 12-2

Integrating the literature

Having specified your core category and outlined the main components of your theory, look through different literatures on the problem you are studying. To what extent do these literatures present a particular worldview that can be problematic for people who are experiencing the substantive concern you have been studying? Make detailed notes about these literatures, reflecting on what your theory can bring to the field and how it can help overcome such negative viewpoints. Make further notes on how your findings related to your own worldview at the start of the study.

Further reading

Ekins, R. (1997) 'Review of the literature from the standpoint of grounded theory', Chapter 2 in R. Ekins, *Male Femaling: A Grounded Theory Approach to Cross-Dressing and Sex-Changing*. London: Routledge.

Glaser, B. (1978) 'Theoretical sensitivity', Chapter 1 in B. Glaser, *Theoretical Sensitivity: Advances in the Methodology of Grounded Theory*. Mill Valley, CA: Sociology Press.

Glaser, B. and Strauss, A. (1967) 'Generating theory', Chapter 2 in B. Glaser and A. Strauss, *The Discovery of Grounded Theory*. Chicago: Aldine.

Wuest, J. (2000a) 'Negotiating with helping systems: an example of grounded theory evolving through emergent fit', *Qualitative Health Research*, 10(1): 51–70.

Note

1   In the work of Wuest (2000), the feminisation of caring has been found to place women at increased risk of illness. In Raphael's (2008) work, a failure to diagnose men with osteoporosis can be life-threatening, therefore failure to classify men as being at risk of osteoporosis can contribute to an increased risk of injury or death. Likewise, in Ekin's (1997) work medical views of cross-dressing and transgender can contribute to increasing morbidity among men who are male femaling.

13

Understanding How to Write Theoretically

Aim: To provide an account of how to write grounded theory for a range of audiences

Learning outcomes

After reading this chapter you should be able to:

- develop skills to enhance your awareness of monograph and paper structure and then apply these skills to your own grounded theory writing
- manage the tendency for grounded theory to use obscure and obfuscating language
- assess in advance the problems that writing for different purposes and audiences can pose
- grasp a sense of urgency for actively developing your skills in understanding monograph and paper structure, including locating where key ideas are presented and arranged

We have already touched on writing in some respects in Chapter 11 when we discussed preparations for sorting in terms of thinking whether or not you will be preparing a book, a PhD thesis or a paper or making a presentation. Writing for publication is really a burden we all carry. Think about it. You have just conducted a grounded theory study. If the claims of the methodology are correct, then you should be aware that your study will provide the field you are working in with a new perspective. You might have discovered how marginalisation occurs and how groups are treated unfairly. It is your responsibility, then, to publish your findings to try to get others to see what you have found. You may work in a field that is full of practitioners. If this is the case, it will be very important to communicate your findings to them to help change practice in some way. As you know, grounded theory comes from a time and a discipline that values the production of research monographs over other forms of scholarly activity. There is therefore very little advice on writing a PhD or journal articles. In *Theoretical Sensitivity*, Glaser (1978) focused on providing advice on writing sociological research monographs. His advice is still very pertinent.

Preparing to write: read for structure

The first thing Glaser talks about when it comes to writing is to ask us to read other monographs to discover their 'little logics' and explore how they have been constructed. This kind of reading is something that you should do with real purpose. The way to go about this is pretty straightforward. Look closely at a text that you would like to emulate in some way and explore its 'logic' of construction. He later expanded on this approach stating that what he was doing was more or less engaging in a process termed 'explication de text' (Glaser 1998). You can get hold of the little logic by looking closely for the overall goal of the paper or book. In your reading, you are really seeking to establish *how this is achieved and if the book manages to deliver it*, and then you should explore the table of contents and the larger structure of the text. Look at how it has been constructed, where are the main ideas, and so on? Go through the book. How are paragraphs formulated? Sometimes a paragraph has an opening line that indicates what the paragraph means. Then the ideas are embedded in the middle of the paragraph before the closing sentence of the paragraph takes you to the next idea. Look at how examples are used. Most examples are introduced. How extensive is the introduction? How far does the example relate or support the claims being made? How does the book handle sources? What general area of enquiry does it relate to? Finally, Glaser suggests going through the book when you have discovered what it promises to deliver and rather than reading the whole thing, read to see if it manages to carry off its promise, and if so how? By making notes on the structure of other publications you can prepare yourself for your own writing.

The same thing holds for journal articles and indeed PhDs. If you are writing a journal article it often pays to explore similar types of article in the journal you are aiming at. Look at their standards of publication. Do they use dense text with few examples? Or are the papers in the journal full of examples and less dense in terms of theory? The latter point is often the case in practitioner journals. If you are targeting a practitioner audience, you may need to think very carefully about the degree to which you densify the presentation of your theory, what this means is that you will have to think carefully at all times just how many categories you can present at any point in time. Glaser (1978) indicates that his preferred style of writing for a research monograph is to produce dense theory. It might be the case that your audience will be less tolerant of this kind of style. As Strauss and Corbin (1990) indicated, often it will be enough to present a few categories alongside details of what your findings might mean for practice. Before you start writing, take time to explore the kind of text you would like to produce and think through carefully how you will achieve something similar. You can then explore your memos and sort according to the goals you have set yourself.

Skills and tips 13-1

Reading for structure

Take a key text in the field you are working in. Read it not for its content but for how it has been written. Take time to explore how the paper or book has been structured. Identify the 'little logic' by locating the overall goal of the book (try it with this text). Explore the table of contents and the larger structure of the text. Where are the main ideas? What are its main conclusions and how are these constructed? How does the book convince? Look closely at each chapter. Where are the main ideas in each chapter? How are the paragraphs constructed? Is there more than one idea per paragraph? How does the writer move from paragraph to paragraph? Are there linking sentences that lead from one paragraph to the next? How is the supporting evidence presented (make notes on the way the examples are introduced and if they fit the claims being made)?

By reading a text to see how it has been constructed, you will be able to think carefully and in detail about how you will achieve the same thing with your text.

Avoiding obscure language

As grounded theory involves building concepts that closely articulate what is going on in the field, it is quite possible that you might struggle to build names for the concepts that have grab and which fit. It is worth taking the time to get the names of your categories right. Language that is overly complicated can be very off-putting and can put people off reading your research. An important tip is to use gerunds sparingly and only when no other conceptualisation is available. This issue has been covered by Birks and Mills (2012), who cite Sandelowski (2007) in discussing the problem of an 'acute attack of grounded theoryitis'. Sandelowski (2007) refers to the use of jargon to over-complicate the description of data analysis but also the presentation of findings in research. Her biggest complaint seems to be with the use of the word 'emerged' to describe the process of data analysis when there really is no need to over-complicate things. Her message is to try to reduce the burden on your reader. Enable them to understand your work rather than hinder them and, wherever possible, use plain language. There are, of course, times when technical language is required, but these times depend on your audience.

Writing the research monograph

Glaser (1978) advises that writing in grounded theory is a careful job of construction. His advice is to follow through your own little logic or goal carefully and in a sustained way throughout the text. He suggested that you start by introducing the nature of the problem and then outlining the most general properties of the core variable. After this, he suggested that you continue by selecting different aspects of your core variable and discussing these in turn by burrowing down into the various different variables that are related to the core variable. Strauss and Corbin (1990) likened this to walking around a statue and looking at it from different angles. If you remember, you will hopefully by now have sorted your memos into a developed framework. You will have memoed on important aspects of the literature and placed these memos at appropriate places within your memo bank. It is a case then of working through this outline, introducing your concepts and illustrating them where necessary with appropriate examples from your data. It is important to pay attention to the meaning of your categories, make sure they are clearly introduced and that they are clearly specified.

There are a number of ways to structure a research monograph. Ekins' (1997) approach is to explore the worlds of cross-dressers and to juxtapose these worlds to other 'worlds'. He begins by discussing the fact that his 'book is about males who make us hesitate. It is the outcome of seventeen years of sociological and social psychological research with males who either wear the clothes of the opposite sex for the pleasure it gives them (cross-dressers), or who wish to change sex and are actively going about it (sex-changers)' (Ekins 1997: 1). This is what Glaser (1978) would call his little logic. Ekins' theory is about the instability of gender as a social category and his approach is to show how his participants vary dramatically in their approach to cross-dressing and transgendering. His introduction outlined his approach in general and he then went on to provide a map for his book. As you can see, often the starting part of the book is where you outline the logic of the book and then provide a conceptual map for your reader to explore.

Another strategy of Ekins (1997) was to split his book between theory and practice. This is because his book was written with two audiences in mind: first, there were the sociologists interested in gendering practices; then there were those from the subculture that he was exploring. The first group is provided with an in-depth discussion of the key problems that confronted him in conducting his grounded theory. The second group is provided with an outline of the findings of his study. These findings explore the variation in strategies and experiences of the men in his study. It is when you are presenting your theory in your monograph that you will have to 'carry forward' (see Chapter 11) different concepts. In this respect you will be seeking to build up your theory by carefully taking time to relate your categories to the core category. Throughout your book, you need to provide clear examples that support your theory.

But you might also be seeking to justify your approach, as Ekins (1997) did at the start of his text. All of these logics and interests will have a varied impact on how you construct your manuscript and it is here that you will need to pay particular attention to *how* you construct your paragraphs. In the next section we will show how the audience and goals of different sections of Ekins' (1997) work affect his paragraph construction.

Pay close attention to paragraph construction

A key aspect of all writing is to pay close attention to paragraph construction. Here, there is a mini logic that you can follow and if you try to stay consistent, this can enhance the clarity of your writing. Take the following example from Ekins (1997):

> In making sense of self, identity and world, there is a constant interplay between private experiences and public knowledge. The third central theme of this book is the exploration of this interplay. Rooted, as it is, in a sociology of knowledge approach, informed principally by symbolic interactionism, this book considers the impact of publicly available knowledge about sex, sexuality and gender on the developing senses of self, identity and the world of cross-dressers and sex-changers. In particular, it considers the interrelations between scientific, subcultural and lay conceptualisations and theorisations of cross-dressing and sex-changing, and their impact on the selves, identities and worlds of male cross-dressers and sex-changers themselves.
>
> Following Goffman, Mead and Schutz, I take it that meaning frames (Goffman 1974), their constituent objects, and knowledge of both, emerge from a world 'taken for granted' (Schutz 1967), a 'world that is there' (Mead 1938). I then find it instructive to distinguish the meaning frames of science from those of 'members' (in my case cross-dressers and sex-changers themselves) and those of lay people. The empirical task then becomes to plot the interrelations between three meaning frames – more specifically to plot the interrelations between three 'knowledges': 'scientific' or 'expert' knowledge (the latter term includes legal knowledge, for example); 'member' knowledge (which would include subcultural knowledge); and 'commonsense' or 'lay' knowledge. (Ekins 1997: 20)

Note how Ekins juxtaposes the private and public dimension of his analysis in the first sentence. He then goes on to elaborate what this means and how this is thematised in his book. Note that he is writing about an 'interplay' which is then clarified in terms of the 'impact of publicly available knowledge about sex, sexuality and gender' on those who are involved in sex-changing. In other words, he is not just giving us a sense of how males female, he is also discussing his theory within this public knowledge. At the end of the first paragraph he then focuses on three worlds. In the next paragraph Ekins goes on to explain how he takes these meaning frames as clashing with those of his participants. He is quite explicit that the task of his writing is to plot the relationships between these meaning frames. The second paragraph then expands on the theoretical justification and explanation of what he is doing. This is not a descriptive passage of text; it is clearly meant for social scientists as it presents his analysis and underlying theoretical approach. The writing is dense and abstract. In the later parts of his book his writing changes. There is no need to justify the approach because here the audience is quite different. Here the writing focuses on developing the theory. The stage of consolidating male femaling is introduced and defined. Then the category is specified more in the second paragraph by linking it with the different processes of male femaling (body femaling, erotic femaling or gender femaling). One paragraph ends by specifying that consolidating femaling moves towards focusing on a particular aspect of male femaling for the future. This is then picked up in the next paragraph and the category of consolidating male femaling is further specified and we are told that some male femalers eventually go for the operation to physically become women (see Ekins 1997: 131). The culmination towards the ultimate goal of becoming female is presented as a liberation of the self and identity.

Writing up a grounded theory involves getting yourself to think theoretically, to then present the categories of your theory and illustrate them. If you are effective, you will hopefully be able to get your readers to also think through the eyes of your theory since the primary goal of writing in grounded theory is to give a theoretical account of the area under study. As you can see from the examples presented here, Ekins (1997) presents the categories and then *builds up a conceptual picture*.

All of this indicates that the audience for your work is a central determinant of the nature and style of the way you must prepare and write your grounded theory. In these examples, an academic audience is clearly being addressed in the first part of the book. This involves Ekins (1997) in a justification of his approach and a discussion of the general theoretical nature of his findings. There is a need to engage in broad debates about the status of a grounded theory and you may well find yourself having to engage in some form of justification for your categories. We stated in Chapter 11 that you can in fact prepare for your audience by asking the appropriate questions during sorting, as you integrate your theory. Asking yourself why your category is justified and preparing to provide some statements about that can, in fact, be useful. Like we said, it all depends on your audience. This could never be truer than when it comes to writing up a PhD.

Writing up PhDs

The audience of a PhD can be as varied as the audiences of books and papers. The problem you will face, however, is that the typical PhD thesis is often formalised in very specific ways. Knowing in advance what is expected will be critical in making sure that you write to those expectations. It may be that important compromises have to be endured for you to secure your PhD. As we stated previously (see Chapter 11), you need to be clear before you start your study and, critically, before you start sorting and preparing for your write up what the expectations of your examining faculty are concerning the structure and content of the PhD thesis. This involves assessing the degree of flexibility you can have for the traditional sections of the PhD, including the literature review, methodology, materials and methods, and findings and discussion sections. Remember the assessment criteria for a PhD are usually that *you must demonstrate a contribution to knowledge*. This means you will have to go beyond some of the guidelines given by Glaser (1978) in *Theoretical Sensitivity*. You will have to write your thesis with a degree of justification, despite Glaser's later complaints about worrisome accuracy (Glaser 2001, 2009). Grounded theory was originally designed to discover theory from data. The methodology tends not to focus on criteria of justification and yet you may need to engage in such activity as you write up your PhD. Do not assume that the contribution of your PhD to knowledge will be obvious. It is your task to demonstrate this.

As we have already discussed in Chapter 11, Raphael (2008) was able to compromise pretty easily by conducting and writing up a very brief literature review that highlighted several features about the topic she was investigating. She focused on the nature of her topic (osteoporosis in men) as a public health problem, highlighted through a search of the literature regarding the degree to which men had been excluded from research on the subject area, and then went on to establish the kinds of impacts the condition could have. This exercise was relatively uncomplicated but provided her with an important source of justification for her study. In addition, because she focused on the area and its features, she did not engage with any categories derived from other studies and therefore this review would not really impact on her ability to generate her theory. By conducting this review, she was then readily able to show that her theory of gendered positioning and gender shock was a meaningful contribution to the literature on gender and illness.

The presentation of her findings follows a clear logic. She begins by showing how her theory emerged by gradually building up her categories. This then prepares the way for a chapter at the end, in this chapter she proposes a theory of gendered positioning that seeks to integrate her findings (Raphael 2008). The style of presentation in a PhD is quite common, with statements illustrating her cases. These statements were taken from interviews with a sample of men who struggled to come to terms with the categorisation of their condition as that of osteoporosis. So, rather than beginning with the presentation of her theory, she gradually justifies it's development and in the end presents it as a dense theory fully integrated to explain how men come to terms with having an illness that, on the face of it, only affects women. The journey they go through becomes the focus of her theory. Her style all the way through is to provide plenty of examples, something that Glaser (1978) might have called 'incident tripping', but remember her task is to present a contribution to knowledge that is well justified. By providing her examples she was able to demonstrate that her categories were well developed and fully grounded in the data. In her discussion and conclusions Raphael (2008) went on to link her theory to other substantive areas and in doing so was able to demonstrate the general relevance of her theory by comparing her findings with those of other studies looking at gendered illnesses, such as breast cancer in men. All the way through her thesis she supported and extended her theory by drawing productively on the appropriate literature.

Writing journal articles

While the research monograph is the favoured approach to publish grounded theory, it is not the only approach in all disciplines. Some research areas place a much greater premium on journal articles. As you will know by now, the work of Wuest (1997a, 1997b, 1998, 2000a, 2000b, 2001) can be seen as a great example of how to develop a grounded theory and contribute to an area of interest. As others have advised, you should focus on one or two categories and explain how they vary, and then detail their main dimensions while at the same time outlining how they contribute to knowledge. A good starting place for publishing from your grounded theory might be to start by providing an in-depth analysis of the problem your participants are experiencing. Wuest (1997b) explored the problem as follows:

> What emerged as most problematic for women caring was the competing and changing nature of caring demands within the larger sociocultural and political structure. Women's caring demands are both internal and external, emanating from partners, children, parents, extended family and self. The basic social process, found to be employed by women to manage the problem of competing and changing demands, was named precarious ordering. Precarious ordering is a dynamic, recursive, two-stage process of moving from relative disorder in the reactive caring stage of fraying connections to the relative order of the proactive stage of setting boundaries, negotiating and repatterning care. (Wuest 1997b: 50)

As you can see, Wuest (1997b) introduces the problem of women's caring demands, outlines their nature and then specifies that they have an internal/external dimension related to 'partners, children, parents, extended family and self'. She then talks about the basic social process that was 'employed by women' to manage these demands. We are told that this was a two-stage process, moving from disorder to 'setting boundaries, negotiating and repatterning care' (Wuest 1997b). Wuest focuses on one or two core problems and this enables her to expand on the details of these aspects of her grounded theory. This theory was then extended through the theoretical sampling of women from a range of backgrounds in numerous papers.

Wuest (1997a, 1997b) clearly followed the advice of Glaser. She began by specifying the general problem and then, over time, gradually burrowed into her theory to produce greater and greater detail. You should consider doing likewise. Take time to think through your theory. Can you begin by highlighting your problem? How has this been explored elsewhere? How does the experience of it vary? By exploring this, you can go towards specifying in general terms how your theory can explain the ways in which people manage the problem.

As you can see, your strategy for journal articles needs to be thought through. The big advantage of grounded theory is that you can target very specific kinds of outputs by re-sorting your memos according to the goal you set yourself. As you do this, you can integrate your grounded theory around different categories and for different purposes by asking yourself key questions that can help you develop the paper in the direction of a specific contribution (see Box 11-1 in Chapter 11).

Skills and tips 13-2

Writing up

1. Take one of your categories and sort it for writing up by organising in a detailed plan what your key ideas are in this category.
2. Outline carefully how you will present it, including what examples you will use and why. Then draft the section, paying particular attention to where you introduce new ideas and making sure all new concepts and ideas are introduced clearly.
3. Try to use plain language and avoid strange terms.
4. Substantiate a particular claim with illustrations from your data set. Do not assume that the data speaks for itself. Rather, take time to introduce any observations and quotes by carefully locating them for your reader.
5. After drafting the section, re-read it. This time try to read it as though you have never seen it before. Is it easy to follow? Is the order right? Are the ideas introduced appropriately?

Key points about writing up

The literature on grounded theory is full of useful advice on how to write up and present your findings and you should embrace all of this advice. Birks and Mills (2011) provide excellent guidelines on how to go about presenting your theory for a thesis, monograph or journal article. Likewise, Strauss and Corbin (1990) provide lots of useful advice on how write grounded theory for different purposes. Each of these authors offers useful tips for writing, such as paying attention to detail and making sure you get the right style of presentation. In addition, Charmaz (2006) gives excellent advice on making your mark in your writing. A particular strength of Charmaz's work is her writing, which is widely read because it is so good. Her impact on the chronic illness literature has been enormous. So do pay attention to her advice. Yet despite all these wonderful contributions, there remains something missing.

One of the important things about writing up that we have uncovered in our rediscovery of grounded theory is that it is important to *develop your skills at reading how monographs, papers and books are constructed*. This involves more than thinking about your audience, as we have seen in this chapter. In redis-covering grounded theory, we have discovered that before you begin to write you might want to learn how to read for structure.[1] It is with the development of the skill and the sensitivity to explore a text for its structure that you will begin to develop your own skills for organising and presenting your grounded theory. Once you do this, you will discover that there are several ways to 'make your mark', as Charmaz (2006) has put it.

We have subsequently applied these techniques and skills to our exemplars to uncover how these have been developed to make a contribution to their respective literatures. Hopefully, you will see that this skill involves becoming sensitive to the unfolding logic of your categories, their relationships and how they are presented. It also involves paying attention to the way you move from one paragraph to the next and how you link the flow of your text. It is about the way you strategically position your findings for your audience.

The main points about writing up are therefore as follows:

- Learn to read books, papers and monographs for structure. This involves:
  - following the logic of the book's construction
  - following the 'little logics', which means exploring where the main ideas are located
  - establishing how the author moves from paragraph to paragraph. Do they link the last sentence of one paragraph to the first sentence of the next, and so on?
  - exploring how the author relates their findings to the literature. Do they critique it or add to it by adding substantive findings?
  - establishing the density of the text. Does it involve lots of examples or is it characterised by a detailed discussion of categories and their relationships?
- Pay attention to paragraph construction
- When writing a PhD, pay close attention to the regulations of your faculty.

Summary

This chapter has invited the reader to consider the challenge of writing up. It began with a look at motivations for writing grounded theory. An important motivation in grounded theory must be to change practice or to widen rele-vant audiences' access to the findings of research. The chapter then looked at

Glaser's advice regarding the construction of texts: to take the time to study how texts have been constructed and to adopt a conscious approach to writing. The chapter then provided an analysis and discussion of the sentence and paragraph construction of several texts designed for different audiences. Here we discussed the necessity to be clear when communicating grounded theory and offered some practical advice on avoiding obscure language. The chapter covered writing for monographs, PhDs and research papers.

Further reading

Birks, M. and Mills, J. (2011) 'Presenting a grounded theory', Chapter 8 in M. Birks and J. Mills, *Grounded Theory: A Practical Guide*. London: Sage.

Charmaz, K. (2006) 'Writing the draft', Chapter 7 in K. Charmaz, *Constructing Grounded Theory: A Practical Guide through Qualitative Analysis*. London: Sage.

Glaser, B. (1978) 'Theoretical writing', Chapter 8 in B. Glaser, *Theoretical Sensitivity: Advances in the Methodology of Grounded Theory*. Mill Valley, CA: Sociology Press.

Strauss, A. and Corbin, J. (1990) 'Writing theses and monographs, and giving talks about your research', Chapter 13 in A. Strauss and J. Corbin, *Basics of Qualitative Research: Grounded Theory Procedures and Techniques*. Thousand Oaks, CA: Sage.

Note

1   Birks and Mills (2011) provide some useful references to the broader debate on how to present qualitative research. This work is useful. However, it does not include details of the specific skills Glaser (1978) was talking about in *Theoretical Sensitivity.*

14

Rediscovering Formal Theory

Aim: To discuss and evaluate the development of formal grounded theory

Learning outcomes

After reading this chapter you should be able to:

- describe the range of strategies you can use to develop formal theory
- have a practical understanding of how these strategies might be deployed in developing formal theory
- have an appreciation of the importance of thinking about and developing formal theory as a fundamental part of the integrated package that is grounded theory

There is nothing more indicative of the location of grounded theory within North American sociology than the idea of generating formal theory. It is with this idea that you can begin to grasp the historical significance of *Discovery* and *Theoretical Sensitivity* as the development of a particular line of reasoning in sociology. Right from the outset, in the preface of *Discovery*, Glaser and Strauss (1967) *saw their project **as a decisive step away from a conjuncture between three different approaches***: Merton's middle-range theory, Lazarsfeld's quantitative sociology and the Chicago School. Glaser and Strauss stated that:

> [none] of these traditions – nor any other in postwar sociology – has been successful at closing the embarrassing gap between theory and empirical research. The gap is as wide today as it was in 1941, when Blumer commented on it, and in 1949, when Merton optimistically suggested a solution. (Glaser and Strauss 1967: vii)

Merton's suggestion was to produce 'middle-range theory'. By the time *Discovery* was produced, this endeavour had already gathered momentum.

There were studies of the concept of commitment (Becker 1960), social integration (Blau 1960), role strain (Goode 1960) and expressive and instrumental group structure (Marcus 1960), among other things (Bressler 1961). Glaser and Strauss (1967) placed both substantive and formal grounded theory as another version of this kind of theory (see Glaser and Strauss 1967: 32). But it is critical to note that they also broke with this tradition and the polemic at the heart of *Discovery* is very much a response to claims Merton made in *Anomie and Deviant Behavior* (Clinard 1964).

In objecting to Merton, Glaser and Strauss (1967) reacted to several claims. The main thrust of their objections was against what they felt was his desire to preserve 'speculative theory' and the undermining of qualitative research methods as unsystematic. In contrast, they believed that their approach was a much more efficient way to generate theory that would fit and work. They clearly felt that Merton's approach to the generation of theory was 'speculative' and unsystematic, and that they had hit on a method to close the theory–data gap. Their break from these traditions has implications for the way they subsequently approached both the generation of substantive theory and formal theory. The goal was not to operate with speculative theory, but to build formal 'middle-range' theories from facts towards substantive and then formal theory. Their approach, then, was contrasted with that of Merton and Parsons because they felt it was a much more systematic method than those that had gone before. They clearly had in mind a sociology of the same areas that Merton had envisaged (for example, they talked of sociological studies of loneliness, brutality, debating, bidding systems, collusion, diplomacy), but they argued for a very different approach and detailed this in *Discovery*. So what did this look like and how did it shape their specification of formal theory?

The principal difference between substantive and formal theory in grounded theory was said to be on 'levels of generality by matter of degree'. But what does this actually mean? The concept has been challenged as vague (Dey 1999). Indeed, Glaser more recently attempted to clarify the situation (Glaser 2007a). What Glaser and Strauss (1967) meant was that you might develop a substantive theory of dying as a status passage in hospital wards, and this theory might then be extended into a formal theory of status passage (Glaser and Strauss 1971). How can this be achieved? We have analysed the relevant texts where formal theory has been discussed by Glaser and Strauss (1967, 1971) and subsequently elaborated by Glaser (1978, 2007a). Although the texts themselves are full of polemical analyses, there are some positive strategies that can be developed. We have outlined these strategies in Figure 14-1.

Strategy 1: Analytical rewriting

- Can you drop the substantive content of your core category and is it relevant to other areas of research?
- Example: if you drop the 'male' from 'male femaling', is the category of 'femaling' likely to occur in other settings?

Strategy 2: Testing the generalisability of your core

- Does your core category apply elsewhere?
- What effect does applying your core category to a radically different field have on its dimensions?
- Example: If you take awareness contexts and apply them to other substantive fields, do they maintain their relevance?

Strategy 3: Generality and scope

- By selecting a different sample, how does this affect the conceptual generality of your formal theory?
- Collecting examples and data from different sources can improve the conceptual scope of your theory. Do new concepts emerge that are relevant to your theory?
- Example: Wuest (2001) extended her theory of precarious ordering to other groups of mothers and this improved the conceptual generality of her theory. She also discovered that the conflicts mothers had varied by variables such as disability and social resources.

Strategy 4: Extending and de-densifying the core

- Does shifting your core to a formal level result in the elimination of some dimensions of the core category?
- Does moving the core category to a more formal level enhance its key dimensions?
- Example: Strauss (1970) noticed one of his categories, *Status Passage* (Glaser and Strauss 1971), had general relevance beyond *Mirrors and Masks* (Strauss 1970). He combined his interest with observations in Glaser's (1964) *Organisational Careers* and the study of *Awareness of Dying* (Glaser and Strauss 1965) demonstrated that there were other kinds of 'careers', all of which had different status passages. Do the dimensions of your core category extend beyond relevance to that core?

Strategy 5: Theoretical sampling

- Are there a wide variety of sources for theoretical sampling that you can mine for comparisons?
- By taking your core category and placing it within different sets of observations, how does this modify your theory?
- Example: Femaling placed within Riot Grrl culture results in the generation of a new mode of femaling called subversive femaling. The mode of femaling involves a subversion of female stereotypes and can be expressed in body femaling. The comparisons we derived from the literature suggested that body femaling as a consequence of subversive femaling tended to be less permanent than in male femaling, although other examples might extend our analysis further.

Figure 14-1 Strategies for developing formal theory

Generating formal theory

In *Discovery*, Glaser and Strauss (1967) were very careful to point out that formal grounded theory was very much something they were developing. This was something that was later picked up by Glaser (1978, 2007a). In what follows, we will go through each of the analytical techniques that they suggested would be relevant for developing formal theory. Some of these techniques have been extended from the basic techniques of grounded theory, such as data slicing and theoretical sampling. Others are new suggestions that we feel are nonetheless relevant for the development of theory at this level.

Analytical rewriting to formal theory

The first thing Glaser (1978) suggested was to remove the substantive reference of the theory. For example, in their study of dying in hospital wards, they clearly had a substantive focus on status passage as dying. By removing the dying reference, Glaser and Strauss (1967, 1971) were able to justify studying status passage more generally in terms of its impact on other areas of social life, such as working in organisations or going through formal education. Likewise, comparative failure in a scientific career could also be seen as comparative failure in marriage, religion, and so on. Clearly, one possible first step in generating formal theory is analytical. It involves exploring if the substantive focus of the original category can be deleted and if the resulting category can be substituted, at least in thought, to other substantive areas. So the first stage of analysis to generate a formal theory is to simply remove substantive references and then think carefully about where you might find similar processes.

Have a look at our exemplars. You can very quickly see that many of them have general categories that may be used to develop a formal theory. A particular theme seems to cut across many of them, that of gender. Ekins (1997) indicated that his substantive theory of male femaling could be developed into a formal theory of 'gendering'. Indeed, perhaps a more formal theory of 'gendering' lies behind Raphael's (2008) theory of gendered positioning in illness. Certainly her concept of 'gender shock' could be interpreted as one possible conceptual contribution to such a theory. It is not hard to see how the reactions of revulsion and curiosity of the general public to cross-dressing and sex-changing in men could be a manifestation of such 'gender shock'. Finally, isn't the whole social structural process of 'caring' (Wuest 2001) related in some way to formal processes of gendering?

A good way to test the process of analytical rewriting would be to explore Wuest's (2001) concerns about the claim that her theory of precarious ordering can be seen as a formal theory of coping with caring demands. We feel she is right to express reservations about expanding her theory in this way. If we adopt the approach suggested by Glaser and Strauss (1967, 1971) and Glaser (1978), then clearly she has not quite achieved the analytical step necessary to break out of the substantive area of 'caring' into a more general theory of pre-carious ordering. That step can be taken, however, by simply removing the reference to 'caring' and 'women' and asking if we might be able to see similar processes elsewhere. We think the answer would be a resounding 'yes'. Much of the stress of working in an academic institution could be explained by setting boundaries, negotiation and repatterning relationships. Part of the reason for this is because the structure of the job requires each academic to perform several roles, usually teaching, administration and research. Trying to balance these roles can be quite demanding and much of the stress of the job is not unlike the kinds of fraying connections we see in Wuest's theory. But we certainly agree with Wuest and Glaser and Strauss that such thought experiments are not enough. A more sustained approach to exploring formal theory generation is of course required. This step was proposed by Glaser and Strauss (1967, 1971) and Glaser (1978) through a modification of the comparative method.

Skills and tips 14-1

Formalising strategies

Take one of your categories and try the strategies outlined in Figure 14-1, Strategies for developing formal theory. Can the category be generalised beyond the substantive area you are working on? Does it have potential to form part of a more formal theory?

Constant comparative analysis and formal theory

Glaser and Strauss (1967, 1971) and Glaser (1978)[1] continued to generalise the comparative method when they took it beyond the comparison of organisational units towards more general 'conceptual' units:

> As a general method for generating theory, comparative analysis takes on its fullest generality when one realizes its power applied to social structural units of any size, large or small, ranging from men or their roles, through groups, organizations, to the nations or world regions.

> Comparative analysis can also be used to compare conceptual units of a theory or theories, as well as data, in terms of categories and their properties and hypotheses. Such conceptual comparisons result, as we have seen, in generating, densifying, and integrating the substantive theories into a formal theory by discovering a more parsimonious set of concepts with greater scope. (Glaser 1978: 150)

As you can see, what Glaser was talking about was comparing 'conceptual' units of theory as well as data so you can compare different status passages, patterns of loneliness, and bidding systems, among other things. The argument is that you need to consider the main categories of your theory and see if they have relevance beyond the area you are working in. Glaser (1978) outlined a number of further procedures for theoretical sampling for formal theory. The first stage was to sample from *any* groups that might be relevant. Theoretical sampling was therefore radicalised beyond the substantive field, the goal being to generate as many ideas as possible. Here again, the idea of 'slices of data' that had first been developed in *Discovery* returned to enable the process of generation of theory. Slices of data might be formed from a wide variety of cases. These slices would not have been directly comparable, something that would have been necessary in a verification study. For generating formal theory, however, this variety would be highly beneficial because it would yield more information on categories. Glaser went on to say that slices of data that could be used in formal theory as opposed to substantive theory would be the 'anecdotal comparison' (Glaser 1978: 151). Comparisons of the latter kind were clearly seen as useful for generating ideas.

Comparisons between different groups were encouraged for the generation of formal theory. Indeed, it was made clear that the principle use of these should be to generate ideas about how a category might vary. The researcher was to avoid worrying if groups were comparable and to focus on sources of variation, including important qualifying conditions for different categories (Glaser and Strauss 1967, 1971; Glaser 1978). The idea was to focus on comparisons that would (a) help develop the generality of the emerging theory, and (b) improve the conceptual scope of the theory by making it apply to a much broader range of populations. This is all well and good, but what might it actually look like?

Thankfully, we already have some excellent examples of just how you can achieve this. Wuest (1997a, 2000a, 2000b, 2001) expanded the conceptual scope of her developing theory by sampling progressively more diverse populations. She was able to explore how groups with few resources might be faced with being able to handle increasing caring demands. The scope of her theory was therefore extended. But as she sampled and analysed more and more data, the 'conceptual generality' of her emerging theory was also enhanced by, for example, collecting data from a sample of mothers who were caring for children with increasing physical and mental needs. By improving the scope and generality of her sampling, she was able to see how increasing physical demands could lead to negative health impacts. The generality of her theory was therefore expanded to include more theoretical categories than previously. These relationships were also discovered to have a much greater variety. So, for example, the conflicts experienced by middle-class mothers who were caring for physically and mentally disabled children tended to be directed at securing adequate health and educational services whereas mothers from deprived backgrounds tended to be in conflict with services in order to satisfy basic needs, such as food and clothing (Wuest 2001).

We can ask more questions of Wuest's (2001) approach. It is not hard to see that perhaps this theory might have been greatly enhanced by collecting data from a sample of men who were involved in caring. This kind of sampling would have enabled much more dramatic comparisons that may have exposed more about the gendered nature of caring and how gendered assumptions can impact on handling caring demands. Another comparison might have been along the dimension of formal and informal caring, for example, comparing how professionals involved in caring (e.g. nurses) cope with the demands of caring compared to informal carers (e.g. spouses).

Glaser and Strauss (1971) go on to talk about the comparison of non-comparable groups as a possible technique for generating formal theory. They argued that you can compare fire departments and emergency wards because both deal with emergencies. Such comparisons must often 'be explained on a higher conceptual level. For example, one could start developing a formal theory of social isolation by comparing four apparently unconnected monographs: Blue Collar Marriage, The Taxi Dance Hall, The Ghetto, and The Hobo. All deal with facets of "social isolation"' (Glaser 1978: 152). Here we can see that the suggestion is to engage in a systematic comparison of existing research in the published literature. This is where the flexibility of grounded theory, *as a process for generating theory*, comes into its own.

Another associated process of generating formal theory involves the reduction in density of theoretical categories as you move from substantive to the formal level. What Glaser (1978) meant by this was that as the theory becomes more abstract, it will become necessary to dispense with dimensions of your categories that no longer apply to the level that you are specifying your theory. A key aspect of generating formal theory is the process of 'de-densification'. This is something that Glaser and Strauss experienced when they developed their formal theory of *Status Passage*. An important consequence of de-densification, they argued, meant that it would be impossible for a formal theory to be fully saturated. Rather, the implication was that such theory was useful for others to enable them to develop their theory (see Glaser and Strauss 1971: 190–191).

It should be clear by now that Glaser and Strauss (1967) had in mind a process of working to a greater degree of generalisation from substantive to the formal theory. Glaser (2007) later revisited this idea and specified some more aspects of this process. He argued that your goal should be to generalise the core category, not to discover a new core category. Therefore, you should seek to conduct each of these operations on the core category as you seek to improve its generality by conducting each of the techniques above and looking at the category within different substantive areas. In this way, the core category can act to control the process of abstraction by de-densifying and extending your analysis. So what does he mean?

> We shall illustrate by outlining what can be more fully seen about a rather 'dense'
> analysis in one of our books. If we conceive of dying as a passage between sta-
> tuses, then its major properties appear to be: dying is almost always unscheduled;
> the sequence of steps is not institutionally prescribed; and the actions of the vari-
> ous participants are only partly regulated. Quite relevant also is that dying (though
> not necessarily death itself when it comes) is usually defined as undesirable and is
> usually involuntary. (Glaser and Strauss 1971: 8–9)

As we can see, Glaser and Strauss (1971) discuss how previous work had hinted that status passage may have more general implications (Strauss 1970). This work included *Awareness of Dying* (Glaser and Strauss 1965), *Mirror and Masks* (Strauss 1970) and *Organizational Scientists* (Glaser 1964). By comparing each of their previous studies, they were able to discover that the category of status passage could be written as a formal theory. They combined their observations from each of these studies and discussed how to develop status passage. They discovered, for example, that when they were studying dying patients in hospitals they were dealing with an organisational career, but at the same time an illness career. By comparing the different types of career, they discovered that the status can be either scheduled or non-scheduled.

Theoretical sampling and formal theory

The key point about theoretical sampling for the generation of formal theory is to seek out wide sources of data. Once again the maxim is comparisons for the development of ideas. In this respect, Glaser (2007) indicated that reading wide sources of data and studies on similar categories would be permitted as sources for comparison. In other words, getting hold of a good reader that related to the category was permitted (Glaser 2007: 85). In doing so, pay attention to the impact of transferring categories from one theoretical context to the next. Your catego-ries will need to be modified and this means you may have discovered an impor-tant dimension of such categories in the new context. When such comparisons generate further dimensions for categories, it is necessary to check these dimensions for their generality.

There are two ways this can be achieved. First, you can follow your core category while comparing and contrasting how it behaves in different contexts. Second, you can follow the main dimensions of your core category derived from your substantive theory and see how they behave in different contexts. The best way to explain this is with a few examples. Let's take the concept of 'male femaling'. In Ekins (1997) study it is part of a substantive theory. As we have seen, we can analytically rewrite the theory by removing the male refer-ence. That is one strategy to see if the category has the potential to be applied in other substantive fields. The category of femaling, if it has general potential, should perform differently in different contexts. The following comparisons will enable us to illustrate this point. Take the following incident from Ekin's monograph:

> In this case the erotic femaler gets maximum sexual excitation by becoming the stereotypical erotic female, the 'sexy hooker'.
>
> The gender femaler, on the other hand, tends to move in the opposite direction. Residual fetishisms may recede. In this case his fascination with the whole world of the feminine now knows no bounds. He wants to look like and behave like a 'real' woman (as he sees women), not some stereotypical male fantasy of one. This may entail the steady development of his femme self with her own personality, tastes and enthusiasms. (Ekins 1997: 132)

Male femalers vary in the way that they handle the female stereotype: body femaling has an erotic component and an attraction to the stereotype whereas gender femaling is directed at being female and often rejects the stereotype as superficial. Both approaches have material consequences for doing femaling: erotic femaling involves sexual excitement from role-playing whereas gender femalers get excitement from being female. Now take this concept of femaling and apply it to a completely different subculture – 'Riot Grrls'. Riot Grrls are a third-wave feminist punk rock movement who also do things with female stereotypes. Their main goal is to subvert these in an attempt to re-express femininity (Belzer 2004; Krolokke and Sorensen 2005). Here we searched through the literature on Riot Grrls. This literature is literally full of incidents that can be used for constant comparative analysis to develop femaling as a category that can be placed outside the context of the original substantive theory on male femaling. A few examples should help us illustrate the point. On the one hand, the term 'grrl' is an attempt to reclaim the formerly derogatory term 'girl':

> giving it growl and bite, and thereby transgressing the connotations of 'girl'. ... 'Grrl' cannot be separated from 'girl', because it involves criticism of the other term ('girls' are weak, emotional, immature, etc.) but also an identification that again implicates a generational and philosophical distancing to 'woman' ('Women' are mature, second-wave feminists, older, etc.). This doubled identification and opposition gives rise to a new term with an entirely different meaning ('grrls' are strong, assertive, feminine, empowered, etc.). Thus the use of the word 'grrl', we would say, articulates a performative desire of agency and action, while at the same time performatively delivering a criticism of both sexism and feminism. (Krolokke and Sorenson 2005: 139–140)

By drawing on this analysis, we can see that femaling, for some groups of women, also involves rejecting aspects of the female gender stereotype. The elements being rejected are the perceived aspects of femininity, such as passivity and weakness. We can then suggest an extension of the category of femaling by articulating these relationships and knowing that people do things with stereotypes. Femaling in a more general sense then involves either an active engagement with female stereotypes, as in erotic male femaling, rejecting female stereotypes, as in gender male femaling, or a *subversion of female stereotypes*, as in Riot Grrl culture. By taking the category of femaling we are able to see how it performs within a different context and, as a consequence, we can see how it might be developed into a more general category. This analysis can be extended. Ekins (1997), drawing on the spirit of grounded theory, argues that male femaling is not simply a way of communicating. It is also a way of being. By searching through the literature on the Riot Grrl subculture, we found another incident that can enable us to extend femaling further.

> Perhaps the most interesting and subversive way Riot Grrrls used their bodies to overturn gender norms was their practice of writing traditionally negative words used to describe women on their bodies. This technique has several purposes: first, it provided a way for girls to connect; and second, it was a way to preempt the thoughts of a male-dominated society about assertive women. ... 'Women are on constant display, everywhere, as semen receptacles. The 'gaze,' when it comes to women, is real; Riot Grrrls write BITCH, RAPE, SLUT and WHORE on their bodies because that's what a lot of men already see there,' says one scholar. Indeed, Hanna claimed that writing such words on her body was akin to 'holding up a mirror to what [guys] were thinking.' In this way Riot Grrrls were able to destabilize the objectifying gaze, directly challenging the men who looked at them. (Belzer 2004: 86)

This is a fascinating example and shows that subversive femaling can have the added dimension of body femaling. Like Ekins (1997), males who female also engage in body femaling, but in contrast to some males who female, those subverting femaling 'write' on their bodies. But we should note that such changes are less permanent than having surgery to become a woman. Is this always the case? After all, would subversive femaling involve permanent tattoos with the words like 'SLUT', 'WHORE' on their bodies? Only further sampling could help us modify this category further. Nonetheless, the incident suggests that there might be more dimensions to subversive femaling, such as the degree of play involved in this mode of femaling, and political statements are always in some senses contingent or temporary.

Some preliminary conclusions

We hope that Figure 14-1 and the examples given here can show you how to move your core category out of its substantive area and explore how it might hold or perform under different circumstances. Also note how moving it out of the substantive context *modified* the core rather than refuted it. Another consequence is that often comparisons using incidents taken from different literatures cannot be controlled as easily as, say, further theoretical sampling. Glaser (2007) noted that this had unavoidable consequences for our ability to integrate formal grounded theory. This last point is particularly important and one worth exploring in more depth.

Status Passage is full of fascinating examples of comparisons of diverse incidents derived from many different contexts. While the approach to develop the comparisons was controlled, Glaser and Strauss (1971) were not able to show that the theory was fully integrated. Instead, they presented the formal theory as a series of different, interrelated themes. The guidance they gave was that in thinking about the integration of your formal theory you might want to consider formal models (process, structure) as the basis on which to build your integration (see Glaser and Strauss 1971: 180). They discovered that one additional advantage of their formal theory *Status passage* was that it could in fact be coded down into a new substantive theory. In Chapter 8 they turned to comparisons that focused on status passage and its relationship to social mobility. According to them, when it comes to an analysis of social mobility, three principal issues need to be considered: the time spent trying to achieve or prevent mobility; the rate of movement up or down; and the frequency with which people engage in actions to try to modify their mobility. The following excerpt is a good example of a comparison that was aimed at specifying male mobility and status passage:

> Those who remember Budd Schulberg's What Makes Sammy Run will easily recognize that one characteristic of this driven man was his continuous, round-the-clock, effort to 'reach the top.' In committing himself to that goal, Sammy simultaneously committed himself to unceasing total effort. Virtually every act was subordinate to his enterprise. All contradictory impulses or desires were sternly repressed. Even time that he spent with acquaintances or women was converted into a means for getting ahead; that is one reason why he could be read as excessively manipulative, calculating, and self-centered. If, now, we change direction downward and consider how a working class family manages to keep its balance just above 'the poverty line,' we see that a similar commitment of virtually total time may be necessary. Commitment of time can range from total to negligible, and vary tremendously for different phases of climbing and falling (or standing still). Different persons who are implicated in a man's mobility may agree or disagree about the necessity for amounts of time committed. And everyone concerned may rethink decisions about temporal commitments. (Glaser and Strauss 1971: 158)

In this example, both men show total commitment to maintain their status but one has fewer resources than the other and, as a consequence, may find himself struggling to maintain his low status. This comparison then leads to the statement that describes how commitments of time vary (from total to negligible) in totality, but also for different 'phases' of either 'climbing' or 'standing still'. They lead into the next phase of their analysis and show how the 'different persons' mentioned above can affect someone's mobility by drawing on an example of how someone may be forced to 'juggle' a demanding home life and how this might hold him back. But then how do other people avoid such commitments so they do not have to juggle (Glaser and Strauss 1971: 162–163). Here, then, the frequency through which people attempt to engage with climbing the status ladder can vary and be limited by their commitments. The use of the theoretical samples enabled them to describe how these aspects of the theory interrelate. The important point about this is that clearly a formal theory can be 'coded down' into a substantive theory and we should also note how such coding down can modify and change our categories.

A few things remain to be said about generating formal theory. First, you can see theoretical sampling involves collecting comparative incidents from the literature. In this respect the literature becomes an important source of incidents for integration into your theory rather than a source of comparison for similarities and differences (Glaser 2007). You can also see that the primary technique you will be engaging in when generating your formal theory will be writing memos on the incidents derived from reading the literature. You will be less likely to be involved collecting data and analysing it, although further data collection is not ruled out. Writing these memos can be challenging. You are working at a very different level of generality and, as a result, will find that the comparisons can be counter-intuitive; it may take some time to integrate them into your theory. Other comparisons might be easy to make, but the less obvious comparisons are often the most revealing. Finally, it is important when engaging in comparisons at this very general level that you do not 'redescribe' the incidents but that you make a genuine effort to develop the categories. It is all too easy to become obsessed with the accuracy of comparisons and then fail to adequately compare.

Skills and tips 14-2

Moving categories

Take your core category and remove any reference from it that applies to your theory. Now, can your category be transferred to another unit, organisation or setting? Now make notes on what happens to the category when you do this. Now take the main relationships that exist to your core category. Which dimensions can be moved to the new context and survive? Which no longer apply? Write about your observations on this. What happens in relation to the overall position of your theory when you move it in this way?

Key points about formal theory

The desire to build formal theory is perhaps the most promising but least understood aspect of grounded theory.[2] Throughout this book we have made repeated references to formal theory *as an integrated part of doing grounded theory*. The very idea of 'data slicing' that is central to developing theoretical sensitivity and improving your skills in analysis is as fundamental to building a substantive theory as it is to building a formal theory. We do not think it is possible to separate formal theory off from substantive theory. On reading Strauss and Corbin (1990), you will find that formal theory is only mentioned in passing. It is as though the intention of Glaser and Strauss (1967) to suggest a more systematic way to build 'middle-range theory' has been forgotten. Perhaps the increasing operationalism of the grounded theory literature in recent years has served to take the method out of its context and present it as a series of rules? In the process of doing this, it appears that we have forgotten that a key aspect of grounded theory, as it was intended, was to participate in building a particular kind of theory. This barely gets a mention today.

The key points about formal theory are that:

- considerations of formal theory are part of the integrated whole of grounded theory; thinking about formal theory is fundamental to building substantive theory
- data slicing is a key technique for generating formal ideas about substantive theory, but it is not satisfactory on its own
- formal theory is built out of a process of constant comparative analysis involving:

  o removing the substantive reference point of the theory and checking to see if the same phenomena can be seen in other substantive fields
  o establishing if the main categories of your theory can be applied to other fields
  o exploring if the theory and its categories can be applied to other groups; such comparisons are done with the goal of theory generation in mind, not verification

- it involves theoretical sampling in different substantive fields to see if the same phenomenon can be observed in the field, such observations involve:

  o carefully monitoring of how the categories that are moved in this way behave under the new conditions and memoing about this behaviour
  o carefully watching how the dimensions of your categories behave in the new context. Do the dimensions survive or are they removed when the category moves substantive field?

- formal theory will more often than not involve reading other literature or documents from a different field to secure different incidents for analysis
- there are key strategies for developing formal theory and these are detailed in Figure 14-1.

Summary

There is no more neglected an area in grounded theory than the issue of formal theory. This chapter has attempted to resurrect formal theory as a workable strategy integral to the grounded theory project as a whole. It has placed formal theory back within the context of Merton's middle-range theory, although here we have also demonstrated that grounded theory sought to move beyond middle-range theory. The chapter then sought to provide the interested reader with a range of practical strategies for the development of formal theory. These strategies range from activities such as removing the substantive reference of the theory to enable the researcher to observe how the core category might behave if it was moved into another formal field of research. The chapter demonstrated that a principal effect of formalising a grounded theory is de-densification, where dimensions of the theory are dropped as the categories become more general. It also showed how these strategies can be used to critique and extend existing grounded theories and provided a way to enable the recombination of existing grounded theories by comparing existing theoretical categories across substantive fields.

Further reading

Glaser, B. (1978) 'Generating formal theory', Chapter 9 in B. Glaser, *Theoretical Sensitivity: Advances in the Methodology of Grounded Theory*. Mill Valley, CA: Sociology Press.

Glaser, B. and Strauss, A. (1967) 'From substantive to formal theory', Chapter 4 in B. Glaser and A. Strauss, *The Discovery of Grounded Theory*. Chicago: Aldine.

Glaser, B. and Strauss, A. (1971) *Status Passage*. Mill Valley, CA: Sociology Press.

Wuest, J. (2001) 'Precarious ordering: toward a formal theory of women's caring', *Health Care for Women International*, **22**(1–2): 167–193.

Notes

1   It is worth noting that Glaser (1978) more or less copied Chapter 9 out of *Status Passage* for his chapter in *Theoretical Sensitivity*.

2   Dey (1999) explores formal theory for the degree to which it handles the distinctions between nomothetic and idiographic analysis, between intensive and extensive analysis, and discovers that neither really apply. What he failed to analyse sufficiently was that one key reaction within grounded theory was to Merton's desire to see much more theory of the middle range. Beyond this, we have also demonstrated throughout this book that when you do grounded theory, thinking about formal theory is integral to how you do it. There is therefore no real justification for artificially separating formal and substantive theory.

15

Rediscovering Grounded Theory: Back to the Future

In some senses this book represents a bit of an adventure. In undertaking this adventure we hope to reinvigorate grounded theory by rediscovering the context within which it was developed. In doing so, we have been seeking to present grounded theory in a new way, one that seeks to capture what made the method so refreshing at the time when it was written. In some respects *this book is an act of forward looking preservation*. Sure, it looks back, but our view is firmly to the future of grounded theory. In this final chapter, we would like to make a few, albeit brief, observations.

Throughout this book we have stated that methodological pluralism in grounded theory is something that should be welcomed. While this perspective does carry risks, we feel that the advantages outweigh the risks. A pluralist approach to grounded theory will ensure the method survives as standards of scientific enquiry change. It will also enable the application of grounded theory methods to new forms of data analysis, for example, visual data (Konecki 2009), and alternative theoretical frameworks, for example, feminism (Wuest 1995). In this respect, grounded theory approaches can meaningfully contribute to the use of new and emerging forms of data by using these data and commenting on them. It can also contribute critically to the use of numerous theoretical perspectives. It is not hard to see that this has already been happening. There is little reason to believe that the situation will be any different in the future.

In adopting this approach, however, we also have sympathy for anxieties concerning 'method slurring' (Baker, Wuest et al. 1992) and a perceived slip into postmodernism (Annells 1996; Mills, Chapman et al. 2007). The fact that there are a multitude of studies that claim the grounded theory label but bear little resemblance to grounded theory is something everyone working with grounded theory recognises as a problem. So while we embrace the advantages of methodological pluralism, we in no way condone an anything-goes approach. The debate within grounded theory concerning what it is, is a serious debate, and one that needs to be resolved. We hope this might be done *without* having to resort to developing some kind of 'grounded theory police'. How might this be achieved?

One way to resolve the tensions within grounded theory is to encourage a positive debate about quality. There is a need for consensus on what grounded theory is. This consensus should not try to construct 'straw man' versions of grounded theory, but should engage in a positive process of specification and definition. We have already taken some tentative steps towards this in Chapter 2, but we would never claim that the process can end there. Tools such as the crib sheet in Box 6-2 might be developed into a more generally agreed tool that could be applied in systematic reviews of the quality of grounded theory studies. In a second sense, then, we are arguing for the development of an appreciation of exemplary grounded theory research and systematic reviews of the overall quality of the field. This approach can be applied to each of the different versions of the method. We are mindful, however, that these kinds of activities require some form of consensus. It might therefore be necessary to have a consensus conference on grounded theory. This brings us to our next point.

We firmly believe that alternative versions of grounded theory should be encouraged. In Chapter 3, we have sought to demonstrate how this might be achieved through a critical evaluation of constructivist grounded theory. We took as our starting point the work of Charmaz (2000) and Bryant (2003) and sought to extend their analysis through a discussion of the ontological and epistemological aspects of constructivism. This included an appreciation of the problem of universals and a reflection on what this means for how we might conduct grounded theory differently. We also explored the compromises and dilemmas involved in developing a constructivist grounded theory and proposed a detailed framework for developing this. While our approach is critical, it is also positive, and results in the proposal of a framework for constructivist grounded theory (see Table 3-1). We achieved this by proposing that the adoption of the method to other approaches can be achieved. This means there is a more general sense within which we can understand grounded theory. By exploring constructivist grounded theory in this way and embracing methodological pluralism, the task of clarifying and rediscovering grounded theory becomes even more urgent. We then moved forward from this by engaging in a sustained rediscovery of grounded theory.

The sociological imagination and rediscovering grounded theory

It should now be obvious that one of our core inspirations for rediscovering grounded theory is that it emerged from the sociological imagination. This book is the first sustained analysis of the origins of the method from this perspective.

In re-examining the method within the context from which it was developed, we can see for the first time that grounded theory owes a lot of its language and approach to a debate it was having with those writing in *Sociologists at Work* (Hammond 1964). It also owes a lot to the comparative tradition in sociology – something not many authors appear to have recognised.

One of the key innovations of grounded theory was the radicalisation of the comparative method. Our analysis goes beyond this, however. For the first time we can address some of the widely accepted views about grounded theory and attempt to provide a more detailed diagnosis of the origins of the method. For example, there is a commonly held argument that grounded theory contained seeds of the later split between Glaser and Strauss because it was developed out of a compromise between the Columbian and Chicago Schools (Dey 1999). This is only part of the picture. Our analysis has shown that *Discovery*, as a text, was written *against* certain approaches to building theory. It was *discontinuous* in very important respects with both the Columbian and Chicago Schools of thinking. It is in *the breaks with these previous traditions that grounded theory becomes distinctive.*

We have found that the techniques of theory building in grounded theory derive their main inspiration from the sensitising approach to the concepts of Blumer rather than the definitive conceptual approach of Lazarsfeld. Nonetheless, grounded theory was inspired by Lazarsfeld's concept indicator model, although, as we have seen, Glaser and Strauss (1967) reversed the direction of analysis in their newly proposed constant comparative method. Instead of beginning with concepts and deductively seeking out indicators, as Lazarsfeld advised us to do, Glaser and Strauss (1967) argued for categories to be developed out of rigorous comparisons of indicator to indicator. This was to be achieved by exploring the commonalities and differences that could be observed in such comparisons – from the ground up.

While we set out to analyse the original texts and to study the writing context at the time, we have also conducted an analysis of what has been written about grounded theory since. In this analysis we would like to suggest that the discontinuities in grounded theory developed, not because the original method was inspired by different schools of thinking, but because it was generalised beyond its context. Strauss and Corbin (1990) deliberately wrote about grounded theory as a general qualitative method and, as such, it became increasingly characterised by operationalism. It became associated with techniques and procedures rather than a way of thinking. This had two effects. First, it resulted in the 'forgetting' of certain aspects of the original method. The sociological imagination was dropped. One consequence of this is that data collection and analysis became less focused on social units of analysis. A kind of methodological individualism emerged. Gone were the references to social units of analysis and gone was the social dimension. Second, by removing the context of the operations and procedures in grounded theory the method seems to have taken an objectivist appearance. It is this objectivism that Charmaz

(2000), in particular, was reacting against. We have argued, however, that this objectivism should not be attributed to the original method. Grounded theory was developed at the time when the influence of positivism was declining and methodological pluralism developing. Grounded theory is part of the latter movement, not the former.

So for us, no matter how much grounded theory has been generalised beyond its original context, an essential aspect of the heritage of the method is its sociological origins. What we have shown in this book is that, by forgetting these origins, some of the practical inspiration behind the techniques of grounded theory has been lost. This, we feel, is to the detriment of grounded theory as a method. It makes for poorer grounded theory. In large part, then, our rediscovery of grounded theory also involves a rediscovery of a whole set of procedures and techniques of theory building that appear to have been ignored or lost as the method was developed. As the context of grounded theory was stripped away, so were important figures of thought that were fundamental to it.

So, for example, we have shown the value of paying close attention to the unit of analysis. In recent years too many grounded theory studies consider only individuals with different characteristics for sampling. While this might be an efficient method for sampling, it is less good for enabling us to think theoretically. We would like to push this point further. The generalisation of grounded theory to the point where it was moved beyond its original context also risks removing particular forms of theoretical sensitivity from grounded theory. In this respect there is too little discussion of sensitivity to the kinds of data one might collect and, indeed, what constitutes data when building theory in the grounded theory literature. Innovations such as those proposed by Konecki (2009) are to be welcomed. In addition, virtually no one demonstrates sensitivity to the technique of data slicing as fundamental to building categories. We hope that by rediscovering aspects of grounded theory such as these that we have opened up some of the lost art of the method and that these techniques are found to be especially helpful for building your own categories.

If, however, forgetting the sociological legacy in grounded theory has been to the detriment of it as a method, it has also been to the detriment of grounded theory as a project. Part of our rediscovery of grounded theory has uncovered that it was developed as a new way to theorise in sociology. The main goal of the method was not to produce ever more refined techniques for the collection and analysis of data. These techniques are of course important, but they are not more important than the knowledge the method was supposed to generate.

Grounded theory has produced research findings and outputs that have been counted among the most fundamental in their respective fields. The work of Charmaz (1991a, 1991b, 1992) is a case in point. Charmaz has produced some of the most widely cited and used empirical studies in the accounts of illness litera-ture. Likewise, the work of Ekins (1997) is also considered fundamental to the transsexual and transgender literature. This point should not be taken lightly. In the relatively recent *Sage Handbook of Grounded Theory*, Anthony Bryant and Kathy Charmaz (2007) argued that grounded theory had become the pre-eminent qualitative research method despite the fact that it remains heavily contested (Bryant and Charmaz 2007). But is grounded theory's legacy only to be articu-lated in relation to its usefulness as a method? Surely the contribution of grounded theory should be understood through the status of its findings and its position on theory and theorising?

Can we speak of a 'grounded theory' perspective?

There has been so much conflict in grounded theory over the nature of the techniques and the process of doing grounded theory that no one has stopped to ask if there is in fact a discernible grounded theory perspective. Looking closely at the exemplars in this book, it is quite clear that when the grounded theory approach is used, it can contribute a distinctive perspective. This should not be jettisoned without careful consideration of what we might lose. What, if anything, is distinctive about the grounded theory perspective?

If you go back through our analysis of constructivist grounded theory in Chapter 3, you will see that we have made a number of important observa-tions about what might be lost if we only focus on the meaning of phenom-ena for individuals. What we might lose is that people are *frequently acting towards and reacting against the meanings things have for them*. Society pro-duces categories of, for example, what it means to be female. Such categories generate a myriad of problems for those who do not identify with these forms of categorisation, or who are excluded from them (Ekins 1997). They can also produce a kind of 'gender blindness' to the point where people who develop diseases that are only associated with one or other gender fail to recognise that they have a condition. This can often have life-threatening consequences (Raphael 2008). Grounded theory, as it was originally intended, seeks to articulate these encounters and to generate theory that exposes the relationship between social categorisation and strategic action. The grounded theory perspective exposes much of what people do for and against the cat-egories that society generates. Social categories generate or perhaps reflect problems that people attempt to constantly resolve by typically engaging in a series of practical strategies. A method that enables us to access this world is worth preserving.

Taking this general inspiration, then, perhaps we should take much more seriously the development of a unified grounded theory perspective? One way to achieve this might be to develop a reflection process in grounded theory by enabling reviews of quality. But this approach would also enable reviews that seek to synthesise findings from numerous grounded theory studies. The goal of synthesising the myriad of findings from grounded theory studies may well produce what could be called a formal grounded theory perspective. To this end, we have taken the time to carefully distil the positive strategies that can be used to generate formal grounded theory. It is hoped that this distillation will enable the eventual discovery of a grounded theory perspective. In doing so, we might in fact find that much more remains to be discovered about grounded theory.

Glossary

Axial coding is associated with Strauss and Corbin's book, *Basics of Qualitative Analysis* (1990). It involves attempting to 'put the data back together' by making connections between categories. This happens through the use of a coding scheme that involves specifying the causes, consequences and conditions of a category.

Category a stand-alone element of a theory.

Code a word or set of words used to summarise what is going on in data. Codes are used to group together similar incidents during coding.

Coding the process of breaking data into incidents and grouping them together under codes.

Comparative method a general approach in sociology associated with the work of classical writers such as Durkheim and Weber. It is associated with the analysis of social processes across different social units compared to each other on the basis that they hold key characteristics in common. By varying some aspects of the comparison, the method tries to establish what makes such social processes vary.

Concept a general entity used to specify or define an element of a scientific theory. Concepts in grounded theory have two major features. First, they should be linked to concrete entities; this is their *analytic* function. Secondly, they should enable the reader to have a direct link to the area under question; this is their *sensitising* function.

Conceptual definition involves defining categories by giving them a precise meaning that is restricted to a clear set of criteria with clear dimensions.

Conceptual specification involves gradually adding to the meaning of a concept as new features of that concept are encountered during the study.

Constant comparative method is the method used to summarise the essential elements of grounded theory analysis. Grounded theory was described as this to distinguish it from the comparative method. The constant comparative method involves comparing incidents to incidents, categories to categories, with the goal of establishing similarities and differences and enabling the researcher to write about these when memoing.

Core category the central category of the theory that helps to integrate and organise all other categories.

Data slicing is a flexible technique of theoretical analysis that is used to create thought experiments with emerging categories to enable the researcher to test the general relevance of a category. Data slicing is also used to identify where to go for new information to continue to develop the categories in the theory.

Deduction is based on the idea that a hypothesis is put forward that proposes consequences for a category or a relationship between categories, it then involves collecting data in order to see if those consequences emerge. If they do, the hypothesis is corroborated; if not, it is falsified.

Definitive concepts are concepts that are well defined. They have clear attributes, cover individual instances of the concept and are prescriptive in that they tell us what to see.

Epistemology is an element of the philosophy of science that is concerned with answering questions about how we can know what we know.

Formal theory is a type of grounded theory that has relevance to more than one substantive group or area of study.

Incident a chunk of data. Incidents are typically grouped together under codes.

Induction a process of formulating hypotheses that involves generating a hypothesis from direct observation and subsequently seeking out negative cases to challenge the hypothesis. When negative cases are found, the hypothesis is reformulated and you start looking for new negative cases.

Logic of discovery refers to the debate about how scientific theories and hypotheses are generated in order to be tested or explored in more depth.

Logic of justification refers to the criteria that can be used to establish if a scientific theory is true or false.

Memoing is a core process of grounded theory analysis that involves building a bank of memos recording the observations of the researcher in relation to the development of their theory.

Memos are notes that are used to describe how categories in the theory have been developed, how they vary and how they relate to each other, including how they have been modified.

Ontology is a branch of philosophy that addresses questions about what exists.

Open coding is a stage in grounded theory analysis that involves coding for as many categories as possible in order to summarise what is happening in the field of interest.

Preconceptions are the set of hidden assumptions and professional baggage a researcher will bring to any study. They can be problematic during grounded theory analysis because they can lead to a selective blindness in coding.

Prior interests are the motivations that a researcher brings to a particular study. These can be productively used during grounded theory to enable the development of the theory.

Realism involves the belief that the world we live in consists of things such as human beings, horses, chairs and rocks, and that these entities have a nature that is independent of human thought.

Saturation is a goal of coding. The theory is saturated when the collection of any further data will yield very little additional information that can be used to continue specifying the categories in the theory.

Selective coding   a phase in the process of doing grounded theory that involves sampling, collecting data, theoretical coding, saturation, and reading and integrating the literature.

Sensitising concepts   are concepts that have relaxed benchmarks and well-defined attributes. They tend to indicate where they may be observed and are characterised by not specifying exactly what to look for.

Sorting   is the process of organising memos into a specific order, usually with the goal of presenting the theory in mind. Sorting is dependent on the presentation format being considered, where this can be for a lecture, seminar, PhD, book or research paper.

Substantive theory   is a grounded theory that has been applied to a limited range of groups and areas of analysis.

Theoretical pacing   involves planning the process of doing a grounded theory study from asking the right question and starting out through to writing up. It also involves an awareness that a flexible approach will be needed to the use of each of the techniques of grounded theory, such as sampling, open coding, selective coding and analysis.

Theoretical sampling   refers to the process of collecting and analysing data for the purpose of theory generation. Specifically, it refers to a process of combining several different slices of data for the purpose of comparison in order to develop the theory by, for example, specifying a dimension of a category.

Theoretical sensitivity   the title of the second book on grounded theory written by Glaser (1978), it refers to the two essential attributes of the researcher who undertakes grounded theory: (1) the researcher should have the skill to understand and know what theory is, how it varies and how it is constructed; (2) the researcher should also adopt an attitude of openness to the alternative ways to build theory.

Theoretical specification   is a strategy for theory building that involves the development of categories continually through constant adjustments in their description rather than a process of rigid definition. Theoretical specification primarily involves the use of sensitising rather than definitive concepts.

Unit of analysis   grounded theory analysis involves analysing how phenomena occur and vary in different kinds of units. Different units might include different social organisations, such as hospital wards and classrooms, or social psychological units of analysis, such as open- and closed-awareness contexts, or it may involve different units of time, such as the beginning, middle or end of a process.

Bibliography

Adorno, T.W., Frenkel-Brunswik, E., Levinson, D.J., Sanford, R.N. (1950). *The Authoritarian Personality*. New York: Norton.

Annells, M. (1996) 'Grounded theory method: philosophical perspectives, paradigm of inquiry, and postmodernism', *Qualitative Health Research*, 6(3): 379–393.

Aristotle (1924) *Aristotle's Metaphysics*. Oxford: Clarendon Press.

Artinian, B., Giske, T. et al. (2009) *Glaserian Grounded Theory in Nursing Research: Trusting Emergence*. New York: Springer.

Baker, C., Wuest, J. et al. (1992) 'Method slurring: the grounded theory/ phenomenology example', *Journal of Advanced Nursing*, 17: 1355–1360.

Bazeley, P. (2002) 'Computerized data analysis for mixed methods research', pp. 385–422 in T. Tashakkori and C. Teddlie (eds), *Handbook of Mixed Methods for the Social and Behavioral Sciences*. London: Sage.

Bazeley, P. and Richards, L. (2000) *The NVIVO Qualitative Project Book*. London: Sage.

Becker, H. (1960) 'Notes on the concept of commitment', *American Journal of Sociology*, 66(1): 32–40.

Belzer, H. (2004) 'Words + Guitar: the Riot Grrrl Movement and Third-Wave Feminism', Master of Arts in Communication, Culture and Technology, Faculty of the Graduate School of Arts and Sciences of Georgetown University, Washington, DC.

Bendix, R. (1963) 'Concepts and generalizations in comparative sociological studies', *American Sociological Review*, 28(4): 532–539.

Birks, M. and Mills, J. (2011) *Grounded Theory: A Practical Guide*. London: Sage.

Blau, P. (1960) 'A theory of social integration', *American Journal of Sociology*, 65(6): 545–556.

Blumer, H. (1940) 'The problem of the concept in social psychology', *American Journal of Sociology*, 45(5): 707–719.

Blumer, H. (1954) 'What is wrong with social theory?', *American Sociological Review*, 19(1): 3–10.

Bressler, M. (1961) 'Some selected aspects of American sociology, September 1959 to December 1960', *Annals of the American Academy of Political and Social Science*, 337: 146–159.

Bringer, J.D., Johnston, L.H. and Brackenridge, C.H. (2007) 'Using computer-assisted qualitative data analysis software to develop a grounded theory project', *Field Methods*, 18(3): 246–266.

Bryant, A. (2003) 'A constructive/ist response to Glaser's "Constructivist grounded theory?"'*Forum: Qualitative Sozialforschung/Forum: Qualitative Social Research*,

4(1): 15. Retrieved on 13 June 2013 from http://www.qualitative-research.net/index.php/fqs/article/view/757/1643.

Bryant, A. and Charmaz, K. (2007) 'Grounded theory in historical perspective: an epistemological account', in A. Bryant and K. Charmaz, *The Sage Handbook of Grounded Theory*. London: Sage.

Burr, V. (2003) *Social Constructionism*. London: Routledge.

Charmaz, K. (1991a) *Good Days, Bad Days: The Self in Chronic Illness and Time*. New Brunswick, NJ: Rutgers University Press.

Charmaz, K. (1991b) 'Identity dilemmas of chronically ill men', *The Sociological Quarterly*, **35**(2): 269–288.

Charmaz, K. (1992) 'The effects of intrusive illness on self-concept: adult patients' perspectives', *Pediatric Pulmonology*, **14**(S8): 230–231.

Charmaz, K. (1994) 'Discovering chronic illness: using grounded theory', pp. 65–93 in B. Glaser (ed.), *More Grounded Theory Methodology: A Reader*. Mill Valley, CA: Sociology Press.

Charmaz, K. (2000) 'Grounded theory: objectivist and constructivist methods', in N. Denzin and Y. Lincoln (eds), *Handbook of Qualitative Research*. Thousand Oaks, CA: Sage.

Charmaz, K. (2006) *Constructing Grounded Theory: A Practical Guide through Qualitative Analysis*. London: Sage.

Charmaz, K. (2008) 'The legacy of Anselm Strauss in constructivist grounded theory', pp. 127–141 in N. Denzin, J. Salvo and M. Washington (eds), *Studies in Symbolic Interaction (Volume 32)*. Bingley UK: Emerald Group Publishing Limited.

Charmaz, K. (2009) 'Shifting the grounds: constructivist grounded theory methods', in J. Morse, P. Stern, J. Corbin et al. (eds), *Developing Grounded Theory: The Second Generation*. Walnut Creek, CA: Left Coast Press.

Charmaz, K. and Mitchell, R.G. (1996) 'The myth of silent authorship: self, substance, and style in ethnographic writing', *Symbolic Interaction*, **19**(4): 285–302.

Chenitz, W.C. and Swanson, J.M. (1986) 'From practice to grounded theory: qualitative research in nursing.' Menlo Park, California: Addison-Wesley, Health Sciences Division.

Chiovitti, R. and Piran, N. (2003) 'Rigour and grounded theory research', *Journal of Advanced Nursing*, **44**(4): 427–435.

Clarke, A. and Friese, C. (2007) 'Grounded theorizing using situational analysis', in A. Bryant and K. Charmaz (eds), *The Handbook of Grounded Theory*. London: Sage.

Clinard, M. (ed.) (1964) *Anomie and Deviant Behavior*. Glencoe, IL, and New York: Free Press.

Coleman, J. (1961) *The Adolescent Society: The Social Life of the Teenager and its Impact on Education*. Glencoe, IL, and New York: Free Press.

Coleman, J. (1964) 'Research chronicle: the adolescent society', Chapter 8 in P. Hammond (ed.), *Sociologists at Work: The Craft of Social Research*. London and New York: Basic Books.

Creswell, W. (1998) *Qualitative Inquiry and Research Design: Choosing among Five Traditions*. London: Sage.

Dalton, M. (1964) 'Preconceptions and methods in Men who Manage', Chapter 3 in P. Hammond (ed.), *Sociologists at Work: The Craft of Social Research.* London and New York: Basic Books.

Denzin, N. (2007) 'Grounded theory and the politics of interpretation', in A. Bryant and K. Charmaz (eds), *The Sage Handbook of Grounded Theory.* London: Sage.

Denzin, N.K. and Lincoln, Y.S. (eds) (2005) *The Sage Handbook of Qualitative Research.* (Third Edition) London, Sage.

Dey, I. (1999) *Grounding Grounded Theory: Guidelines for Qualitative Inquiry.* London: Academic Press.

Durkheim, E. (1938) *The Rules of Sociological Method.* Toronto: Collier-Macmillan.

Ekins, R. (1997) *Male Femaling: A Grounded Theory Approach to Cross-Dressing and Sex-Changing.* London: Routledge.

Fernándcz, W.D. (2005) 'Issues and design', in D. Hart and S. Gregor (eds), *Information Systems Foundations: Constructing and Criticising.* Canberra: Australian National University ePress.

Feyerabend, P. (1975) *Against Method: Outline of an Anarchistic Theory of Knowledge.* London: New Left Books.

Ford-Gilboe, M., Wuest, J. et al. (2005) 'Strengthening capacity to limit intrusion: theorizing family health promotion in the aftermath of woman abuse', *Qualitative Health Research*, 15(4): 477–501.

Gadamer, H. (1976) *Philosophical Hermeneutics.* Berkeley, CA: University of California Press.

Garfinkel, H. (1967) *Studies in Ethnomethodology.* Englewood Cliffs, NJ: Prentice-Hall.

Gibson, B. (1997) 'Dangerous dentaling: a grounded theory of HIV and dentistry', Doctorate dissertation, School of Clinical Dentistry, Queen's University of Belfast.

Gibson, B. (2007) 'Accommodating critical theory', in A. Bryant and K. Charmaz (eds), *The Handbook of Grounded Theory.* London: Sage.

Gibson, B., Gregory, J. et al. (2005) 'Grounded theory and systems theory: the emergence of the grounded systems observer', *Qualitative Sociology Review*, 1(2): 3–21.

Gilgun, J. (2010) 'An oral history of grounded theory: transcript of an interview with Leonard Schatzman', *Current Issues in Qualitative Research: An Occasional Publication for Field Researchers from a Variety of Disciplines*, 1. Amazon Kindle Edition.

Glaser, B. (1964) *Organizational Scientists: Their Professional Careers.* United States of America, The Bobbs-Merrill Company, Inc.

Glaser, B. (1965) 'The constant comparative method of qualitative analysis', *Social Problems*, 12(4): 436–445.

Glaser, B. (1978) *Theoretical Sensitivity: Advances in the Methodology of Grounded Theory.* Mill Valley, CA: Sociology Press.

Glaser, B. (1992) *Emergence versus Forcing: Basics of Grounded Theory Analysis.* Mill Valley, CA: Sociology Press.

Glaser, B. (1996) *Gerund Grounded Theory: The Basic Social Process Dissertation*. Mill Valley, CA: Sociology Press.

Glaser, B. (1998) *Doing Grounded Theory: Issues and Discussions*. Mill Valley, CA: Sociology Press.

Glaser, B. (2001) *The Grounded Theory Perspective: Conceptualization Contrasted with Description*. Mill Valley, CA: Sociology Press.

Glaser, B. (2002) 'Constructivist grounded theory?', *Forum: Qualitative Social Research*, 3(3) ART 12. Retrieved on 13 June 2013 from [http://www.qualitative-research.net/index.php/fqs/article/viewArticle/825]

Glaser, B. (ed.) (2005) *The Grounded Theory Perspective III: Theoretical Coding*. Mill Valley, CA: Sociology Press.

Glaser, B. (2007) *Doing Formal Theory: A Proposal*. Mill Valley, CA: Sociology Press.

Glaser, B. (2009) *Jargonizing: Using the Grounded Theory Vocabulary*. Mill Valley, CA: Sociology Press.

Glaser, B.G. and Holton, J. (2004) Remodelling Grounded Theory, Forum Qualitative Socialforschung/Forum: Qualitative Social Research, 5(2). Retrieved 13 June 2013 from [http://www.qualitative-research.net/fqs-texte/2-04/2-04glaser-e.htm]

Glaser, B. and Strauss, A. (1964) 'Awareness contexts and social interaction', *American Sociological Review*, 29(5): 669–679.

Glaser, B. and Strauss, A. (1965) *Awareness of Dying*. Chicago: Aldine.

Glaser, B. and Strauss, A. (1967) *The Discovery of Grounded Theory*. Chicago: Aldine.

Glaser, B. and Strauss, A. (1968) *Time for Dying*. Chicago: Aldine.

Glaser, B. and Strauss, A. (1971) *Status Passage*. Mill Valley, CA: Sociology Press.

Goffman, E. (1959) *The Presentation of Self in Everyday Life*. Harmondsworth: Penguin.

Goffman, E. (1961) *Stigma: Notes on the Management of a Spoiled Identity*. New York: Doubleday Anchor.

Goffman, E. (1968) *Stigma: Notes on the Management of Spoiled Identity*. Harmondsworth: Penguin.

Goffman, E. (1974) *Frame Analysis: An Essay on the Organisation of Experience*, New York: Harper and Row.

Goode, W. (1960) 'A theory of role strain', *American Sociological Review*, 25(4): 483–496.

Gregory, J., Gibson, B. et al. (2005) 'Variation and change in the meaning of of oral health related quality of life: a "grounded" systems approach', *Social Science & Medicine*, 60(8): 1859–1868.

Hacking, I. (1999) *The Social Construction of What?* Cambridge, MA: Harvard University Press.

Hammond, P. (ed.) (1964) *Sociologists at Work: The Craft of Social Research*. London and New York: Basic Books.

Hanson, N. (1958) *Patterns of Discovery*. Cambridge and New York: Cambridge University Press.

Hempel, C. (1965) *Aspects of Scientific Explanation*. New York: Free Press.

Henwood, K. and Pidgeon, N. (2003) 'Grounded theory in psychological research', in P. Camic, J. Rhodes and L. Yardley (eds), *Qualitative Research in Psychology: Expanding Perspectives in Methodology and Design*. Washington, DC: American Psychological Association.

Hesse-Biber, N. and Leavy, P. (2006) *The Practice of Qualitative Research*. Thousand Oaks, CA: Sage.

Jenkins, R. (2002) *Foundations of Sociology: Towards a Better Understanding of the Human World*. New York: Palgrave Macmillan.

Kelle, U. (1997) 'The development of categories: different approaches in grounded theory', in A. Bryant and K. Charmaz (eds), *The Handbook of Grounded Theory*. London: Sage.

Kempner, J. (2006) 'Gendering the migrane market: do representations of illness matter?', *Social Science and Medicine*, **63**(8): 1986–1997.

Konecki, K. (2008) 'Grounded theory and serendipity: natural history of a rescarch', *Qualitative Sociology Review*, **4**(1): 171–188.

Konecki, K. (2009) 'Teaching visual grounded theory', *Qualitative Sociology Review*, **5**(3): 64–92.

Krolokke, C. and Sorensen, A. (2005) *Gender Communication Theories and Analyses: From Silence to Performance*. London: Sage.

Kuhn, T. (1962) *The Structure of Scientific Revolutions*. Chicago: University of Chicago Press.

Lazarsfeld, P. (1958) 'On evidence and inference', *Daedalus*, **87**(4): 99–130.

Lazarsfeld, P. (1959) 'Problems in methodology', Chapter 2 in R. Merton, L. Broom and L. Cottrell (eds), *Sociology Today: Problems and Prospects*. New York: Basic Books.

Lempert, L. (2007) 'Asking questions of the data: memo writing in the grounded theory tradition', in A. Bryant and K. Charmaz (eds), *The Sage Handbook of Grounded Theory*. London: Sage.

Lijphart, A. (1971) 'Comparative politics and the comparative method', *American Political Science Review*, **65**(3): 682–693.

Lindbekk, T. (1992) 'The Weberian ideal-type: development and continuities', *Acta Sociologica*, **35**(4): 285–297.

Lipset, S. (1964) 'The biography of a research project: "Union Democracy"', Chapter 4 in P. Hammond (ed.), *Sociologists at Work: The Craft of Social Research*. London and New York: Basic Books.

Locke, J. (1732) *An Essay Concerning Human Understanding*. (Tenth Edition) London: Printed for Arthur Bettesworth and Charles Hitch; Edmund Parker; John Pemberton; and Edward Symon, 1731 London: Dent.

Marcus, P. (1960) 'Expressive and instrumental groups: toward a theory of group structure', *American Journal of Sociology*, **66**(1): 54–59.

Marsiglio, W. (2004) 'When stepfathers claim stepchildren: a conceptual analysis', *Journal of Marriage and the Family*, **66**(1): 22–39.

Mead, G.H. (1938) *The Philosophy of the Act*, University of Chicago Press: Chicago.

Merritt-Gray, M. and J. Wuest (1995) 'Counteracting abuse and breaking free: the process of leaving revealed through women's voices', *Health Care for Women International*, **16**(5): 399–412.

Merton, R., Broom, L. and Cottrell, L. (1959) *Sociology Today: Problems and Prospects*. New York: Basic Books.

Mills, J., Chapman, Y. et al. (2007) 'Grounded theory: a methodological spiral from positivism to postmodernism', *Journal of Advanced Nursing*, **58**(1): 72–79.

Mruck, K. and Mey, G. (2007) 'Grounded theory and reflexivity', in A. Bryant and K. Charmaz (eds), *The Sage Handbook of Grounded Theory*. London: Sage.

Nathaniel, A. (2012) 'An integrated philosophical framework that fits grounded theory', in V. Martin and A. Gynnild (eds), *Grounded Theory: The Philosophy, Method, and Work of Barney Glaser*. Boca Raton, FL: Brown Walker Press.

Neill, S. (2006) 'Grounded theory sampling: the contribution of reflexivity', *Journal of Research in Nursing*, **11**(3): 253–260.

Nozick, R. (1981) *Philosophical Explanations*. Cambridge, MA: Harvard University Press.

Parsons, T. (1959) 'General Theory in Sociology', in R. Merton, L. Broom and L.S. Cottrell (eds), *Sociology Today: Problems and Prospects*. New York: Basic Books.

Peters, V. and Wester, F. (2007) 'How qualitative data analysis software may support the qualitative analysis process', *Quality & Quantity*, **41**(5): 635–659.

Plato (1966) *Plato's Republic*. Cambridge: Cambridge University Press.

Popper, K. (1959) *The Logic of Scientific Discovery*. London: Hutchinson Education.

Popper, K. (1970) *Normal Science and its Dangers*. Ed. I. Lakatos and A. Musgrave. Cambridge: Cambridge University Press.

Raphael, H. (2008) 'A grounded theory study of men's perceptions, understanding and experiences of osteoporosis', Doctorate dissertation, School of Nursing and Midwifery, University of Southampton.

Reichertz, J. (2007) 'Abduction: the logic of discovery of grounded theory', in K. Charmaz and T. Bryant (eds), *The Handbook of Grounded Theory*. London: Sage.

Rich, P. (2012) 'Inside the Black Box: revealing the process in applying a grounded theory analysis', *The Qualitative Report*, **17**(49): 1–23.

Richards, T. and Richards, L. (1995) 'Using hierarchical categories in qualitative data analysis', pp. 80–95 in U. Kelle, G. Prein and K. Bird (eds), *Computer-Aided Qualitative Data Analysis: Theory, Methods, and Practice*. London: Sage.

Sandelowski, M. (2007) 'Words that should be seen but not written.' *Research in Nursing & Health* **30**(2): 129–130.

Schütz, A. (1967) *The Phenomenology of the Social World*. Evanston, IL: Northwestern University Press.

Searle, J.R. (1998) *Mind, Language and Society: Philosophy in the Real World*. New York: Basic Books.

Seedhouse, D. (2005) *Health: The Foundations for Achievement*. London: John Wiley and Sons Ltd.

Stern, P. and Porr, C. (2011) *Essentials of Accessible Grounded Theory*. Walnut Creek, CA: Left Coast Press.

Strauss, A. (1970) *Mirrors and Masks*. San Francisco, CA: Sociology Press.

Strauss, A. and Corbin, J. (1990) *Basics of Qualitative Research: Grounded Theory Procedures and Techniques*. Thousand Oaks, CA: Sage.

Strauss, A. and Corbin, J. (1998) *Basics of Qualitative Research: Techniques and Procedures for Developing Grounded Theory*. (2nd ed.). Thousand Oaks, CA: Sage.

Udy, S. (1964) 'Cross-cultural analysis: a case study', Chapter 7 in P. Hammond (ed.), *Sociologists at Work: The Craft of Social Research*. London and New York: Basic Books.

Urquhart, C. (1997) 'The evolving nature of grounded theory method: the case of the information systems discipline', in A. Bryant and K. Charmaz (eds), *The Handbook of Grounded Theory*. London: Sage.

Walker, D. and Myrick, F. (2006) 'Grounded theory: an exploration of process and procedure', *Qualitative Health Research*, 16(4): 547–559.

Weber, M. (1904/1949a) 'The meaning of "ethical neutrality"', in E. Shils and H. Finch (eds), *The Methodology of the Social Sciences*. New York: Free Press.

Weber, M. (1904/1949b) '"Objectivity" in social sciences', in E. Shils and H. Finch (eds), *The Methodology of the Social Sciences*. New York: Free Press.

Weiner, C. (2007) 'Making teams work in conducting grounded theory', in A. Bryant and K. Charmaz (eds), *The Sage Handbook of Grounded Theory*. London: Sage.

Wittgenstein, L. (2001) *Tractatus Logico Philosophicus*. London: Taylor & Francis.

Wuest, J. (1995) 'Feminist grounded theory – an exploration of the congruency and tensions between two traditions in knowledge discovery', *Qualitative Health Research*, 5(1): 125–137.

Wuest, J. (1997a) 'Fraying connections of caring women: an exemplar of including difference in the development of explanatory frameworks', *Canadian Journal of Nursing Research*, 29(2): 99–116.

Wuest, J. (1997b) 'Illuminating environmental influences on women's caring', *Journal of Advanced Nursing*, 26(1): 49–58.

Wuest, J. (1998) 'Setting boundaries: a strategy for precarious ordering of women's caring demands', *Research in Nursing & Health*, 21(1): 39–49.

Wuest, J. (2000a) 'Negotiating with helping systems: an example of grounded theory evolving through emergent fit', *Qualitative Health Research*, 10(1): 51–70.

Wuest, J. (2000b) 'Repatterning care: women's proactive management of family caregiving demands', *Health Care for Women International*, 21(5): 393–411.

Wuest, J. (2001) 'Precarious ordering: toward a formal theory of women's caring', *Health Care for Women International*, 22(1–2): 167–193.

Wuest, J., Ford-Gilboe, M. et al. (2003) 'Intrusion: the central problem for family health promotion among children and single mothers after leaving an abusive partner', *Qualitative Health Research*, 13(5): 597–622.

Wuest, J. and Merritt-Gray, M. (2001) 'Beyond survival: reclaiming self after leaving an abusive male partner', *Canadian Journal of Nursing Research*, 32(4): 79–94.

Wuest, J., Merritt-Gray, M. et al. (2004) 'Regenerating family: strengthening the emotional health of mothers and children in the context of intimate partner violence', *Advances in Nursing Science*, 27(4): 257–274.

Yuen, H.K. and Richards, T.J. (1994) 'Knowledge representation for grounded theory construction in qualitative data-analysis', *Journal of Mathematical Sociology*, **19**(4): 279–298.

Zetterberg, H.L. (1954) *On Theory and Verification in Sociology*. Stockholm: Almqvist & Wiksell.

Znaniecki, F. and Thomas, W.I. (1918/ 2007) *The Polish Peasant in Europe and America* (5 volumes). Whitefish, MT: Kessinger Publishing.

Index

Adorno, T. W., 87–88
analytical rewriting, 226–227
Anomie and Deviant Behavior (Merton), 224
Aristotle, 53–54, 55
articles and papers
    sorting for, 195–196
    writing and, 213, 219–220
Artinian, B., 17
Authoritarian Personality (Adorno et al.),
    87–88
Awareness of Dying (Glaser and Strauss)
    awareness context in, 39–40, 135n3
    constant comparative method and, 86
    on core categories, 39–40
    formal theory and, 230
    on grounded theory, 119
    on memos, 177
    units of analysis in, 33
axial coding, 79, 84, 85, 96

Basics of Qualitative Research (Strauss and
    Corbin)
    on coding, 83–84, 85, 96, 97–98, 168
    on concepts and categories, 66–67,
        68, 79
    on formal theory, 234–235
    Glaser and, 30
    on literature, 202, 208
    on memos, 182
    objectivism and, 118
    operationalism and, 99–100n2
    on prior interests and preconceptions, 111
    on research questions, 34
    on sorting, 197
    on theoretical pacing, 149
    on theoretical sensitivity, 106
    view of grounded theory in, 3, 238
    on writing, 213–214, 215
Bendix, R., 75
Birks, M. See *Grounded Theory* (Birks and
    Mills)
Blumer, H.
    on coding, 95, 96, 100n2
    on concepts and categories, 71–72, 73,
        75, 78–79, 238

books
    sorting for, 187, 194–195
    writing and, 213, 215–217
Bringer, J.D., 181
Broom, L. See *Sociology Today* (Merton, Broom
    and Cottrell)
Bryant, A., 32, 238, 241

categories
    concepts and, 66–68
    contemporary views on, 68–69
    discovery of grounded theory and, 73,
        75–80, 77
    properties and, 36
Charmaz, K.
    on coding, 83–85, 96, 97–98
    on Dey, 203
    importance of, 240–241
    on literature, 209
    on main tenets of constructivist grounded
        theory, 45–47, 238
    on meaning, 3, 45–46, 59–60, 84
    on memos, 182
    objectivist grounded theory and, 31–32, 50,
        238–239
    on openness, 48, 59
    on operationalism, 100n5
    on research questions, 34
    on sorting, 197
    on writing, 221
Chenitz, W.C., 203
Chicago School, 68, 70, 78, 223, 238
coding
    definition of, 40, 82
    in *Discovery*, 83, 88–90, *89*, 95, 96
    key points about, 168–169
    in literature, 83–86
    openness and, 36
    theoretical context of, 86–88
    theoretical sampling and, 131–132
    in *Theoretical Sensitivity*, 87, 90–98, *92*
    See also axial coding; open coding; selective
        coding
Coleman, J., 8–9, 10–11
Columbia University, 15, 68, 70–75, 78, 238

comparative sociology, 6–13, *9–10*, *12*, 126–128, 201, 238–239

Comte, A., 13–14

concepts
    categories and, 66–68
    contemporary views on, 68
    discovery of grounded theory and, 70–75, *72*, *74*, 78–79, 238

conceptual elaboration, 73

conceptualism, 55, 56

constant comparative method
    vs. comparative methods, 8, 10–12
    concepts and, 70–75
    constructivist grounded theory and, 49
    development of, 86
    formal theory and, 227–230
    overview, 12–13
    theoretical sensitivity and, *115*

constructivism, 16, 50–58, *52–53*

constructivist grounded theory
    critical grounded theory and, 118–119
    vs. grounded theory, 3, 19–20, 47–50, 62–63
    main tenets of, 44–47, *47*, 58–61, *61–62*, 238
    vs. qualitative research, 63
    universals and, 58

Corbin, J. See *Basics of Qualitative Research* (Strauss and Corbin)

core categories
    in *Awareness*, 39–40
    Birks and Mills on, 31
    explanatory power and, 36–37
    overview, 39
    selective coding and, 163–165
    sorting and, 188, *190*
    theoretical pacing and, 147
    in *Theoretical Sensitivity*, 93–95, *94*

Cottrell, L. See *Sociology Today* (Merton, Broom and Cottrell)

Creswell, W., 32

critical grounded theory, 118–119

critical junctures, 152n6

critical rationalism, 15, 37

cutting point, 97, 142, 152n6

Dalton, M., 7, 11

data collection
    constructivist grounded theory and, 59
    openness and, 35
    See also theoretical sampling

deduction, 2–3, 41, 78, 122–123

definitive concepts, 72, *72*

Denzin, N.K., 18, 118, 209

deviant case analysis, 9

Dey, I.
    on coding, 85–86, 98, 101n12
    comparative sociology and, 24n4
    on concepts and categories, 67–69, 79
    on formal theory, 236n3
    on Lazarsfeld and Glaser, 71
    on literature, 203
    on sorting, 199n1
    on theoretical pacing, 149
    view of grounded theory by, 32

The Discovery of Grounded Theory (Glaser and Strauss)
    on categories, 75–78
    on coding, 83, 88–90, *89*, 95, 96, 164
    Columbia and Chicago Schools of sociology and, 70, 78, 238
    on concepts and categories, 70, 72–75, *74*, 77, 78–79
    on constant comparative method, 12–13, 227–228
    on explanatory power, 36–37
    on formal theory, 229
    on grounded theory, 27–30, 223–225
    Kuhn and, 16
    on literature, 200–202
    on memos, 171–173, *172*, 174, 177
    on openness, 33–36
    philosophy of science and, 19–20
    positivism and, 15, 32
    sociological context of, 5–13, 126–128
    stages of doing grounded theory in, 137, *137*, 143
    on substantive theory, 38–40
    on theoretical sampling, 122, 126–127
    on theoretical sensitivity, 110–111, 113–114, 118

Durkheim, E., 6, 33

Ekins, R.
    coding and, 154–155, 163, 167
    formal theory and, 226, 230–232
    on literature, 204, 206, 207–208
    memos and, 177–178
    overview of research by, 108, 241
    prior interests and, 111
    sorting and, 187, 194
    theoretical pacing and, 141, 144, 147, 148
    theoretical sampling and, 123–124, 125, 129–131, 132, 133, 230–232
    theoretical sensitivity and, 111, 113
    writing and, 215–217

empiricism, 13–14

essentialism, 54, *55*, 56

Essentials of Accessible Grounded theory (Stern and Porr), 17–18

ethnomethodology, 16, 107
explanatory power, 36–37, 49

falsificationalism, 37
Fernández, W.D., 152n5
forcing, 7, 33, 48
formal theory
    key points about, 234–236
    overview, 223–225
    techniques for, *225–234*
Frege, G., 13–14

Gadamer, H., 46
Garfinkel, H., 16
Geer, B., 7
Gerund Grounded Theory (Glaser), 133
Gibson, B., 155–156
Giske, T., 17
Glaser, B.
    Columbia University and, 15, 68
    on concepts and categories, 3, 72
    on constructivist grounded theory, 58
    on forcing, 48
    on formal theory, 229–230, 232
    on reflexivity, 121n3
    on remodelling of grounded theory, 30
    Strauss and, 15, 30, 70
    See also *Awareness of Dying* (Glaser and
        Strauss); *The Discovery of Grounded
        Theory* (Glaser and Strauss); *Status
        Passage* (Glaser and Strauss); *Theoretical
        Sensitivity* (Glaser)
Glaserian Grounded Theory in Nursing Research
    (Artinian, Giske et al.), 17
Goffman, E., 135n4
grounded theory
    comparative sociology and, 6–13, *9–10, 12,*
        126–128, 201, 238–239
    core aspects of, 32–41, **42**
    definition of, 1
    goal of, 2–3
    philosophical context of, 13–16
    philosophy of science and, 17–20
    rediscovery of, 3–5
    sociological context of, 1, 5–13,
        9–10, 12
    views on, 30–32, 237–242
Grounded Theory (Birks and Mills)
    on coding, 83
    on concepts and categories, 66, 68
    on memos, 182
    philosophy of science and, 18
    on sorting, 197
    theoretical pacing and, 142
    view of grounded theory in, 31
    on writing, 214

grounded theory method, 23–24n1
Grounding Grounded Theory (Dey), 67–69

Hacking, I., 56
Hammond, P., 6–11, 86, 126, 201, 238
Hempel, C., 51
Henwood, K., 203
hermeneutics, 36
Holton, J., 30

ideas, 73
induction, 37, 41, 78, 122–123
integration, 187–197, *190*
integrative fit, 189, *190*, 205–206

Kant, I., 50
Konecki, K., 240
Kuhn, T., 16, 17

language, 214
Lazarsfeld, P.
    on coding, 87–88, 92, 93, 95, 96–97,
        101n8, 165
    on concepts and categories, 71–75,
        78, 238
    Discovery and, 223
    Glaser and, 68, 71–75
    lectures, 187, 196
lifeworld sociology, 16
Lincoln, Y.S., 18
Lindbekk, T., 165
Lipset, S., 9, 24n8
literature
    critical use of, 203–208, *207*
    debate about, 200–203
    key points about, 209–210
    theoretical sensitivity and, 114,
        114–115
Locke, J., 55
The Logic of Scientific Discovery (Popper), 15
logical elaboration, 73
logical positivism, 13–15, 16, 31–32, 37, 51
London School of Economics, 15

Marx, K., 33
meaning, 3, 45–46, 59–60, 84
memos
    computers and, 180–181
    in *Discovery*, 171–173, *172*, 174, 177
    key points about, 182
    literature and, 208
    overview, 173–180, *174, 175–176, 178*
    sorting and, 188, *190*
    theoretical sampling and, 133
    in *Theoretical Sensitivity*, 137, 171–172,
        174, 179

Merton, R., 86, 223–225
See also *Sociology Today* (Merton, Broom and Cottrell)
methodological pluralism, 4, 237–238
methodological unity of science, 14, 51
Mills, J. See *Grounded Theory* (Birks and Mills)
Mirrors and Masks (Strauss), 230
Myrick, F., 79

Nathaniel, A., 18–19
nominalism, 54–55, *55*, 56, 58, 59
Nozick, R., 41
NVIVO, 181

objectivism, 51, *52–53*, 57, 118
objectivist grounded theory, 31–32, 46, 50, 238–239
On Theory and Verification in Sociology (Zetterberg), 15
open coding
constructivist grounded theory and, 48
goal of, 162–163
key points about, 169
in literature, 85–86
overview, 154–158
slices of data and, 161–162, 169
techniques for, 158–161, *158*, *159*, *161*
theoretical pacing and, 146–147
in *Theoretical Sensitivity*, 91–93, *92*, 131–132
openness
constructivist grounded theory and, 48, 59
overview, 33–36
theoretical pacing and, 144–146, *145–146*
theoretical sensitivity and, 35, 36, 109
operational relativism, 58
operationalism, 73, 78–79, 97, 99–100n2, 100n5, 238
Organizational Scientists (Glaser), 230

papers and articles
sorting for, 195–196
writing and, 213, 219–220
Parsons, T., 33, 86–87
Peirce, C.S., 19
PhD research
sorting for, 191–194, *193*
writing and, 213, 217–219
phenomenological method, 34, 36, 48
Pidgeon, N., 203
Plato, 53–54, *55*
Popper, K., 15, 16, 37
Porr, C., 17–18

postmodernism, 16, 237
pragmatism, 19
preconceptions
constructivism and, 51
in *Discovery*, 8
literature and, 202–205
theoretical pacing and, 144
theoretical sensitivity and, 111–112, 116–117, 118
prior interests
theoretical pacing and, 143–144
theoretical sensitivity and, 111–112, 116–117, 118
process-theories, 40
properties, 36, 68–69, 76

qualitative research
coding and, 88–90
vs. constructivist grounded theory, 63
quantitative research, 88

Raphael, H.
coding and, 156–158, 159, 163–164, 167
formal theory and, 226
on literature, 203–204, 206, 207–208
memos and, 173–174, 175–177, *175–176*
overview of research by, 108–109
sorting and, 187
writing and, 218–219
rationalism, 14
realism, 51, 53–54
reflexivity, 117–120
relativism, 51, 58
research monographs
sorting for, 187, 194–195
writing and, 213, 215–217
research process, 41, 50, 61
research questions
constructivist grounded theory and, 48
theoretical pacing and, 144–146, *145–146*
units of analysis and, 33–34
resultant grounded theory, 23–24n1
Russell, B., 13–14

Sandelowski, M., 214
saturation, 186
Schatzman, L., 107–108, 122
Schütz, A., 16
scripting, 165–167, *166*
second-generation grounded theory, 3
See also constructivist grounded theory
selective coding
key points about, 169
overview, 163–168

selective coding *cont.*
  Strauss and Corbin on, 85
  theoretical pacing and, 147–148
  in *Theoretical Sensitivity*, 93, 131–132
seminars and lectures, 187, 196
sensitising concepts, 72, *72*
slices of data
  formal theory and, 228
  Lipset and, 9
  memos and, 178
  open coding and, 161–162, 169
  theoretical pacing and, 147
  theoretical sampling and, 125–131,
    133–134
Sociologists at Work (Hammond), 6–11, 86, 126,
  201, 238
Sociology Today (Merton, Broom and Cottrell),
  86–88, 90
sorting
  integration and, 187–197, *190*
  key points about, 197–198
  overview, 186–187
Status Passage (Glaser and Strauss)
  on formal theory, 227–228, 229–230,
    232–234
  on slices of data, 125–127
  sociological context of, 126–128
Stern, P., 17–18
Strauss, A.
  Chicago School and, 68
  Glaser and, 15, 30, 70
  See also *Awareness of Dying* (Glaser and
    Strauss); *Basics of Qualitative Research*
    (Strauss and Corbin); *The Discovery of
    Grounded Theory* (Glaser and Strauss);
    Status Passage (Glaser and Strauss)
structural functionalism, 33
The Structure of Scientific Revolutions
  (Kuhn), 16, 17
substantive theory, 38–40
Swanson, J.M., 203

theoretical pacing
  key points about, 148–149, *150*
  overview, 136–139, *137, 138*
  process of grounded theory and,
    142–148, *143*
  techniques and, 140–142, *140*
theoretical sampling
  categories and, 78
  coding and, 131–132
  Coleman and, 8
  formal theory and, 230–232
  general principles of, 123–125
  key points about, 133–134

theoretical sampling *cont.*
  overview, 122–123
  slices of data and, 125–131, 133–134
theoretical sensitivity
  definition of, 35, 36
  literature and, 114, ***114–115***
  openness and, 35, 36, 109
  overview, 106–114, *107*
  preconceptions and, 111–112, 116–117, 118
  prior interests and, 111–112, 116–117, 118
  reflexivity and, 117–120
Theoretical Sensitivity (Glaser)
  on coding, 85, 87, 90–98, *92*, 131–132, 165,
    167–168
  Columbia and Chicago Schools of sociology
    and, 70
  on concepts and categories, 70–71, 73–75,
    74, 77
  on constant comparative method, 11,
    227–228
  on core categories, 93–95, *94*
  on degree family, 40
  on formal theory, 226, 227–228, 229
  on integrative fit, 189, 205–206
  on literature, 202
  on memos, 171–172, 174, 179
  philosophy of science and, 19–20
  sociological context of, 5–6
  on sorting, 186–190, *190*, 197–198
  stages of doing grounded theory in,
    137–139, *138*, 143
  theoretical pacing and, 142, 147
  on theoretical sensitivity, 106–107, 109
  on writing, 213, 215, 218–219
theory, 2–3
theory structure
  constructivist grounded theory and, 49–50, 61
  overview, 38–40
Time for Dying (Glaser and Strauss), 40
Tractatus (Wittgenstein), 14

units of analysis
  Coleman and, 8
  definition of, 24n5
  operationalism and, 238
  research questions and, 33–34
  theoretical pacing and, 141–142, 144
  theoretical sampling and, 125
universals, 53–57, *55*

verificationalism, 37
Vienna Circle, 14–15

Walker, D., 79
Weber, M., 6, 33, 165

Wittgenstein, L., 14
writing
  key points about, 220–221
  overview, 212–213
  preparation for, 213–214
  theoretical pacing and, 148
Wuest, J.
  alternative approach to grounded theory by, 101n12
  coding and, 154–155, 167
  critical grounded theory and, 118–119
  formal theory and, 226–227, 228–229
  on literature, 204–205, 207–208

Wuest, J. *cont.*
  overview of research by, 108
  preconceptions and, 112
  prior interests and, 111
  sorting and, 187, 195–196
  theoretical pacing and, 140–142, 144–145, 147, 148
  theoretical sampling and, 123, 124, 127, 128–129, 132, 135n2
  theoretical sensitivity and, 111, 112, 113
  writing and, 219–220

Zetterberg, H.L, 15